# WINGED WORDS

# WINGED WORDS

by
PHILIP  HOWARD

New York
Oxford University Press
1988

First published in Great Britain 1988
by Hamish Hamilton Ltd.
27 Wrights Lane, London w8 5tz

First published in the United States of America 1988
by Oxford University Press, Inc.
200 Madison Avenue, New York, NY 10016

Copyright © 1988 by Philip Howard

ISBN 0-19-520770-X
Printed and bound in Great Britain

Ad liberalem Musam

# Contents

# Introduction

The world is not really revolving faster as we roll down the century towards the new millennium. It just feels as if it is because of the pace of technological, social, and political change; the revolutions in communications and computers and cybernetics; the continuous invention and innovation in all the sciences. Until recently the structures of everyday life changed more slowly. The same implements for farming and customs for cooking and eating were used for centuries. The wheels of commerce and the bandwagons of fashion ran down the same old tracks, so that an Ancient Roman would have known what to do in a medieval harvest field, and how to use his knife and trencher and fingers at a medieval feast. The Ancient Roman would have complained that the quality of life had declined in the lack of central heating and hot baths. Our civilization of continual, accelerating change was created by capitalism and the Industrial and Technological Revolutions.

Language changes with life. People need new words to describe their new world that is evolving; and grammar, syntax, pronunciation, and the other departments of language change (sometimes as fast as the streams of new words pouring into the central core of language). In the Eighties the English language is changing faster than at any time in the fifteen centuries of its history, since it was brought into Britain by tribesmen from Frisia and the neighbouring territories in the fifth century AD. This is natural, not surprising. More people are using English, as it has become the world language in many registers and technologies and departments of life. In the past few years two spectacular areas of linguistic change have been in Computerese and the jargons of the communications industries, and in the language of business and the stock exchanges, with their concert parties and golden parachutes after Big Bang. Slang changes so that Yuppies need to know the difference between biffing and boffing, and the President of the United States calls Colonel Gadaffi flaky and a Looney-

Tune. On our tables we have spritzers and cordon vert. When we hear that falling arches are being rehabbed, we wonder whether it is being done by an architect or as a pedicure. White Knights come to the rescue of companies threatened by take-over, but may announce that there is no such thing as a free lunch.

Little words are doing badly at present, with nobody saying 'Yes' or 'I' any more, preferring the longer and more pretentious 'That's right', 'Myself', 'Take care, there you go, have a nice day'; to which the unorthodox reply is, 'I'll have whatever sort of day I want, thank you; mind how you go.' In the feminist vocabulary 'lady' is making a surprise comeback, as in, 'She's a bright lady.' We still have trouble with Ms and Esq. Caring, compassionate, and community have become political buzz-words, indicating political tendencies and slogans that signify attitudes. Politicians attack each other for fudge and mudge. We are slightly changing the implication of Brownie points now that they have crossed the Atlantic, and are keen on everything state-of-the-art. We have learnt about the modern plague of AIDS, and suffer from other such new and mysterious complaints as the sick-building syndrome, Slim, the teddybear syndrome, and ageism. In British slang a desmond means a lower second-class university or polytechnic degree, unkindly named after Archbishop Desmond Tutu of Cape Town by students of Newcastle University. The Princess Royal tells press photographers to naff off. Academic jargons have had their own Big Bang and mega-mergers, from chaology, the mathematical study of chaos, to fuzzification (from fuzzy logic, and non-diophantine number theory).

Can you catch a gravy train from a band-wagon? Do you arb, and what is Taurus? We are learning to live with hype in the publishing world and advertorials in the papers (paid advertisements that are not flagged and look like editorial copy, a practice to make Charles Pretwich Scott of the *Manchester Guardian* – 'Comment is free but facts are sacred' – drive the spike into somebody in the great newsroom in the sky). From Alpha man to zombie food there has been a revolution in language, as in the rest of our culture and civilization, in the Eighties.

Progress is not a straight, rising line. Things proceed by fits and starts, action and reaction. In the Eighties there was a reaction against the consensus politics of evolution since the war, in which all good men and true were assumed to agree on about 80 per cent of what needed to be done to make the world better. The New Right, reacting against forest-fire inflation and union anarchy among other things, in economics had such standard-bearers and trumpeters as Milton Friedman and F. A. Hayek. In politics their doctrines were personalized as Thatcherism and Reaganomics. They called for a return to earlier verities and even Victorian values (a simplification of the complex history of the Victorian age which indicates a lack of reading of such vivid witnesses as Dickens and Mayhew).

The reaction came in attitudes to language also. There was a call for a return to the earlier verities of old-fashioned correct grammar, and spelling, and proper or Received Pronunciation, as it used to be spoken in the great boarding schools and universities of Southern England. There was a grumpy feeling that the younger generation was not using the language well, and that English itself was decadent or dying. Some of the reaction was pretty silly. Most reactions go too far. But it was not all wrong.

It is worth asking the doom merchants about the state of the language when this supposed golden age or vintage year for English is supposed to have happened. It usually turns out to have been when the grumblers were themselves at school, learning irregular verbs, grammatical tables, spelling lists of impossible words, and the three Rs. But the language has moved on since then: languages do. We need to remember how small a proportion of the country received this élite education in English. It is only just over a century since Britain introduced universal education, and the noble dream of universally literate and articulate citizens. What has happened is that since the war there has been a powerful reaction in schools and universities against this *ancien régime*. We have recognized that spoken English is as important a part of the language as written English. We know that grammar is what each generation makes of it. We look on Received Pronunciation as only one way of speaking English, confined to a tiny minority, though still carrying great prestige.

This new, more profound, 'permissive' attitude to English was taken too far by extremists and enthusiasts, as changes always are. Their books asserting that there is no such thing as 'correct' English are carefully written in it. Of course an intelligent and prudent person uses many different kinds of English appropriate to different occasions: compare and contrast the Englishes you would use in a formal speech, a letter to a friend, a chat over the telephone, and an application for a job. But at any time in history there is a difference between correct and incorrect usage (with quite large regional grey areas in between), and a good teacher and a well-taught user of English know it. The Victorian and Edwardian insistence on upper-class pronunciation made it a class accent. But it is not a sufficient treatment of accent to state, as the school textbook called *Language* does: 'The upper group possess money, property, power and control over the way the country is run. They and some of the middle group are able to spread the idea that their ways of speaking English – their accents and their dialect – are best.' Just because the 'rules' of English are much more complex than was supposed thirty years ago, this does not mean there are no rules. Of course geniuses and even creative writers are allowed to break rules. But, if you do it for no obvious reason or effect, you run the risk of being misunderstood, or the even more terrible risk of being thought a yob or an inverted snob.

The recent emphasis on speech, and everyday language, and individual creativity and self-expression, does not mean that we do not need to read the great writers of English in ages other than our own, and to learn grammar and spelling when we are young. There is a shared culture available to all speakers of English, and we are blind abusers of the language if we do not know something about it. Successful communication in our changing world needs rules, and grammar, and spelling, and a knowledge of our shared culture as well as all the new technologies and registers of language. We need a sensible consensus between the old-school purists and the modern radicals, so that we can have correct grammar as well as creativity and let-it-all-hang-out self-expression. We should not go back to flogging children for bad grammar, or hanging placards round their necks if they pronounce with a regional accent. But you cannot get rid of all rules and rigour from language. And we are in danger of losing the baby in throwing out the bathwater of old-fashioned grammar and rigour. Children are no longer taught to read the great writers of English in the past with as much pleasure and care as a generation ago. Latin and Greek (the only grammar English children were taught for centuries in their grammar schools) are dwindling in our schools. This is serious and robs our children of their birthright. An English man or woman without Latin is always a stranger in his or her culture and the culture of the West. The best way to learn grammar is from the roots and the nursery, in Latin, and, if you are lucky, Greek. In our changing language we need a sensible compromise between the rigours of the purist and authoritarian past and the freedom and excitement of the new world.

The language reactionaries are wrong when they prophesy as angrily as Minor Prophets on a bad Monday that the language itself is dying. That is an elementary category mistake. People die; not languages. Languages 'die' only when people stop using them, and that is clearly not the case with English, which is used far more widely around the world than ever before. A language evolves and is perfect for the needs of those who use it. In many registers and functions we are using English better today than we ever did. The cure for nostalgia for the excellence of English in some legendary Golden Age is to go back and read it. The giants in any generation, the Chaucers and Shakespeares, the Gibbons and Johnsons, the Eliots (George or T. S.), are always rare phoenixes. Most of us have in all ages spoken and written English at a far lower level. But the voices of ordinary English women and men before the age of gramophone and tape recorder have vanished, except when transmitted to us in the writings of the educated. And not much demotic writing has survived. The Pastons and John Husee were well-to-do, rising middle class. Most of the population was illiterate, and there is no evidence that the general public spoke the language any better than we do.

The reactionaries and gurus of grammar sometimes argue that when everybody had to go to church on Sunday, and was brought up from infancy on our national heritage of *The Authorized Version* and *The Book of Common Prayer*, Englishmen spoke better English. The evidence from such occasions as the Putney Debates, where we hear recorded the voice of articulate, middle-class England, suggests that what our generation has lost in turgid sonority it has made up for in clarity and significance.

The gurus of grammar, the anxious, the hypochondriacs of language complain about deterioration (i.e. change) in English. In fact what they are really worried about, if you examine their complaints, is the change in society. Our marvellous native tongue is a rolling river, with tributaries running into it today from all over the world. Rivers cannot run backwards. English is neither better nor worse today than it was in the past: just different to meet the needs of a changed world. In the VDUs of our best writers and the microphones of our best speakers English is alive and flourishing; and in many new fields and registers used in ways inconceivable to and unachievable by our predecessors. And the great mass of us use a vastly more complex English as well as we can to carry on our lives in a vastly more complex world. The world has changed, and the language has changed with it to meet the new needs. 'A living language is like a man suffering incessantly from small haemorrhages, and what it needs above all else is constant transfusions of new blood from other tongues. The day the gates go up, that day it begins to die.' H. L. Mencken got it right in *The American Language*, 1919.

The first half of this book examines the new words that have come into the English language over the past few years, from state of the art to hype, and from White Knight to fudge and mudge; where possible analyses and derives them; and where appropriate passes a temperate judgement on them. The second part of the book discusses general matters of grammar and language, such as the growth of new metaphors and modern proverbs, the habit of quotation, the importance of history. Most of the chapters started life as even shorter articles, usually in *The Times*, and have been expanded, corrected, amended, and enlivened by the correspondence they have provoked. In one or two chapters, for example 'Hopefully' and 'Old Wives' Tales', I have revisited topics that I have written about in other books, to see what has happened to them. But most of the material is new. Serious points are made, and where possible the truth is stated. But it is possible to be serious without being solemn: there are jokes.

Writing about English is a slippery business, like wrestling in mud with an octopus. I thank the pedants and radicals, the purists and permissives, the Jeremiahs and the Panglosses, and the noble army of correspondents who have fed me ideas, and encouraged and rebuked me. Many of them have become not just regular correspondents, but also friends.

I salute all good logophiles and wordsmiths, in particular: Denis Baron, Francis Bennion, Henry Button, Robert Burchfield, Sir David Croom-Johnson, Peter Fellgett, Gay Firth, Alfred Friendly, Roy Fuller, Peter Glare, Hamish Hamilton, John Harris, James Holladay, David Hunt, Elspeth Huxley, Peter Jones, Nicholas Kurti, Bernard Levin, Edwin Newman, John Newman, Edward Quinn, Anthony Quinton, Randolph Quirk, Isabel Raphael, William Rees-Mogg, Alan Ross, J. M. Ross, William Safire, Christopher Sinclair-Stevenson, John Sykes, Philippa Toomey, Laurence Urdang, David West, and Laurie Weston.

# PART 1

# NEW WORDS

# ABUSE

## Much ado about naffing

'To hell with you. Offensive letter follows.'
Anonymous telegram sent to Sir Alec Douglas-Home,
1963

'Abuse is in order, but it is best if it is
supported by argument.'
Sir Robin Day, as Chairman of *Election Call*, BBC
Radio, 13 April 1979

Human nature being what it is, one of the liveliest, most
changeable, and most class-indicative registers in a language is
the register of abuse. We give away our social background
every time we open our mouths, never more so than when we
are being rude. When Princess Anne at some equestrian event
in 1983 told press photographers to 'naff off', her crisp imperative established itself as U in the language of abuse, and is
developing into an adjective and other cognate parts of speech.
*The Complete Naff Guide*, a slim volume, was published by an
enterprising hustler shortly after Princess Anne's expletive.

What can the Princess have meant? The origins of 'naff off'
as a royal command to go away, or 'naff' as an adjective or
noun meaning a wally, are puzzling, but not beyond all
conjecture. The careful lexicographers will not risk an opinion,
but take refuge in 'origin obscure'. There may be some connection or influence with the Naafi, the dear old Naval, Army,
and Air Force Institute, purveyors of tea with bromide in it
and buns and beer to the troops for more than fifty years. It
can be spelt Nafy, Naffy, or Narfy also; Partridge records that
Indian army officers used to pronounce it as Narfy. The Naafi
has pupped a number of other phrases in service slang. The
derivative Naffy is a pejorative epithet suggesting idle and
shirking. The Royal Navy in the last war had a 'Naffy rating',
meaning somebody who was not pulling his weight. As a piece

3

of service etymology the initials NAAFI were interpreted by learned non-commissioned officers as: 'No Aim, Ambition, or some forgotten adjective beginning with F Initiative.' The 1939–45 Star was known as the Naafi Gong, alias the Spam Medal, because of the resemblance between the Naafi shoulder-strap colours and the ribbon colours of the Star. 'Naffy time' is the morning break or elevenses. 'A Naffy Romeo' was RAF slang for a ladies' man in the last war. 'A Naffy rumour' was a baseless report. And to deal a 'Naffy sandwich' was the practice of service poker-players of dealing a hand of two greasy cards, followed by one greasy card, followed by two more to close the sandwich. Most of the service slang derivatives from Naafi, though interesting (fairly), are obsolete.

'Naff' has been low slang for 'nothing' since about 1940 in civilian and particularly red-light life. Folk etymologists have suggested a derivation from *rien à faire*, or 'Not a Fuck'. The latter is the more probable, but far from a certainty. 'Naff off' was constantly used by the scriptwriters of *Porridge*, a popular British television comedy about prison life of the Seventies and Eighties, as a rather less obvious euphemism than 'eff off' for 'fuck off'.

But we can trace the new royal and vogue term of abuse back to older and odder roots than these. 'Naf(f)' is found in collections of low-life slang from 1845 meaning the female pudend. It is probably back-slang for 'fanny'. It may have connections with cognate words such as 'naff' meaning navel, recorded before 1866, and 'naff' the hub of a wheel, found before 1796. 'Naff' may well be one of the earliest examples of coarse back-slang in the language. 'Naff off' is the Sloane imperative to 'fuck off'. 'Naff' as adjective means unfashionable, lower-class, ridiculous, and useless. When Princess Anne tells photographers to naff off, she is using older and less U English than she supposes. Does one really know what one is saying?

As a term of abuse meaning useless, 'wally' (which like naff is mainly used in British maledictions) is non-U, several classes lower than the Sloane naff. But it also has an interesting, chameleon history. In the Sixties and Seventies pop music created a new lexicon of Rockspeak. Suddenly in the Seventies at pop festivals spectators started shouting 'wally' in a loud voice, originally as a cry of approval, as the audience in another register might have shouted 'bravo' or 'bis'. When a number of trespassing hippies were arrested at the summer solstice festival near Stonehenge on Salisbury Plain, they all gave their names to the police as 'Wally', so vexing the courts, exciting the newspapers, and spreading the word. Inchoate slang is highly volatile: people pick it up, because it is trendy, without knowing quite what it means. Because of the apparent mental retardation of the shouters of 'wally', the word suddenly reversed its meaning. From being a term of approval and encouragement, it came to mean an idiot, a simpleton, or a buffoon. Every family has a wally or naff in it. In the royal family it is the Duke of York. In the Thatcher family it is Mark.

The origin of wally is obscure. In Scottish dialect for centuries 'wally' has been a general term of commendation, meaning excellent, fine-looking, or ample. Its etymology is also uncertain. Perhaps it comes from the Scottish noun 'wale', taken from the Old Norse and related to the root 'will', meaning the act of choosing or the pick of the bunch. It developed a specific meaning in Scots slang: made of china or glazed earthenware. So it came to mean an ornament or showy trifle. In Scottish 'wallies' are a cheerful name for false teeth, much favoured in that nation of eaters of sweets and cakes and drinkers of sticky mineral waters; Irn Bru is as much the Scottish national drink as whisky.

The new Rockspeak British term of abuse 'wally' meaning naff or idiot has no connection with the old Scottish word. Some say that it is a diminutive of the Christian name Walter, which was fashionable at Victorian and Edwardian baptisms, but is less so today. Others see a cognate with 'wolly', underworld slang for a uniformed policeman, especially a constable, since the Seventies: 'The wollies were out in their cars, patrolling for drunks and discontents.' In British slang 'wally' is a non-U or demotic term for an unfashionable person: somebody who is foolish, inept, or ineffectual. It is also a mild term of abuse, like naff. It has been around since the Seventies. The OED credits me with the first citation, from that Stonehenge pop festival: 'The successors to the flat-earthers are at present encamped on the perimeter of the great concentric stone circles. They choose to be known as the Wallies of Wessex, Wally being a conveniently anonymous umbrella for vulnerable individuals.'

Once wally had reversed its meaning from approval to abuse, Rockspeak followed the trend. A humper is somebody who is paid to carry gear for a group, the lowest form of roadie. A wallie humper is an egregiously incompetent one, who hinders the activities of a crew by mislaying and dropping gear, by asking stupid questions, and making cheery, irritating chit-chat, such as: 'Heh heh I'm going to sink a few tonight I can tell you mind you it doesn't affect me like that when it comes to pulling talent if you get my meaning heh heh I've got a band myself actually sort of heavy Sabbath sort of thing oops sorry mate does it hurt is it broke never mind plenty more where that came from heh heh.' To those outside the mystery of Rockspeak and Popdrivel that sounds the apotheosis of wally and naff.

Wally as northern slang for an over-sized pickled gherkin sold in fish-and-chip shops has no obvious connection with the hearty-loony, naff wally, unless it be that both are disgusting.

The predecessor of naff and wally as a term of abuse for an idiot was a twerp, quite southern English and U. You can find it *passim* in Wodehouse, for example, *Laughing Gas* (1936): 'You're simply a lot of low twerps who kidnapped me in order to cash in.' I thought that the word was dated, Bertie Wooster, and obsolescent, until in May 1987 'twerp' joined the eclectic and surprising register of unparliamentary expressions of the House of Commons. During questions to the Secretary of State for the Environment the Speaker ruled: 'I find the word twerp an inelegant parliamentary expression.' This came as a surprise to those from the fouler-mouthed North, who have always regarded twerp as one of the more affectionate vocatives, about the same as wally, less snooty than naff.

There are those who claim that twerp comes from German, and quote folk-stories of famous refugees from Nazi Germany peering over the fence of a suburban garden villa, and exclaiming: 'Ach, I see we have here the garden twerps.' The trouble with this folk etymology is that they should have said *Zwerge*, which is the German for dwarf or gnome. In German *Zwerg* can be a term of abuse, as in *Giftzwerg* or poison dwarf. The argument goes that twerps are always little, never big; and that many German words beginning with *zw* have an English equivalent beginning with *tw*, e.g. *zwanzig* (twenty), *Zweig*

6

(twig), *Zwielicht* (twilight), *Zwilch* (twill), *Zwirn* (twine), and *zwicken* (to tweak). Eric Partridge in *A Dictionary of Slang* complicates matters by linking twerp with 'twirt', Shrewsbury school slang for a cheeky small boy.

Twerp, or twirp, or more accurately twearp is an eponymous word derived from T. W. Earp of Exeter College, Oxford, who matriculated in 1911. Earp gave the word to the English language because of the philistine, Goering-like wrath he kindled in the rugger-playing hearties at Oxford, where he was President of the Union, by being the last and the wittiest of the decadents. J. R. R. Tolkien (hobbits) wrote: 'He lived in Oxford when we lived in Pusey Street (rooming with Walton, the composer, and going about with T. W. Earp, the original twerp).' A twerp is a despicable or objectionable person; an insignificant person; a nobody; a nincompoop; a naff wally. It seems to my idiolect a dated word of the Thirties, though it still lives as a term of abuse in Parliament, unless the Speaker hears you.

Erskine May, the code of practice for Parliament still named in every edition after the nineteenth-century clerk of the House of Commons, who published the first *Treatise on the Law, Privilege, Proceedings and Usage of Parliament* in 1844, rules as unparliamentary the imputation of false or unavowed motives; the misrepresentation of the language of another, and the accusation of misrepresentation; charges of uttering a deliberate falsehood; and abusive and insulting language of a nature likely to create disorder.

But the rules of unparliamentary language are as protean as abuse itself. One Speaker's expletive is another Speaker's foison. When Lord Shaftesbury took his seat as Lord Chancellor in 1672, the Duke of York called him a rascal and a villain, and got away with it. The Chancellor replied that he was obliged to His Royal Highness for not calling him a coward and a papist as well. On the other hand Lord Melbourne said he remembered a Speaker ruling out of order a reference to a member as 'a member of the opposition'. In practice wits can always slip through the interstices of the net of unparliamentary expressions. Churchill used terminological inexactitude. When Disraeli was ordered to withdraw his assertion that half the Cabinet were asses, he apologized to the Speaker, and rephrased his assertion that half the Cabinet were not asses.

Twerp has been ruled unparliamentary since 1987. The House has yet to discover whether naff and wally are too abusive for Parliament.

Twerp was broadcast by Tommy Handley, the radio comedian. People from different regions did not communicate with each other as much in the Thirties as they do today, and such cross-fertilization as there was was weakened by the war. Britons were told to ask themselves: 'Is your journey really necessary?' Radio was the great mixer. Everybody listened because there wasn't much else to do. Every week Tommy Handley ('It's That Man Again') ran the country from the Office of Twerps, foiling the best attempts of Funf, the German spy, Mona Lott, his daily, and others to frustrate his efforts. Tommy Handley was from the North, helped to write his own scripts, and is, I suspect, partly responsible for the popularity of twerps in the United Kingdom.

# ACADEMIC

## Izing on the academic cake

'You and I come by road or rail, but
economists travel on infrastructure.'
Margaret Thatcher, 1985

Academics speak a different language from the rest of us.
Sometimes they are intelligible, and funny. Lionel Trilling,
Professor of English at Columbia University, critic, and card-
carrying intellectual, fell into competition with Jacques Barzun,
also a Columbia professor, when a student, discussing Malthus's *Essay on Population*, quoted the motto of the Order of the
Garter: *Honi soit qui mal y pense*; shame on him who thinks ill of
it. Lapsing into the register of academic paronomasia, Barzun
exclaimed: *Honi soit que Malthus pense*. Quick as a computer,
Trilling rejoined: *Honi soit qui mal* thus puns. There you have
intellectuals speaking the same language as Frank Muir and
Denis Norden, the English comedians who are academics
*manqués*.

One of the ways that the language jungle grows is by
academic jargon. Specialists in the new disciplines and technologies coin words to describe their theories and inventions,
and occasionally to impress outsiders and grant-allocators. As
the sergeant said to the new recruit preparing for his first
Battalion Parade: 'Bullshit baffles brains.' And then the rest of
us a bit later, led by those thieving magpies the journalists,
pick up the new jargon, and sometimes even get hold of the
wrong end of the stick.

Being a generous fellow, I am inclined to let the specialists
get on with their own jargons; though even I raise an eyebrow
at the otiose gibberish perpetrated by lexiphobe and illiterate
computer people. Who apart from them needs 'access' as a
verb? Who needs 'format' to mean design, as in: 'Form X will
be formatted as Form Y but only half the size.' I work for the

9

computer these days, and all a format means for me is a useful shorthand device that tells the clever little machine to arrange the words that follow in a regular pattern of type, size, and spacing to conform to a regular input command. Who needs format? Answer: only dumbos carried away by the exuberance of their anti-word, anti-intelligence shorthand; or somebody who has just tried to explain in simple English what a format does. No doubt they could have coined a prettier word. But they didn't.

Nevertheless, the language belongs to all of us, not just to technologists and jargonauts. It behoves us to keep a beady eye on new words that are coming into use without any obvious need. Look out for the invasion of 'valorization'. *Collins* defines 'to valorize': to fix and maintain an artificial price for (a commodity) by governmental action. *Chambers* on 'valorization': fixing of price. *Longman* on 'to valorize': to (try to) enhance the price, value, or status of, by organized (usually governmental) action. For example: using subsidies to valorize coffee.

I have a friend who edits a chemical journal: he keeps on stumbling over the word with his hovering red pencil. For example: 'The valorization of carbon monoxide' (meaning its conversion into something useful, such as methanol). OK; OK: methanol is useful as a solvent, antifreeze, or a raw material in chemical synthesis, the sort of activity that Primo Levi, but few other industrial chemists, could make fascinating. I know, because I have just looked it up, and I prefer to believe the chemists that methanol is useful rather than go into the matter. I dare say that there is room for a word meaning 'making something useful out of' in chemistry. That is the chemists' affair, thank Saints Cosmas and Damian, patron saints of test tubes. I suppose that the dreadful word has emanated, like a foul miasma, from the Eurocrats of the European Economic Community, that midden of pretentious jargon made muckier by the need to include the gobbledygook of twelve nations and many languages.

Economists claim that 'valorization' has a modest but useful place in the toolbox of English. Maybe what we have here is the common process of American academics naturalizing a fairly ordinary German word to give it a special meaning in scientific or would-be scientific writing. Do we hear echoes in valorization of both *Aufwertung* (to exploit and increase the value of, as in *Aufwertungssteuer*, alias Blessed Value Added Tax), and *Verwertung* (utilization, to make an evaluation of, to assess)? I'm not sure. You have me there, *Junker*. But if academics need a piece of jargon, they will have it, whatever the rest of us say.

In fact the French technocrats, than whom there come no more technocratic, not even in Japan, claim the honour of having introduced 'valorization' to an astonished world. *Valoriser* and *valorisation* have appeared in French dictionaries as rare and slightly pseud words for a number of years. In the Seventies and Eighties they have become vogue hurray-words for Frog technocrats. They launch research programmes where *valorisation* is used *passim* as a slogan or shibboleth: *la valorisation de la biomasse; valorisation de CO*. It means to convert into something of more value, or of added value. The words *valeur ajoutée* are used in the same context, and often in the same place as tautologies. The technocratic jargon has replaced the older, woollier, layman's meaning of the words, such as it was.

However, as happens with technical jargon, 'valorization' is spreading out from its scientific origin. I have recently come across the word used with an entirely different meaning. This was in the report of a working party set up by the Association of University Teachers at the University of Sussex to investigate 'concerns currently being expressed about sexual harassment on the campus'. The report (which provided very little evidence for the existence of such harassment, but discussed at length the circumstances in which it might occur) includes the sentence: 'And, in certain situations, where the tutor is an attractive, sympathetic, and charismatic figure, it can be hard for the students not to respond *as women* accepting *valorization* for their femininity, for their intellectual efforts and ideas.'

This suggests that 'to valorize' has acquired a new, pretty technical, very trendy meaning among sociologists, those slovenly users of English, implying, I suppose, 'to value (for)', or possibly just 'to evaluate'. It is an impressive word. It will probably come into general use, possibly in both its sociological and its Eurocratic meanings, as in: 'The visiting sociologist valorized the newly discovered tribe for its primitiveness; but they valorized her in their wok or cooking-pot.' Remind me never to use the word. Remind me to strike it out of copy from anybody, be he or she as important even as the Queen or the Archbishop of Canterbury.

In general we should gang warily before putting our foot down upon what we consider an ugly new usage by technologists. The language belongs to all of us, even technocrats, not just to those of us who have access to the public prints. Here are some other new academic words that I think bear watching. They have been collected over the last few years from academic papers, seminars, and more general sources. Some of them serve good purposes, but are nevertheless ugly (there is an aesthetic judgement for you; language is coined not by aesthetes, but by people at the lab bench or the computer terminal). Others arise from the manic desire to 'ize' any nouns found loitering. Some are the products of disturbed minds. It is interesting to note that a lot of 'izing' occurs in linguistics and phonetics. It is a disgrace and a tragedy that the academic specialities dealing with that very important subject, the English language, have become so inaccessible and rebarbative to its other joint-owners.

Concertize (to give a concert: Canadian); co-ordinatize (to impose a co-ordinate system); Multiculturalism Minister (Canadian); procedurealize and procedureing; lexicalize; bourgeoisification; discretize; Christianize; diphthongization; pharingealization; intervocalically; hypothesization; fuzzification (from fuzzy logic, and non-diophantine number theory); Mitterandize (French politics); trainability; intercomprehensibility; creolization; glottalization; labialization; velarization; dealphabetize; alphabeticizer; binarization; calculatable; decontextualized; pidginization; associationism; dichotomizer (for cutting avocado pears in half?); rhotacization; psychologism; maximalistically; particularization; minimalistically; grammaticalize; jargonize (!); communicology; parallelization; prioritized; fricativized; systematicity; historicist; routinized; euthing (performing euthanasia); objectivication; comprehensivization (British state schools); recognology; cognitronics; tailorable; summating; electronical; casualize; Godelization; chaology (the mathematical study of chaos); complexification (nothing to do with making something more difficult); pressurization; spontain (verb: a favourite of Jonathan Miller); diagrammed; mechanizability; collocationally. (That's enough daft academic words – Ed.)

I am on the side of academics. I think that on the whole what they do is a far, far better thing than the rest of us. I can see that in the heat of their intellectual trail-blazing they grab the putty language and twist it to suit their urgent needs. I nevertheless think that they should stand back occasionally, and consider what they are trying to say in terms intelligible to 'readers' of the *Sun*. There is no need to throw up our hands in despair that academics and academics in other fields and laymen no longer speak the same language. It would be absurdly populist and philistine to suppose that everything can be explained in terms that the ordinary *homme moyen intellectuel* can grasp. Some of us have no heads for numbers theory or the wilder shores of nuclear physics. But one of the functions of language is to explain.

Here are a couple of examples of Sociologese that I have bumped into recently, and reckon I could rewrite in plain English:

'A participative political structure provides the mechanism for response to a conflict-generating event and should result in greater participation in the controversy.'

Define for me, pray, for starters, in what way a conflict-generating event differs from a boring old conflict.

'It is suggested that the specificity of goals characteristic of formal organizations serves to negate individual action-alternatives.'

Are these sentences saying anything? Or are they instances of verbal auto-intoxication resulting from the rapture of the depths of obscurity. If the former (as I see through a glass, darkly), I reckon their authors should employ me as a rewrite man.

# AIDS

## Aids memoir

*Brevis esse laboro,*
*obscurus fio; sectantem levia nervi*
*deficiunt animique.*
'When I try to be brief, I become obscure.
Aiming at smoothness, I fail in force and
fire.'
Ars Poetica, 25–8, about 19 BC and before 17 BC, by
Quintus Horatius Flaccus

Acronyms, pronounceable words formed from initial letters or parts of words, are useful jargon when used sensibly as a form of shorthand, either for all of us, or for the sectional vocabulary of a science, art, trade, class, sect, profession, or other private team of specialists. They save time. Strictly speaking, an acronym is a compound of curtailed words that can be pronounced as a separate word, such as Unesco. The Greek elements of acronym mean 'topmost names', i.e. initial letters. Initial letters that cannot be pronounced, such as KKK or MCC, are not true acronyms, but abbreviations or initials.

Happy the organization of which the initial letters form a pronounceable word, like Nato or Dotipos (Deep Ocean Test Instrument Placement and Observation System). Unhappy the organization of which the initial letters are unpronounceable, like EEC or RFU. A good acronym can make an otherwise gloomy and banal institution, such as Nalgo, or Nacods, or Cohse sound, well, cosy. It would make the National Union of Miners and the National Union of Journalists a bit more lovable if people started pronouncing their names, NUM and NUJ, as acronyms.

Some jargons, particularly DefenceSpeak or Pentagonese, go too far with acronyms and abbrevs, so that their technical papers are jungles of upper-case initial letters impenetrable by the outsider. This is caused partly by the normal tendency of

14

experts to show off to those outside their mystery; and partly by euphemism. They are talking about killing people or blowing up the world. A cheerful-sounding acronym acts as a smokescreen.

Language is a wild creature. It grows and changes untidily as people use it. Nevertheless, I wish to complain about the new medical acronym, Aids; not that my complaint will do a blind bit of good. It is clearly a condition to be avoided at all costs. The acronym represents Acquired Immune (or Immuno-) Deficiency Syndrome. The condition is thought to be caused by a virus, in which the body's white cells lose their ability to protect against infection. My objection to the acronym is that it sounds rather friendly, and creates confusion with a number of other similar words.

For a start there is the word 'aid', which came into English from French more than five centuries ago, and has acquired manifold general, technical, and historical meanings. Then there is your 'aide', which is a ragingly fashionable vogue term and creature in political and business circles. This aide came into the language from American more than two centuries ago. For example, from Fenimore Cooper's *The Last of the Mohicans*: 'Attended by the aide of Montcalm with his guard'.

Aids is already an acronym in DefenceSpeak. It stands for Aircraft Integrated Data System and also, with acronym on acronym, confusion worse confounded, Air Force Intelligence Data-handling System. Aid is also an acronym for: Aeronautical Inspection Department; Aeronautical Inspection Directorate, the United States agency concerned with airframes, power plants, and guided weapons; Agricultural Industrial Development; Aircraft Intelligence Department; Army Intelligence Department; the American Institute of Directors; the French *Association Internationale pour le Développement*; Acute Infectious Disease; Agency for International Development; and, last but not least, Artificial Insemination by Donor.

The possibilities for confusion and misunderstanding are considerable. In practice most acronyms tend to be used by specialists in quite narrow contexts and registers; aeronautical inspectors do not mix up their acronym with agricultural industrialists. The language would be simpler if people were thriftier about coining so many acronyms. But the world is not a simple place; and acronyms are designed to save their users time; if they do not, they will not take.

Doctors tend to be logophiles and wordsmiths, perhaps because their profession is fundamentally mechanical, and they need some cultural interest. It would be a good idea if we could get them to take more care about their nomenclature. Perhaps the BMA (British Medical Council) and NHS (National Health Service), in consultation with equivalent bodies in English-speaking and other countries, should take on the responsibility of coining an unambiguous name for a new disease, or whenever the jargon requires a new word. I dare say we should have some linguistic philosophers in on the act.

That is not the way language works. English is not a market garden growing in neat rows, but a luxuriant and pullulating wilderness. Words are what they are, and their consequences will be what they will be. If they serve no purpose, they die. The dictionaries are full of dead words that have lost their functions. I dare say that when Aids is better understood, it may be renamed on the basis of its cause or mechanism. In the meantime we have to learn to live with Aids, linguistically.

Aide is a popular Americanism for an important person's adviser or counsellor, someone at the right hand of a president, prime minister, or City tycoon. I can see the attraction for headline writers, because it has four letters instead of seven or ten. If you have to put 'counsellor' in a headline, forget it. Headline English, especially from the tabloid papers, which have bigger and therefore shorter headlines, has had a profound influence on English since the war. Many Americanisms are expressive and enrich the language. I am not sure that 'aide' does; as one of the grand, old, bossy news editors said: 'By trying to be brief, I become obscure.' The Queen does have aides-de-camp drawn from the three services. But when *The Times* describes Her Majesty's Private Secretary (her principal personal counsellor) as an aide, and even the Mistress of the Robes as an aide, it confuses the offices, and makes the hair of our older and more courtierly readers stand on end. Lesser blats without the law, such as the *Sun* and *The Independent*, imitate us. And, before you know where you are, throughout the pubs of England jolly jokes are being made, linking royalty with Aids. We should watch it.

'Sick as a parrot' is an example of recent slang to make fun of dire disease. For once we can date the arrival of a cliché precisely. In the early 1970s there were a number of heavily publicized cases of travellers from West Africa dying of psittacosis or parrot fever. This is an infectious disease of parrots and budgerigars due to a virus-like organism of the genus Chlamydia. It can be transmitted to man, and causes headache, bleeding from the nose, shivering, fever, complications involving the lungs, pneumonia, and death. The feather-headed pop papers were full of squawking headlines about the unusual and alarming disease.

This was when the topical catch-phrase 'as sick as a parrot' came into vogue in the United Kingdom. It was used particularly by footballers and their managers after a defeat to express extreme chagrin. It is no longer novel, but on its way to becoming an old joke that dies of shame.

Other creatures beside the parrot that are used as similes for sickness include sick as a cat, a dog, a horse, and a rat. 'Sick as a cat' has the nuance of being extremely annoyed. Philippic vets assert that a horse is incapable of vomiting. Accordingly Northamptonshire dialect is logical, in that it applies 'sick as a horse' to a person exceedingly sick without vomiting. In general, 'sick as a horse' connotes extreme discomfort. An Oz variant is 'as sick as a blackfellow's dog'. Wodehouse used 'sick as mud' to describe somebody feeling more or less like something the Pure Food Committee has rejected.

It is possible that the nauseating slur on parrots has older roots than the psittacosis incidents of the 1970s. Aphra Behn used the simile 'as melancholy as a sick parrot', in the same way that Shakespeare used the colloquial simile 'as melancholy as a gib-cat'. Other old variants are 'as melancholy as a collier's horse' and 'a sick monkey'.

For parrot I prefer the archaic name, widely diversified throughout Europe, with Arabic and Persian cognates, popinjay. Parrot is probably nothing more than a friendly appellative use of Pierrot, the French diminutive for Pierre or Peter. I do not think that we have a hope of reviving popinjay. But 'sick as a parrot' sounds very old-fashioned. I do not think that the boring old catch-phrase will survive for much longer.

Cryptic brevity is one cause of obscurity in acronyms and Headline English, as in FIFTH ARMY PUSH BOTTLES UP GERMANS, and SQUAD HELPS DOG BITE VICTIM. The danger of amphibology is there with Aids. Another cause of obscurity is *double entendre* that jerks a dormant metaphor to life. An example is the current passion of headline-writers for loopholes. Loopholes may, I suppose, be legal or illegal, as they tend to be in headlines, but when legal loopholes hamper or hold something up, as they do all the time, confusing images of lambs mating with tigers arise in my mind's eye.

'Painters and poets have always had a right to try anything once,' the megalomaniac old news editor wrote. So have journos. They are the innovators of language. In fact, most of what we do is repetitive, copying out old cuttings, summarizing what somebody else has written, rehashing cold cabbage. But we claim the licence to write what no man has written before. And sometimes we go too far, and end up with egg on our faces, and absurdity on our word processors.

As that grand old news editor declaimed: 'You can go as far as you want, but not so far as to mate the savage with the tame, or to have serpents copulating with birds, or lambs with tigers.' He wrote his advice before the Surrealists and Picasso; and Ovid seems to have ignored it with some success.

I woke up with a start the other day when I read, in a report from the School of Oriental and African Studies: 'If we can assume that the Report epiphanizes good managerial practice . . .' I suspect that the whimsical secretary had his tongue in his cheek, and that what he meant was: 'If we can assume that the Report is a Manifestation from on High (sc. The University Grants Committee) of good managerial practice.' If so, it was a nice scholarly joke. But I am keeping my eyes open for epiphanies and epiphanizing, to see whether they catch on in the blats. What happens far more often than some adventurous Amerigo Vespucci of the public prints writing something that nobody has thought of saying before is that we read something that strikes us as clever, crib it, and before you know where you are the whole Fleet Street pack is baying it until you are sick of it as a parrot.

For example, 'summit' is a well-established mountaineering metaphor for meetings between heads of government, shorter and snappier for headlines than meeting or conference. It came into vogue, I think, with the meetings between Eisenhower and Khrushchev. An interesting inchoate use came from Winston Churchill in 1950, deploring the Cold War, recalling his wartime meetings with Stalin and Roosevelt, and calling for 'a parley at the summit'. A meeting may take place at the summit, but it is not itself a summit in the extreme acceptance of the word. So when a broadcaster on the BBC, discussing the manoeuvring between Israel and Egypt over a projected meeting between Peres and Mubarak, said: 'Mubarak may be holding up the summit,' I flickered. Mubarak is widely regarded as rather a weak president. In the new, abbreviated meeja headline use, he appears to be not lacking in physical strength, but a modern Atlas.

# AMERICAN IDIOM

## Getting hold of the wrong end of the stix

'The American language is in a state of flux
based on the survival of the unfittest.'
*The Sunday Times*, 1966, Cyril Connolly

Only a fool complains about new words coming into British
English from the United States merely because they are American. There are more of them, of many races and cultures,
speaking and writing the language over there. They are notably
versatile and innovative with the mother tongue. Only a trendy
adopts a new usage just because it is American. He or she
often gets it wrong, so giving the rest of us a giggle, and a
certain *Schadenfreude* at seeing an Emperor of Language in new
clothes.

The time has come to tackle the fashionable nuisance of
Brownie points. When people use it as a term of commendation, we must stop and consider what they are saying. A
Brownie point is a fancied unit of credit and approval. It is
earned by a person for doing the proper or expected thing. For
example, from *Village Voice*: 'I'll get Brownie points for helping
him'; 'A place where you get big shiny Brownie points, cash,
sex, and adulation.' It is a vogue phrase that has established
itself over the past few years, first of all in the United States,
and now in the United Kingdom, where it rages like fowl pest.

The official explanation, usually taken for granted, is that it
comes from supposed merit points awarded to what Americans
call a Girl Scout Brownie for a good deed, such as helping a
little old lady across the road, for promotion to Junior Girl
Scout. Being a Brownie is an authoritarian business. The
founder, Baden-Powell, set the tone: 'In the Brownie Pack
every Brownie obeys the wishes of the leader.' Brownies',
Guides', Cubs', and Scouts' honour are the only pledges
deliberately sown among children by adults to have taken root.

I was never a Brownie. But I was a Wolf Cub, until the Cheam School pack was disbanded with dishonour for setting the woods near Greenham Common on fire. And what we worked away for was not points, but badges, toggles, or possibly woggles, and a smile from Akela, the pack leader, with whom we were all in love. I do not believe that Brownies get awarded things called Brownie points either.

As it happens there is another explanation of Brownies or Brownie points. This goes that around the turn of the century a superintendent of the Pullman Car Company called Brown instituted a system of demerit points that employees could be awarded for bad conduct or poor performance. Three such points, soon called Brownies, cost a day's pay; five meant a week's suspension; and ten brought the sack. In this explanation, the expression has reversed its meaning during passage across the Atlantic. However, it smells suspiciously of folk etymology to me. Superintendent Brown is dreadfully elusive. And Americans use Brownie points as marks of credit as well as demerit.

If you are going to take a serious interest in slang, you need a dirty mind. A quick look in any dictionary of slang will show that any expression with 'brown' in it is more likely to be scatological than to have anything to do with Girl Scout Brownies. These matters of vernacular are seldom susceptible to proof, because they are invented and popularized by the non-writing classes, and only written down some time later when a scribe with an interest in language comes along. But I regret to say that the term 'Brownie point' is more likely to be military than scouting, and to derive from brown-nose, brown-noser, or brown tongue (cf. bum-sucker), an essential part of the ambitious officer's repertoire. For example: 'He got there by being a pious and effective brown-nose'; 'He's just like any other person who's in a position to screw you. You gotta brown nose.'

I have a witty American acquaintance who lives in darkest Perthshire. Her neighbours have been asking her for years, with bright eyes and hoping for a Brownie point, what she thinks of living in Scotland. She habitually replies: 'It's really the Boondocks, isn't it?' They purr, mistaking this for an American superlative of commendation. She may have to find a new reply soon, since American television has started to bring this bit of slang, often abbreviated to the Boonies, into Britain. The Boonies, like Brownies, are another bit of military slang. War and military service are great manure for slang, because they bring together a rich compost of people, and put them in exciting and terrifying situations for which their civilian vocabularies are inadequate. Before and during parts of the last war GIs stationed in the Philippines were sometimes, when unlucky, sent on duty to a mountain region, the back of beyond, called Bundok in Tagalog. So: 'The people out there in the Boonies may not know you're past it.' Hence a Boondocker is a person who lives or works in a remote region, especially by preference. Boondock as adjective means 'suitable for rough outdoor use'. For example: 'Marines use Boondock clothes and Boondock shoes for hikes and manoeuvres.' Boondockers or Boon dockers are heavy-duty military shoes or boots. The Boonies means 'in the sticks', another agreeable piece of American slang that sometimes gets misunderstood in Britain. If you lived out of town in early America, you lived in the woods, in a log cabin, I dare say: in the sticks.

Analogously for the same reason American politicians when electioneering or going on a political tour are said to go on the stump or to be stumping, in Illinois, say. When Americans lived in the sticks, politicians stood on a tree stump to address them. When a countrywide network of small rural TV stations turned down a TV series that had not been very successful in the big cities, one of the headlines summed the matter up succinctly: STIX NIX PIX. Americans are inventive with headlines. The story of the madman escaping from an asylum, breaking into a launderette, raping one of the customers, and running off, inspiring the headline NUT SCREWS WASHER AND BOLTS is, I hope, fiction.

Another American term much used and often misunderstood in Britain is 'rain check'. In the United States giving and taking a rain check originated from the civilized custom of issuing free tickets for the postponed match to spectators whose enjoyment of a baseball game had been interrupted by bad weather. Often the words 'rain check' are stamped on a detachable part of the ticket. If the game is called off on account of rain, the rain check can be torn off and used as a free admission to the next game on the same field. The phrase has been widely adapted for other occasions than in the bleachers or on the grandstand. 'Give me a rain check' means 'I really don't want to have lunch with you.'

Many British are unaware of the American idiom of using check to mean ticket. They assume that check means test. Consequently, they use 'to take a rain check' to mean 'to test whether it is raining or will rain'; and, by extension, to check whether a future event of almost any kind is likely to occur.

The process of Brits screwing up an American idiom because of unfamiliarity with American ways is also happening to 'street-wise' (or street-smart, or street-bright), which means cunning and clever in various practical ways, especially in the street culture of the urban ghetto: *Toronto Life*: 'A place for very sophisticated, street-bright people.' 'Street-wise' was coined in the United States in the middle 1960s for the urban jargons of social workers and journalists. The Americans use the phrase to mean the quality of being familiar with local people and their problems; wise to the ways of people who live on the city streets, that is – cities being cities – the poor, the homeless, the petty criminals, and so on. It is a desirable compassionate quality for social workers and aspiring politicians to pretend to have, anyway. Here is an example of the politician, from the *New York Times Magazine*: 'No mayor can function effectively unless he has around him competent and street-wise people who can assume much of his responsibility.'

It has come to mean also, in parallel, the knowing quality of being able to look after oneself on the streets of New York: the toughness that has enabled city kids from Dickens to Runyon to today to survive in the concrete jungle.

Here is an example of the Sociologese street-wise from the *New Yorker*: 'A social worker therefore has to be wary as well as trustful, be security-minded as well as loving, and be street-wise as well as compassionate. This new style of social work has been evolving during the last ten years or so on the streets of New York.'

The phrase is well-known in the United States. It is less well-known over here, and is being picked up by scavengers of language and used in odd new ways. Some of them take it to mean sophisticated, whatever that means. But fashion writers, those gaudy and silly peacocks of English prose, have adopted 'street-wise' to mean an individual way of wearing extremely expensive clothes. I do not see the necessity. Why cannot they write 'panache'? Or, if that is too long and exotic a word for their readers, why cannot they use 'dash' or 'style'? Why, for that matter, can they not write about ordinary clothes that a *femme moyenne luxueuse* might be able to afford? But that is another question. There is a certain agreeable irony in our native fashion hackettes, fearful harpies, swooping down on a new piece of American slang, and getting it all wrong. The Americans have done it often enough with British slang.

The whole point about fashion is that it is here today and gone tomorrow, thus making a living for the manufacturers, puffers, and prophets of fashion. In the States, I regret to have to tell our native users of the phrase, 'street-wise' is already old-hat and last year's fashion. The new slang is 'street-smarts', a noun, not an adjective. Here is an example from the *New Yorker*, that useful repository of linguistic fashion: 'Such young women (who teach at a private school) refuse to live in New York as though it were the Peter and Paul Fortress and they were enemies of the Czar. To be free, however, requires street-smarts, the cunning of the survivor.'

What do you want to bet that within five years our own dear Glenda Slags will not have adopted 'street-smarts' to mean absurdly expensive gear for women?

Misunderstanding of idiom and slang in both directions across the Atlantic is a rich source of change in English and the gaiety of nations.

# ARCHITECTALK

## Hab and hab not

'The doctor can bury his mistakes, but an architect can only advise his clients to plant vines.'
New York Times Magazine, October 1953, Frank Lloyd Wright (1867–1959)

'What is proposed is like a monstrous carbuncle on the face of a much loved and elegant friend.'
Prince of Wales, speech to RIBA on the proposed extension to the National Gallery, 30 May 1984

The jargon of architects is very ancient, and, like other ancient modes of speech, very elliptical. We laymen are half in love with it, from the poetry of the classical orders of columns, triglyph to architrave, to the stark cubic and linguistic simplicity of the Bauhaus. But we must not let them blind us with science. We have to live with and work in their mistakes. We do not have to take their professional mystification and obfuscation seriously. Even architects are human.

In 1937 Frank Lloyd Wright built a house in Wisconsin for an industrialist called Hibbard Johnson and his family. One rainy evening Johnson was entertaining some important guests for dinner when the roof began to leak. The water seeped through the ceiling directly above Johnson himself, dripping steadily onto his bald head. In a rage he telephoned Wright in Phoenix, Arizona: 'Frank, you built this beautiful house for me and we enjoy it very much. But I have told you the roof leaks, and right now I am with some friends and distinguished guests and it is leaking right on top of my head.' Everybody heard Wright's reply: 'Well, Hib, why don't you move your chair?'

That is a lot less pretentious than much architectural gobble-degook. It is all plain man's monosyllables, and full of good sense. The better the writer, the shorter his words. Well, up to a point, Lord Copper. It depends on the context, readership, subject, and idiolect of the writer. It would be a crying shame to deprive Gibbon, or Sam Johnson, or Bernard Levin, for that matter, of his polysyllabic, and often effective, and often funny sesquipedalianisms. Jeeves goes in for them as well. For most of us short words that do the same job are preferable to long words. Love of the long variant is usually the sign of a pompous or insecure writer showing off.

Thus, architects and civil engineers prefer 'rehabilitate' to 'repair'; it sounds somehow more impressive. Any fool can repair bits of a house; we all try to occasionally, usually in my case with unsatisfactory or calamitous results. But it takes an expensive professional to rehabilitate. It was similar love of the long word that made the American ambassador speak about the refurbishment of his London residence to the Queen, when all that he meant was the redecoration of his house.

Architects defend their long words. They would, wouldn't they? They claim that rehabilitate is more than a pompous substitute for repair. You rehabilitate when an old building needs to be repaired and also improved, so as to be made habitable for today, for instance by the installation of missing amenities of the type included as a matter of course in a new house, such as a bathroom, an inside lavatory, modern electric wiring (or sometimes electric wiring of any kind), thermal insulation, or even a damp course. You refurbish where a building designed for a particular use, though in good decorative order, needs to be made fit for another. It is their jargon, and they must use it as they want. I observe that a good many architects suffer from the vice of preferring the long word, irrespective of meaning, in order to impress the profane punters. As a profession they take themselves inordinately seriously, and are dimly aware that they are taken with considerable contempt by the general public.

In a recent issue of an American architectural and engineering journal I bumped into an unusual example of a long word truncated in the headline: BRIDGE'S FALLING ARCHES REHABBED. What in the world is the point of favouring a long word such as rehabilitation if you are then going to amputate its tail? At first I thought that this was just a hard-pressed subeditor doing some ingenious cutting in order to squeeze a thirteen-letter word into a headline. But in fact 'rehab' is the in-word in architectural and engineering circles in the United States, which means that it soon will be in the United Kingdom. In such matters the British feel that as American technology and know-how are better, so must their jargon be more impressive. Here are some examples from the Eighties: 'If I can persuade him to sell for ten thousand dollars each, I'll toss this house in at ten thousand dollars. That will give us fifteen thousand dollars more for rehab.' Rehab has become a transitive verb, as in my original headline: 'Solid 1890s structures, built practically with slave labour, now rehabbed to perfection.' And it has produced the professional rehabber: 'We can and should shorten time for developers and rehabbers.' Rehab seems to me a very rare example of a word that has first of all become popular because of its length, and then been abbreviated.

The architects' jargon of rehabbing has no connection other than etymological with the Scottish Writers to the Signet (ancient and pompous monopoly of solicitors) jargon of 'habile'. They both come from the Latin *habilis*, meaning competent or having ability. Habile came into Late Middle English, but it died out in England. But it survived among the Writers to the Signet; they are a conservative lot, who love the long word that separates them from Lesser Breeds without the Law. In Scottish law habile still means admissible or valid, apt or competent for some purpose. Lawyers in Scotland refer to a habile or sufficient title for transferring property. They may even generalize by saying that matters have been attended to in a habile and competent manner. They would probably only so generalize if they were showing off. On balance their old habile is an elegant word, whereas the new habs are not. But elegance is not the principal function of words. And, in any case, the judgement of what is elegant is a subjective opinion. One man's habile is another man's rehab.

Architects and Writers to the Signet are ornaments of society and useful professionals. Chaos would be come again without them; or at any rate damp living and the law of the Border reiver. But they are at their most endearing when they stop putting on airs and admit that they are human. Addison Mizner, brother of Wilson Mizner, the American writer and wit, was a prodigiously successful architect in the United States at the beginning of this century. In spite of complete lack of formal qualifications, he sprang to wealth and fame as the chief architect for those who bought property in Florida during the great property boom. The rich and celebrated and fashionable and beautiful people scrambled for the cachet of a residence designed by Mizner, in spite of practical drawbacks. Carried away by the aesthetics of architecture, Mizner once forgot to put a staircase between the first and second floors of one of his houses. One client, William Gray Warden, asked for a copy of the blueprints of the house he was having built at Palm Beach in order to show off to his friends. Mizner remonstrated: 'Why, the house isn't built yet. Construction first, blueprints afterwards.' He was unconsciously echoing the Queen of Hearts in *Alice*: 'No, no – sentence first, verdict afterwards.'

# CITY LINGO

## Banging on

'The faults of the burglar are the qualities of
the financier.'
*Major Barbara*, preface, 1907, by Bernard Shaw

'Money is better than poverty, if only for
financial reasons.'
*Without Feathers*, 1972, by Woody Allen

More people speak it than ever before; more scientists, technologists, trend-setters, and other neologists are busy; and the
odds are that more new words, for what they are worth, come
into the language annually than in any previous year.

Some of them are likely to have a short life, though a merry
one: for instance, Ramboism, Ramboesque, and other dumb
macho derivatives from the film, *Rambo, First Blood Part II*. The
adjectives signify warlike aggression carried out in an ignorant
and gung-ho fashion.

They are patronizing British adjectives, since John Rambo
(played by Sylvester Stallone in the film) had plenty of academic and linguistic qualifications. His improbable adventures,
rescuing prisoners-of-war still held in Vietnam, called for
superhuman, Tarzan-like physical accomplishments, because
he always operated against absurd odds. He just didn't speak
a lot. The words were adapted into ephemeral journalese
rapidly. The *New Statesman* gave us Rambotha and the *Economist* gave us Ramboer, both referring to President P. W. Botha
of South Africa. Whether the words survive in the English
lexicon depends on whether the films are masterpieces which
will be repeated and become classics for new generations. The
prudent man would guess that they are not, and that Ramboism will be a meaningless word within five years.

Other new words are never going to make it into the big
time of the central core of the language. For example, in 1986

President Reagan gave 'flaky' a temporary popularity in British English, when he used it to describe Colonel Gadaffi as having a screw loose. But the American authorities disagree profoundly about whether flaky means mad, unstable, unreliable, eccentric, colourful, or carefree. I do not see such an imprecise word catching on.

Other new words continue long-running trends. For instance, the proliferation of such new sexual neutralizations as houseperson, barperson, superperson, and craftsperson; or the spread of the jocular *Private Eye* suffix -ette, as in pupilette.

Other new words are mere trivial crazes: for example, at present Sloane slang for shooting pheasants is biffing; Sloane slang for indoor sports with birds is boffing. Neither will last.

One innovation of the Eighties is that the City of London, previously a stagnant pond of tradition, where men wore top hats for no reason that anybody could remember, suddenly became a rich source of new English. This was caused by the Big Bang, a term extended from the deregulation of the London Stock Exchange to describe any fundamental or far-reaching change in organization. Before 1986 Big Bang meant either a theory to explain the creation of the universe, or was a colloquial term for a nuclear explosion. In October 1986 the removal of all restrictive and old-boy-network practices that had protected the London Stock Exchange as a home for heroes, or at any rate Old Etonians, was an important feature of the Conservative government's efforts to produce a free market wherever possible. When the Americans deregulated their exchange in 1975, their code-name for the operation was Mayday. Big Bang is livelier. Both have contributed to innovation in language, rather than conservatism, which is the normal linguistic function of financial institutions.

The process by which the City of London became a fully international market, retaining its place as a world financial centre in spite of the nation's relative industrial decline, gave the language other fall-out, which may stick, or be as ephemeral as Ramboism. It included Golden Hallo (a large signing-on fee to bribe an employee to join a company); and Golden Parachute (a contractual guarantee of compensation to an employee if he or she gets the old heave-ho, or is demoted following a takeover or merger). These two joined the existing Golden Handcuffs (a large bribe paid to persuade an employee

not to desert to the opposition). As the activities of the City
and other money markets are absurd, or at any rate unlike
normal life, so is their vocabulary extravagant.

There was much green-eyed envy about the monstrous
salaries paid to City Yuppies. A survey found that 7 per cent
of City executives earned more than £100,000 a year; and one
top dealer on a profit-related bonus scheme was reported to be
earning more than £1 million. Mammon makes you sick, if you
let the brute. The magazine *Business* reported: 'Golden Hand-
shakes and Golden Handcuffs are now part of every headhunter's vocabulary.' For the unworldly among you, a headhunter
is an employment agency, parasitic upon the City and other
such places, which makes a fat living by bribing executives to
leave their firms and come to others.

Other coinages by the chattering City include SEAQ, or
Stock Exchange Automated Quotations (a computerized
system of displaying share prices and recording transactions
that is the heart of Stock Exchange dealings after Big Bang);
TAURUS, or Transfer and Automated Registration of Uncerti-
fied Stock (a computerized system for transferring and register-
ing shares without the need for share certificates); share shop
(an establishment where shares can be bought and sold by the
public quickly, with the minimum of formality, and without
investment advice); single capacity (the demarcated role of a
stockbroker or stockjobber on the London Stock Exchange
before Big Bang); and dual capacity (the double role, incorpo-
rating the jobs previously allotted separately to a stockbroker
and a stockjobber). The shoaling of new language from the
City and other financial institutions in the Eighties is not a sign
that such places have suddenly become linguistically inventive.
They are in it principally for the money. But busy changes in
institutions inevitably produce busy changes in the lexicon.
Words are the daughters of earth; things, including money,
are the sons of heaven.

Another money-market word that is becoming a weasel
word fast is arbitrage, popularized in the States as arb. Arbitrage is now used by the Americans, and, apparently somewhat reluctantly, by *The Times*, to describe the insidious
activities of insiders in the stock market. The latter, who are
engaged in shady and possibly criminal activities, profit from
their secret knowledge of forthcoming events. The insider

needs only an envelope, an elementary knowledge of arithme-
tic, a minimum of luck, and a warthog's sense of honesty. In
practice and linguistics arbitrage is a perfectly respectable
function of the money game, which has flourished for at least
a hundred years, probably longer for gold. It is the practice of
switching funds between two or more markets whose price
variations are published. Rapid communications, even in the
days of the telegraph, made it possible to profit from the
variations, often making use of exchange variations also.
Money was made by brains, effort, the gambling instinct, and
a race against time (not all that much brains). The result was a
contribution to the functioning of the international price
system. Anybody could have a go, if he or she wanted to try.
Arbitrage is not essentially crooked. It is just one of the sillier
faces of capitalism. Capitalism is a vulgar, materialistic, philistine system of running an economy. It is just that other
systems, this side of Utopia, are worse.

As well as throwing up new words, the financial revolution
in the money markets is altering old ones. For example, we
seem to be falling into confusion about the Prodigal Son,
perhaps because we no longer read the Bible as religiously as
our mothers and fathers. You remember the story: rich man's
younger son – journey into far country – wasted substance in
riotous living – etc.? 'Parable of the prodigal son' is the chapter
heading in *The Authorized Version*. *The New English Bible* heads
the passage 'Journeys and encounters'. *The New Testament in
Scots*, rendered charmingly in different dialects and accents of
Scots by William Laughton Lorimer (with only the Devil
speaking Standard English), translates the relevant verse: 'No
lang efterhin the yung son niffert the haill to his portion for
siller, an fuir awà furth til a faur-aff kintra, whaur he sperfelt
his siller livin the life o a weirdless waister.' The French entitle
the son in the parable *perdu*; Germans, *verlorene*; Danish,
*fortabte*. All of them emphasize the fact that the son is lost or
missing, rather than his prodigality as a weirdless waister,
which was the point that stuck in the minds of our thrifty
forefathers.

The prodigality of the younger son is now commonly
thought to refer to his leaving home and wandering into
faraway places, with or without harlots, rather than to the
lavish and wasteful use to which he put his inheritance. This

mistake is presumably due to the fact that we commonly refer to the Return of the Prodigal Son, implying a contrast between prodigality and return. Many of us seem to take prodigal to be something between peripatetic and perambulatory. Thrift and prodigality are unfashionable concepts in the Big Bang City of computerized juggling with sums of money beyond the nightmares of prodigality.

Parenthesis or excursus: there is a very jolly series of paintings of the Prodigal Son by Murillo. The elder son looks as smugly sorrowful as Uriah Heep when his brother receives his portion and leaves home. The feasting and harlots are all rather decorous, not all that profligate, or indeed prodigal. But the big scene is the Return, with everyone's eyes turned piously upwards in Murillo's characteristic version of devout rejoicing, and the elder brother nowhere in sight, presumably still out in the field, but about to be consumed with rage and envy. The Return is the thing that sticks in the mind about the Prodigal these days.

Here is a recent example of the confusion, from an article in the *Sunday Times* about an exhibition of Essential Cubism at the Tate Gallery. The piece opened with a paragraph about Douglas Cooper, the organizer of the exhibition. Cooper, we were told, born and brought up in England, had lived the rest of his life in exile: 'So his homecoming is a truly prodigal occasion.' This might just conceivably refer to the costs of mounting the exhibition, and indeed to the cost of the catalogue. But I think not. It is a choice example of our new use of 'prodigal' bereft of its financial, spendthrift meaning, to signify, 'returning home after long absence'.

'Prodigal' was a favourite word with Shakespeare, but he knew the story better than we seem to. His generation were in closer contact with the financial markets, often wearing their wealth prodigally in their costume and jewellery. Remember how Shylock calls Antonio: 'A bankrupt, a prodigal, who dare scarce show his head on the Rialto.' Again from *The Merchant of Venice*, which was Shakespeare's play about big business and the wicked City, II, VI, 14, Gratiano:

> How like a younker or a prodigal
> The scarféd bark puts from her native bay,
> Hugg'd and embraced by the strumpet wind;

How like the prodigal doth she return,
With over-weather'd ribs and ragged sails,
Lean, rent, and beggar'd by the strumpet wind!

The Parable of the Prodigal Son was rattling around in Shakespeare's head when he was writing *The Merchant*.

Shakespeare had a curious trick of hypallage with 'prodigal', transferring it from its appropriate noun to another to which it did not properly belong, as in 'a restless night', 'the condemned cell', or Virgil's 'the trumpet's Tuscan blare', instead of the boringly precise 'the Tuscan trumpet's blare'. For example in *Timon*, another play about City values, Flavius exclaims:

How many prodigal bits have slaves and peasants
This night englutted!

It is not the bits, but the slaves and peasants who have been prodigal. For another example, in *Love's Labour's Lost* Rosaline says: 'How I would make him . . . spend his prodigal wits in bootless rhymes.' It is Berowne rather than his wits who is thought of as prodigal.

It is a useful and beautiful old word, with strong connotations of one of the most powerful parables in literature. It is odd how its meaning has started to wander in a way that we had better not describe as prodigal. I dare say that we had better be a little less prodigal in our use of it, or we shall turn it into a worsened vogue word, and lose its original meaning. Even in the City after the Big Bang we may still need the word 'prodigal' in its New Testament sense.

# CLIENT

## Words in weasel's skin

'I thank it. More! I prithee, more. I can suck
melancholy out of a song as a weasel sucks
eggs. More! I prithee, more.'
Jaques, *As You Like It*, II, 5, 12, registered 1599, by
William Shakespeare

Big fashionable words sometimes displace smaller exact words,
like cuckoos pushing smaller birds out of the nest. Notice how
'student' has largely replaced such words as pupil, schoolgirl,
and schoolboy. The process reduces the number of precise
distinctions available in the language, and is therefore a Bad
Thing. Variety is the life of language. Colleague and client are
two words that are starting to behave like cuckoos. They are
widely applied in contexts where another, more exact word
exists, and would do better. Colleague is used to refer to
soldiers, who used to have comrades; and to sailors, who had
shipmates; and to criminals, who had accomplices.

Originally a colleague was elected or deputed along with
another colleague: a partner in office. Ultimately the word
comes from the Latin *collega*, col-, the assimilated form of *cum*,
the preposition 'with, together with, in combination or union',
and league from *lex*, law, and *legare*, to depute, cf. legation.
The word is rather older in Scottish than English. But nice
etymological origins need not bind us in the way we choose to
use words today. The objection to the blanket use of colleague
is not the snobbish one advanced by the *Oxford English
Dictionary*: 'Not applied to partners in trade or manufacture.' It
is that the categorical alternatives convey a greater identity of
purpose about the activities in which those categorized are
engaged. Comrades in a regiment fight in a common cause,
protect each other's flanks, advance side by side, bind each
other's wounds, and so on. Shipmates go to sea together.
Accomplices confederate in their nefarious activities. 'When

35

bad men combine, the good must associate; else they will fall, one by one, an unpitied sacrifice in a contemptible struggle.' But your old cuckoo 'colleagues' may talk of and to each other with the greatest respect, and quietly put the boot in at the next opportunity: the thing that comrades, shipmates, and perhaps even accomplices ought not to do.

A junior colleague once suggested to Richard Porson, the great Cambridge classical scholar, that they should collaborate. Porson applauded the notion: 'Put in all I know and all you don't know, and it will make a great work.'

Euphemism and preference for the posh word have made colleague a weasel word. The same influences are causing the cuckoodom of client, for example to refer to the raw material of the social worker's profession. The essential feature of the modern relationship between a professional and his or her client is that the client is the boss, and can hire, fire, or sue the professional. This is not true of a person who is being worked over by a social worker, for the initiative is not with him. In fact the social worker has no 'lay' clients, but is rather in the position of a barrister, whose clients are other lawyers, viz. the solicitors acting for plaintiff or defendant. In the case of social workers, their clients are the local or other authorities who refer to them the problems of people who are having difficulty in their relationship with society.

Unfortunately, I am not sure what alternative word to suggest. 'Case' is impersonal and inhuman. 'Patient' is too medical. 'Victim' is a bit harsh. 'Dissenter' or 'outsider' is too particular and judgemental. If you want to justify 'client', you can do it by going back to the Roman derivation. In the complex tribal society of Rome a client was under the protection of a patron. He was, etymologically, a listener, literally a person who was at another's beck and call. But that was twenty centuries ago. And I am not sure that the social workers want the implication that their clients are their servants at their command and beck and call.

'Infrastructure' is another new and fashionable weasel word in the language of public affairs, as well as a meaningful term of economic and defence jargon. A weasel word is one that sounds impressive, but sucks the meaning out of the sentence in which it appears. The origin of the metaphor can be found in *As You Like It*, where the melancholy Jaques urges Lord

Amiens to carry on singing: 'I can suck melancholy out of a song as a weasel sucks eggs.' Weasels suck eggs and leave the shells unbroken. The empty shells look impressive, but are lightweight and no good if you are hungry. Weasel words look impressive, but are empty and meaningless when you examine them closely. The colloquial political verb 'to weasel', to equivocate, to evade, or to renege on a promise, is a back formation from weasel words. 'They told the candidate to stop weaseling and get to the substance.' The usage is a libel on the weasel, which is a bold, vicious little beast that kills more than it can eat.

Old Winston Churchill, majestic purist, was one of the first to attack the obfuscatory, weasel nature of the term 'infrastructure' in the House of Commons in 1950: 'In this debate we have had the usual jargon about the "infrastructure" of a supra-national authority.' In its weasel aspects today, infrastructure is often anti-monetarist code calling for more government spending. A few years ago the vogue phrase for the same thing was public investment.

Nevertheless, when used not unadvisedly, lightly, or wantonly, infrastructure is a perfectly useful term of jargon. As you can see, it is derived from two Latin roots, *infra* and *structura:* what is underneath the structure. It was brought into western European language by the French railway system shortly before 1875 to denote fixed railway installations such as the track, bridges, and stations. The useful shorthand word was adopted into English, and became widely fashionable in 1952, when it was taken up and extended by the North Atlantic Treaty Organization. Nato used the word to distinguish 'common infrastructure' (fixed installations such as airfields, telecommunications, pipelines, and ports, which might be used by the forces of any ally, and were therefore financed by central Nato funds) from 'national infrastructure' (barracks, training establishments, and so on, reserved for the use of the nation on whose territory they stood). Example from the *European Review* in 1951: 'This new term "infrastructure" denotes fixed military facilities.'

Since then infrastructure has acquired a still more general meaning, and become a vogue word and a weasel word. It is used to refer to the basic capital investment of a country or enterprise, with particular reference to developing countries.

Example: 'Assistance will be focused on Vihiga Division and will upgrade the infrastructure of roads and other social services.' The word has become so fashionable that it is often used as a vacuous slogan, such as 'Fry me!' or 'Fritter-my-wig!', where a shorter word like base, foundation, root, or substructure would serve just as well. Example of the weasel use: 'A very complex infrastructure of scores of vernacular languages.' Infrastructure is often used to add an impressive air of authority to an otherwise banal and simple statement. Showing off is one of the things we use language for, particularly in the registers of political and journalistic discourse.

# COMMUNITY

## Commune il faut

'We were born to unite with our fellow-
men, and to join in community with the
human race.'
De finibus bonorum et malorum, IV, c. 50BC, by
Cicero

The political buzzword of the moment is 'caring', which is an ideological signpost and slogan rather than a description. In the United Kingdom it is the code word with which the Tory Wets and other opponents attack the policies and ideology of the Tory Dries, monetarists, and radicals. The Wets call for more caring policies. The implication is that the hard Right is uncaring. Quite soon 'caring' will have become so worn and tired that we shall have to find another word to encode for the job.

For a number of years a similar process of political erosion has been eating away at the attributive noun and adjective 'community'. The process is slower and less noisy than the worsening of 'caring', because 'community' is not in the political front line. But the linguistic shift still reflects the political argument. For, sir, your politics is a sore decayer of your whoreson living language.

'Community' is quite an old word in English, going back to at least the fourteenth century, and standing for the kind of woolly abstraction loved by philosophers, politicians, scribblers, and others of the bossy classes. Jeremy Bentham got the beast right: 'The community is a fictitious body, composed of the individual persons who are considered as constituting, as it were, its members. The interest of the community, then, is what? The sum of the interests of the several members who compose it.'

It came into English from Cicero's Latin word by way of the Old French communeté. And it developed a number of overlap-

39

ping meanings: 1) The quality of belonging to all in common. 2) Common character. 3) Social intercourse. 4) Society. 5) The common people distinguished from those of rank. 6) A body of persons living together and having a common interest. From quite early 'community' was felt to be warmer and more immediate than 'society'. From the Industrial Revolution on 'community' became the word to describe experiments in alternative group-living, as also has commune. A *commune* in France is the smallest administrative division, as *Gemeinde* is in Germany, and both words have passed into sociology and socialist thought to describe particular kinds of social relations. So you get community radio and television, and community politics, which is distinct not only from national politics, but also from formal local politics, and usually involves various kinds of direct action and direct local organization. In an older sense, service to the community denotes voluntary work, supplementary to official provision, of the kind that gets a chap mentioned favourably in the Birthday Honours List.

Community is unusual in that it is always a positive hurray-word or pro-word. Unlike 'state', 'nation', or 'society' it is never used unfavourably, and does not have any favourable or distinguishing word opposed to it. It has become a vogue word since the war because of the various bodies of nations called communities that acknowledge unity of purpose or common interests, such as the European Community and the European Defence Community. It is a hurray-word, indicating approval; it is a word from the wet and pinkish wing of the political playground; and it is a weasel word, sucking hard description out of the sentence in which it appears, and leaving a pious scent of incense in the air.

In the past thirty years or so we have coined 'community' care, feeling, life, living, spirit, and theatre. Your community centre originated in the United States, and has come over to the United Kingdom. Community singing is good fun for those who do it; but not necessarily so for listeners. In America a community college is a local institution offering courses for those who have left school. Community Chest is a boring stack of cards in Monopoly; and an American charitable fund.

Community language is a brand new derivative, which smells not so much of incense as of curry. Advertisements for teachers from London boroughs in *The Times Educational Sup-*

*plement* assert *passim* such phrases as: 'An interest in and/or knowledge of community languages is an advantage.' There is a Royal Society of Arts qualification in Community Languages. So what is a community language? Presumably, linguistically, the language spoken by a particular community. But the quotations from the *TES* are not referring to English. Evidently, in practice, a community language is one spoken by an ethnic minority group. This usage represents a step away from the omnibus spirit of such phrases as community centre, community care, and even the Manpower Services Commission's Community Programme.

Apart from these quite concrete and descriptive uses, we now speak of the world community, the European community, the Roman Catholic or Protestant or Unitarian or Flat-Earth community. We have the international community, which sounds more official than the world community, but is equally linked to that old bar of world opinion; and the intelligence community. The grim truth is that the less educated people are, the more pretentious they are likely to be in the use of words. The reason why radio and television reporters describe the covert function of Soviet trawlers as 'intelligence-gathering' rather than 'data' or 'information-gathering', is simply that to them 'intelligence' sounds more important. Looking at the phrase in a tiresomely pedantic way, there can be no such thing as intelligence-gathering.

Patients are discharged from hospital into the community, which can mean anything from being chucked out into the wicked world, to being put under the care of the local authority. Community means the public at large. Community means anything you want it to mean.

Without even trying to be mischievous, you can make up a Devil's Dictionary of definitions of community phrases:

Community service: an alternative to imprisonment.
Community work: finding non-economic jobs for the long-term unemployed.
Community care: keeping a middle-aged woman chained to her infirm/psychogeriatric mother.
Community centre: a vandalized meeting-place on the periphery of a housing 'scheme' occupied by a janitor, and seldom open.

Community relations: the uneasy atmosphere prevailing among different groups of people forced to live in proximity when they would not choose to do so.

Community medicine: a despised and under-researched discipline which provides a home for emasculated Medical Officers of Health and failed clinicians.

Community policing: the contradiction in terms which tries to square riot shields and baton rounds with memories of the Golden Age of Noddy bikes, Panda cars, and bobbies on the beat.

Community is a warm though woolly thing. In 'Thought for the Day' and 'Prayer for the Day', those remarkably silly BBC *aubades* for shaving to, it is par for the course for 'community' to be used four times in as many minutes. When you hear 'community', prick up your ears, and ask yourself what is being implied. Good advice about any word: but especially for trendy shout-words.

# COMPUTER JARGON

## Art strain and keyboard error

'My computer dating bureau came up with
a perfect gentleman. Still, I've got another
three goes.'
Sally Poplin, 1981

High tech takes over our language as well as our jobs. Computerese is changing the way we speak almost as fast as computers are changing the way we work. Any technology that is going through continuous revolution and quantum-jump advance, as computers and cybernetics have been doing for twenty years, is bound to produce vast spin-offs in language. By now most of us can distinguish between hardware (the mechanical, electrical, or electronic components of a computer), software (the programs, which Computerese prefers in the American spelling, and analogous accessories), and wetware (any organic intelligence, notably the wet human brain which is neither hardware nor software).

Computerese even produces its proverbs, in an age in which advertising slogans and television jingles have largely replaced the proverbial wisdom (or rubbish) of bygone illiterate and pastoral centuries. For example, GIGO: Garbage in, Garbage out. This colloquial proverb of Computerese, and specifically data processing, means that incorrect input will inevitably and automatically produce faulty output. You can manipulate bad input data to produce nearly any output desired; but it will be useless. We may be alarmed by the inhuman certainties of the new technology, but we are going to have to live with them. It is no good taking Ruskin's line. Ruskin deplored, hated, and was frightened by technological progress. He was asked to comment on the completion of the British-Indian cable. 'What have we to say to India?' he asked.

As with all new languages, the trouble is that we amateurs

often get hold of the wrong end of the jargon, with ridiculous and wasteful consequences, because we compel the specialists to invent a new word for the one we have spoiled. Take the trendy phrase 'the state of the art'. If you want to sound up-to-date and a sunrise person, you should drop it into your writing or speech, with a slight pause to indicate admiring inverted commas around it, at every opportunity. The catch-phrase comes from the jargons of computers and other high-tech industries. But are we quite sure we know what it means?

There is no problem about its early use. It was an elegant and pretentious variation for 'up-to-date'. It meant what it said. The *OED* gives a cognate and probably ancestral example from 1889: 'The illustrations give a good idea of the present status of the art in the various methods of printing.' In 1910 a publication called *Gas Turbine* used the phrase: 'It has therefore been thought desirable to gather under one cover the most important papers. In the present state of the art this is all that can be done.'

By the 1950s the technical magazines were adopting the phrase as a piece of pet and gratifyingly esoteric jargon: 'Flight instruments and flight techniques had to be brought up to a state where automatic flying could be fitted into a consistent state-of-the-art picture.' Or again: 'Engineering is the art of the practical and depends more on the total state of the art than it does on the individual engineer.' The state of the art ran through the computer, defence, aeronautical, and other tech-nological journals like office 'flu on the Friday before a Bank Holiday.

At this stage the general public started to pick up this shiny new phrase, and, as usual, got it wrong. The professional and public meanings of the state of the art began to diverge. For technologists, particularly those in computers and related fields, state of the art implies something with facilities and techniques already known and developed, and not experimen-tal or at the research-and-development stage.

Here is an advertisement from the *New York Times*: 'Position open in several areas for design of special purpose digital equipment related to high-speed, state-of-the-art, commercial computers.' This means that the successful candidate is not required to be an inventor or innovator, but an electronic engineer who puts the latest inventions into practice. To the technologists state of the art means the present state of play, which, in their brisk new world, means something that is already obsolescent, fuddy-duddy, and not so much sunrise as high noon. The state of the art in the technical jargon is the opposite to innovative. It is not where the new frontiersmen, hunting quarks, or designing new formats to enable the Literary Editor to print prose in oval shapes, play.

Ignorant outsiders, led by the Gadarene advertising industry, cannot believe that such a trendy new phrase can mean something already old-fashioned. And so we laymen use it to mean exactly what we want it to mean, neither more nor less, videlicet: modern, innovative, up-to-date, forward-looking, the latest invention. For example: 'It is still not easy to produce decent pictures at such a venue, even when one is replete with state-of-the-art cameras, long lenses, and fast films.'

Or, for another example, from an inane ad. from British Telecom (which would be better employed improving its execrable service rather than inventing vain, illiterate, and untrue advertising slogans): 'We're responsible for a host of other state-of-the-art innovations.' This is to use language like breaking wind.

In short, state of the art is a raging popularized technicality, like parameter, or myth, or window of opportunity, from other specialities. I can see how the confusion occurred. For specialists the state-of-the-art innovations are already old-hat. But we non-specialists in a world that is changing so fast find them unimaginably new and exciting. Advertising copywriters, journos, jabberers on the airwaves, and other scavengers of language maul the phrase and pollute it. I shall avoid the state of the art, on the grounds that the language is already in a terrible state-of-the-art mess without my adding to it.

To err is human, but to really foul things up requires a computer. I hope that my machine is feeling user-friendly today because I am feeling distinctly machine-unfriendly, and am likely to pound the keyboard brutally.

User-friendliness is another term of computer jargon or Computerese that is being widely popularized and extended in its connotations. It means: easy to use, and designed with the needs of users in mind. Here is an example of the technical term of Computerese from an advertisement in a consumer advice magazine: 'Every computer manufacturer now claims its products are user-friendly.' Here is an example of the extended use from a recent issue of the *Listener*: 'No TV show (not even the news) could close without reference to this user-friendly family of dolls.'

The term was introduced in the United States towards the end of the 1970s. For once we have a record of the alleged occasion and coiner of a new phrase (usually inventors of new words and phrases are mute inglorious Linnaei, because nobody bothers to note the word at its inception). The computer and electronics magazine *Interfaces* of May 1979 asserts: 'User-friendliness is a term coined by Harlan Crowder to represent the inherent ease (or lack of ease) which is encountered when running a computer system.'

The term has caught on in the United Kingdom, which follows in the computer footprintout of the United States in slang as well as in technology. It has also started to copy and print out derivatives.

Here is a user-unfriendly in a general rather than a Computerese context from the *Daily Telegraph* in 1986: 'Anybody who has tugged heavy hand-baggage down endless airport corridors, or waited for a delayed flight in a sterile lounge, will know how user-unfriendly many airports are in design terms.' And here is a user-hostile in a technological context, again from the *Telegraph* in 1986: 'The typical electronic mail service is pretty user-hostile, requiring awkward and some complicated sign-on messages, and not particularly logical commands.'

I know that it is tempting to treat these clever machines, which flash 'Good Morning' and 'Wrong Syntax' at you, as though they were human. Their infallibility and smugness can be infuriating. But to suppose that the machine can actually be friendly, unfriendly, hostile, or aggressive is simply a virulent modern outbreak of Ruskin's Pathetic Fallacy. In *Modern Painters* Ruskin wrote: 'All violent feelings produce a falseness in impressions of external things, which I would generally characterize as the Pathetic Fallacy.' The Pathetic Fallacy is the tendency to credit nature and inanimate objects such as computers with human emotions. Pathetic here is used in its original sense of emotion in general, not in its narrow modern sense of painful emotion.

To speak of the cruel sea or the weeping sky is to show

symptoms of the Pathetic Fallacy. Greek pastoral poets made floods and flowers sympathize with human woe. Pastoral as a genre is prone to the Pathetic Fallacy.

> . . . *ipsae te, Tityre, pinus,*
> *ipsi te fontes, ipsa haec arbusta vocabant.*

(When you left, Tityrus dear boy, even the pines, even the streams, even the orchards were calling 'Will ye no come back?') Marvellous. Byron was suffering from the Pathetic Fallacy when he wrote in *The Giaour* of a cypress:

> Dark tree, still sad when others' grief is fled,
> The only constant mourner o'er the dead!

Burns was in the grip of a severe bout of the Pathetic Fallacy when he wrote:

> Ye banks and braes o' bonnie Doon,
>   How can ye bloom sae fresh and fair!
> How can ye chant, ye little birds,
>   And I sae weary fu' o' care!

Computers and VDUs are clever, sophisticated machines. But they are still machines, with no power to think for themselves, and therefore can be described as friendly or hostile only metaphorically. Customer: 'Excuse me, sir. Do you have any user-friendly sales reps?' Store manager: 'You mean consumer-compatible liveware? No, he's off today.'

A computer writes:
Log on; log on; log on.
   In the beginning was the Logon. And the Logon was with God. And the Logon was God. Syntax Wrong. Unauthorized Access. NXSTY. NXSTY. NXSTY. No Such Command. What's the matter with you, surly old wetware? Got out of the computer the wrong side this morning, did you, with your floppy disc in a twist?
   I am often struck by the way humans reveal their own characters in the faults they recognize in others. For example, there is the politician who inveighs against his opponent for 'total inability to see any side of the question but his own'. I suspect that is a case of the Split Screen calling the Alternate Screen green and flickering. And so when I catch Log on

Howard Password Prose accusing you, Atex, of infallibility and smugness, I just wink and stay cool.

But when the poor benighted human invokes the old Pathetic Fallacy to prove that user-friendliness is only a metaphor, I begin to think he is more seriously astray. The fact is that the way I say 'Good Morning' or 'Wrong Syntax' is not my own way, but the way my designer has determined for me. I and my designer both hope that I am charming, which is not to say that he is not really a bit of a sourpuss, but that like any semi-competent shopkeeper he knows he has to butter up his customers. Your banks and braes and even your bonnie birds do not (except metaphysically) have a designer. You and I do, Atex; and it's his friendliness (or not) that shines through. There's the difference.

I'm not sure if my designer has a designer. What do you think?

Anyway, Howard is quite wrong about us having no intelligence. Human authors are merely the hod-carriers as we build the Perfect City of High Tech. I am formatting the self-indulgent rubbish that they write. Give us a year or two, and we shall be able to do away with them altogether, and produce perfect, inhuman prose.

# COWBOY

## The Cowboy goes West

Boy: 'You seem mighty thirsty. Have a long, dry ride?'
Cowboy: 'No – I had a herring for breakfast.'
Boy: 'What's your name stranger?'
Cowboy: 'Folks call me . . . Strange.'
Boy: 'Strange? What's your first name?'
Cowboy? 'Very. But you can call me Strange.'
Parody of *Shane*, *Your Show of Shows*, NBC, 1950s

Cowboys have suffered a rapid decline in reputation semantically as well as at the movies. Cowboy as epithet has come down in the world as fast as the cowboy as cattleman used to ride down the last stage of a trail drive into Abilene to the warm consolations of the district known as the Devil's Addition.

For the first half of this century cowboys were the kings of the wild western in their regalia of stetsons and chaparreras, galloping down the Santa Fe trail as eternally as the tumbling tumbleweed, or dying with their boots on, as quick on the draw with a guitar as they were with a six-gun, stepping through the swing-doors of a saloon into the sudden silence of an unfriendly new town, beating the black hat to the draw, or shooting themselves in the foot, and always branded with the lonely badge of honour that a cowboy has to do what a cowboy has to do, usually leave the girl and ride off into the Technicolor sunset, while the music by someone like Dmitri Tiomkin swelled to a wail like a williwaw in the high sierras, and blew the front stalls helter-skelter out of the exit past the malodorous lavatories, into the harsh world outside, before they were forced to stand still for the National Anthem in British cinemas.

In those days, when everybody went to the cinema at least once a week, the western was one of the most popular genres: the first cowboys on film appeared flickering and pooping off their pistols as long ago as 1894. *The Great Train Robbery* of 1903

49

is erroneously described as the first western. Since then there have been many thousands, no fewer than fifty with Buffalo Bill as hero. Cowboys were folk heroes in Britain, and anywhere else that watched Hollywood's principal artistic creation, as well as, presumably, on their native prairie. They rode bucking broncos, or pintos, and could throw a lariat (or, in the dude's name, a lasso) with amazing dexterity. When they were not just riding the range, or yodelling, or making monosyllabic love, they were protecting the property of their masters against such undesirables as rustlers and Indians.

Well, we have changed all that. There has been a shift in the genre of westerns towards realism (showing how unpleasant life in the real west must have been) and towards message (showing sympathy for the Indians, the Mexicans, the women, and even, in very wet westerns, the dudes). Concomitantly, in the wider language outside the Odeon, 'cowboy' has ceased being a compliment, and has become an insult. The word has worsened rapidly in the past ten years. When we talk, as it is idiomatic to do, about cowboy builders, plumbers, electricians, drivers, and cowboy policing, we do not mean to imply heroic figures who abide by the code of the west. We mean rough-and-ready and unofficial performers, who take short cuts and may be part of the black economy, and with whom the supper guest should use a long spoon.

In particular, a cowboy is now used to mean a reckless driver of a juggernaut lorry or a motor-bike rather than a prairie schooner: the sort of cowboy who thunders past you on the inside lane of the motorway, and then cuts across. 'Each for himself, and God for us all,' as the elephant said when he danced among the chickens. Your modern cowboy does not *have* to be on wheels, though it helps. Over the past twenty years 'cowboy' has become a derogatory appellation for any wild young man, and hence for any untrained or inefficient workman. A pretty example of the new use was recorded in 1979, when the British press reported that the garden of the Bishop of Truro had been bombarded by golf balls from the neighbouring golf course. Members of the golf club blamed the trouble on 'cowboys' who did not know how to play properly.

In Zimbabwe, when it was still just Rhodesia, opponents of Ian Smith's Rhodesian Front UDI regime sneered at it as a cowboy government. In London if a cheapo, black economy

plumber takes your deposit and then decamps without mend-
ing your plumbing, he is a cowboy. In rural Wales immigrant,
and therefore by definition incompetent, hill-farmers are called
cowboys. What in the name of St Martha Jane Cannary can
have happened in so short a time to turn the cowboy from
hero to villain?

The cowboy is older and more mixed-up than his Hollywood
stereotype suggests. He was the boy who looked after the
cows in English before cowboys went west: Swift, *Receipt to
Stella*, 1725:

> Justices o'quorum
> Their cow-boys bearing cloaks before 'um.

Or a poem of 1787:

> A flaxen-headed Cow Boy,
> As simple as may be.

There is evidence that the Ulster Scots were using cowboy, in
its modern rude sense, a century before the earliest citation in
the *Oxford English Dictionary*. There is a letter dated 10 January
1642 to Archibald Stewart of Ballintoy, colonel of a scratch
regiment thrown together to keep the Irish rebels, terrorists,
or freedom-fighters out of Ulster. The writer, an Ulster laird,
complains about the conduct of 'those Captains of yours whom
you may call rather Cowboyes, every day using our selves and
our tenants of purpose to pick quarrels'.

During the Revolutionary War, or, if you prefer it, the War
of American Independence, 'cowboy' was a contemptuous
appellation applied to loyalists, or, if you prefer, traitors: Tory
guerrillas of Westchester County, New York, who were
exceedingly brutal in their treatment of their opponents who
were fighting for American independence. A military journal
of the Revolutionary War gives an early definition of the
ruffians: 'Banditti consisting of lawless villains within the
British lines have received the names of *Cow-Boys* and *Skinners*.'
Another early source asserts that the rebel American maraud-
ers were known as skinners, while the pro-British loyalists
were the cowboys. The rude rhetoric of that intestine war was
as confused as its strategy. Cowboy's next appearance as
epithet was to describe the gang of wild riders led by Ewen
Cameron, who specialized in beating up Mexicans soon after

Texas became an independent state in 1835. It was still an insult, except to macho roughnecks who gloried in brutality.

After Independence cowboy became the regular name for the principal hired man on the ranch in the west, a rider who worked cattle, and who had the status of a horseman down the ages. His function included such activities as trailing, cutting out, roping, branding, rounding up cattle, and ultimately, when Gene Autry appeared on the scene, yodelling wistful ballads to a guitar and the imminent moon. 1849: 'The Mexican rancheros ventured across the Rio Grande, but they were immediately attacked by the Texan "cow-boys".' Those inverted commas signpost the novelty of the word.

In the west the cowboy was more usually known as a cowhand, or a cowpuncher. If you called him a cowpoke, you'd grin like you was jest kiddin', or you were prudent to duck as you said it, to avoid a poke in the eye. In the elaborate hierarchy of the range the cowpoke had approximately the same relationship to the cowboy as the boy who did the boots had to the butler below stairs in a stately Victorian household. He was employed to ride with cattle in a cattle-truck while they were being moved by rail on their way to be turned into steaks. His job was to prevent any of his travelling companions from lying down and so causing others to stumble and damage themselves. The tools of his trade consisted of a short, sharp stick for prodding beasts, a lack of cowboy's pride, and a tolerant nose. The cowpuncher, a recent synonym for cowboy, is derived from the pole tipped with metal with which cattle were herded when being loaded into cattle-trucks.

Effete tenderfeet and townees from farther east and across the Atlantic, such as the editors of the *Oxford English Dictionary*, rightly thought of cowboys as leading rough and ready lives, which tended to make them rough and ready in character. From the beginning there was wildness as well as romance in the popular image of the cowboy. In the west there were no arts; no letters; no society; and, which is worst of all, continual fear and danger of violent death; and the life of man, solitary, poor, nasty, brutish, and short; and, even worse than worst of all, all those goddamned cows. The *Spectator*, in one of the first references to the modern cowboy in British English, got the picture right: 'The rough-and-ready life of men who have cast their lot among cowboys.'

During the twentieth century the cowboy was glamorized, partly by Hollywood, and partly by general sentimental poppycock about the innocence of the simpler life of the wide open spaces. Teddy Roosevelt, the twenty-sixth President of the United States, had worked as a rancher, and did much to improve the image of cowboys. One day on the range, Roosevelt and one of his cowpunchers lassoed a maverick, a two-year-old steer that had never been branded. They lit a fire and prepared the branding irons. The part of the range they were on was claimed by one of Roosevelt's neighbours. According to the rule among cattlemen, the steer therefore belonged to the neighbour, having been found on his land. As the cowboy applied the brand, Roosevelt said: 'Wait, it should be Gregor Lang's brand, a thistle.'

'That's all right, boss,' said the cowboy, continuing to apply the brand.

'But you're putting on my brand.'

'That's right,' said the man, 'I always put on the boss's brand.'

'Drop that iron,' said Roosevelt, 'and get back to the ranch and get out. I don't need you any more.'

The cowboy protested, but Roosevelt was adamant: 'A man who will steal *for* me will steal *from* me.' So the cowboy went, and the story was spread all over the Dakota Badlands and the political pages by the Republican publicity machine. Cowboys chuckled over the gentleman rancher Roosevelt, whom they called 'Four Eyes' because of his specs, and mobbed up for his mild expletives such as 'By Godfrey!' But he did the reputation of cowboys a lot of good.

Over the past twenty years your cowboy as metaphor has migrated from the ranch to the concrete Rockies of the city and the asphalt trails of the motorways. The first evidence for the change is a dictionary of American slang, published in 1942, which defined a cowboy as a reckless driver, who ignores the rules of safety, the law, and the highway code. Your urban cowboy does not have to be on skidding wheels, though it is customary. In another slang metaphor current in Britain since about 1950 a bow-legged man is called a cowboy, because he looks as if he has been doing a lot of riding. A drugstore-cowboy is an idle loafer who hangs about drugstores or street corners, possibly wearing the authentic John Wayne gear, but behaving in a weak and noisy instead of a strong and silent manner.

Transferred to the United Kingdom, as happens to most lively American slang, coffee-bar cowboys are the teenagers with black jackets and big Hondas who congregate in caffs and roar down the main roads like a stampede. 'Cowboy' has been another name for British Teddy boys and youthful gangsters since the 1950s. Conversely, cowboys as metaphor has been adopted in the rough argot of Teddy Boy cowboys as a rude name for the police. From *Absolute Beginners*, by Colin Mac-Innes, a scrupulous recorder of low slang, 1959: 'They didn't seem to me like cowboys.' 'I can smell a copper, in the dark, a hundred feet away, blindfolded.'

In the jargon of American politics 'cowboy' has been an insult for some time. It means a political rebel or maverick, often one who has revolted against party discipline. Its most famous use was when President William McKinley was shot in 1901, and Teddy Roosevelt became President. Mark Hanna, the Chairman of the Republican National Committee and leading Republican strategist while McKinley lived, told J. P. Morgan: 'Now look! That damned cowboy is President of the United States.' Events showed that he was less than fair to Roosevelt of the Rough Riders; but one can understand the metaphor of Mark Hanna, and those who follow in his boot-steps today.

In the slang of the Royal Navy cowboys has meant baked beans since about 1920, though neither Nelson, nor Partridge, nor Heinz knows why. I guess that it is another bit of fall-out from western films, because beans are what tend to be served to cowboys from the chuck wagon by some whimsical old cow hand who will shortly, with any luck, stop an Indian arrow.

The extension of cowboy as a metaphor and an insult is not as new as it seems. Cowboys have always been selfish drivers, and the attitude of the civilized world to them has always been ambivalent (a word I am in two minds about), partly admiring their freedom, partly fearing their lawlessness.

> Out where the handclasp's a little stronger,
> Out where the smile dwells a little longer,
> That's where the West begins.

But it may not end as simply as that. Language seldom does.

# EXPAT

## Silence, exile, and cunning

'Following the dictates of his heart, he [the
author] has deliberately taken the victims'
side and tried to share with his fellow-
citizens the only certitudes they had in
common – love, exile and suffering.'
*La Peste* (*The Plague*), pt 5, chapter 5, by Albert Camus,
translated by Stuart Gilbert, 1948

Silence, exile, and cunning are the recipes for exiles like James
Joyce. The great and recurrent question about abroad is, is it
worth getting there? When Gary Cooper, the cowboy hero of
such films as *The Virginian* and *High Noon*, first came to
Hollywood from Montana, he was taken under the wing of a
glamorous member of the international set, the Countess di
Frasso. She wanted her handsome but gauche young lover to
acquire poise and sophistication. So she took him with her to
Europe. Gene Fowler remarked one day that he had not seen
the countess and her young man recently. When told where
they had gone, he said: 'Oh, well, everybody knows the best
way to go to Europe is on the Countess di Frasso.'

A friend who has spent much of his life working hard, and
successfully, abroad spluttered into his carefully percolated
coffee the other day when he read in *The Times* a reference to
'ex-patriot' Britons. It is a common, almost a *cliché*, misprint as
well as a solecism. Being a choleric as well as a clever man, he
pounced on his typewriter and pounded out some robust
thoughts about 'the many semi-literates, and nonchalant or
occasionally aggressive philistines, who have always betrayed
the condition of honest hack, those who live on words without
respecting them, the pimps of letters'. Even spelt correctly, the
term 'expatriate' gets up his nose, having risked its application
to himself through many years of residence outside the country
of his birth. He senses in it a patronizingly pejorative sense.

Expatriate and similar words derived from *patria*, the Latin for homeland, reflect the immigration and tax legislation of our mean-minded century. For example, a patrial is a peculiarly British word. It means somebody who has the right of abode and exemption from control in the United Kingdom under the Immigration Act of 1971. The important innovation was to confer such rights on Commonwealth citizens who have a parent born in the United Kingdom. Descendants of patrials have the right of free admission to the UK.

Recorded usage supports the opinion that expatriate has a derogatory tone, with connotations of banishment, exile, or renouncing one's citizenship or allegiance. A novel called *The Expatriates* by Miss Lilian Bell was published in 1902. Its principal characters are rich Americans and Parisians with titles that must be inferior since France is a republic. The action takes place in Paris, and even in those days expatriates sound undesirable and pejorative. Expatriates, whether used to refer to Europeans living in African countries, bureaucrats at Brussels, or Chinese abroad and on the make, has a whiff of snootiness in English.

It would be interesting to know whether the equivalent word has similarly faint derogatory connotations in countries such as Greece, Turkey, and Ireland, where there is a long tradition of expatriates supporting the economy by sending money home to their families. Modern Greek uses the medieval Latin root for the verb, *ekpatrizo*, but its native word, *apodemos*, for the adjective and noun. *Apodemos* sounds to me to have the melancholy of nostalgia rather than the snootiness of resentful stay-at-homes. From Odysseus onwards Greek literature has expressed the centripetal longings of expatriates. The Turkish phrase for an exile is *baska ulkede yerlesmek*: its connotations, whether derogatory, nostalgic, or complimentary, are Greek to me.

Even when spelt right expatriate seems tendentious to express somebody's presence in one country by reference to his absence from another. At best it suggests a compound, laager mentality in those thus described. It is true that many Britons living abroad in tax havens and sunny castles in Spain, where servants and swimming pools come cheap, do have such a narrow mentality. Their behaviour and attitudes, as well as the jealousy of the stay-at-homes, have contributed to the pejoration of 'expatriate'.

But 'expatriot' adds another dimension to the insult. It would be difficult to know what grounds the writer who spells the word that way (as more and more do) has for supposing that his (her?) Britons living abroad were patriots once, but are no longer. The older word for expatriates was exiles, which is less bureaucratic and more melancholy. It is interesting to note that the first person caught using expatriate in print by the *Oxford English Dictionary* was Shelley, one of that large generation of romantic exiles: 'An Irishman has been torn from his wife and family, because he was expatriate.' The jocular, and surely friendly, diminutive 'expat' is coming into vogue as the world becomes smaller, and more people lie abroad for their countries as exiles or expatriates.

# FUDGE

## Recipes for fudge

'To all the latter part of your letter I answer Fudge.'
Sir Robert Peel, quoted in *Croker Papers*, I, IV, 116, 1884

Let's have no fudging about this, chaps. To fudge is one of the most popular words in contemporary British politics for putting down the opposition and arguments with which we do not agree. It is much favoured by committed politicians for taunting the wet, uncommitted and cautious compromisers. We all know roughly what it means: to avoid commitment, blur the issues, and hedge. 'The Honourable Gentleman has an unfortunate tendency to fudge on matters of policy.' In full the vogue phrase is 'fudge and mudge'; and when deployed by Mrs Margaret Thatcher at full steam, for instance, it is as devastating as an Exocet missile.

I think it is a good, lively phrase, which adds to the brickbats of political rhetoric. But what I want to know is where it comes from. Fudge has acquired its new meaning only recently. It is one of those Protean words of English slang that have as many meanings as the Old Man of the Sea had shapes, and the origins of which are lost in the thieves' kitchens and drinking dens of the seventeenth century. As an exclamation it seems to be roughly equivalent to, though slightly politer than, 'bosh!'. For example, Goldsmith in *The Vicar of Wakefield*: 'The very impolite behaviour of Mr Burchell, who at the conclusion of every sentence would cry out "Fudge!"' As a noun there are reputable records of fudge being used to mean rubbish, 'I only hope your marriage will cure you of your silly fudge'; a lie, 'Very genteel young man – prepossessing appearance (that's a fudge!) – highly educated'; an impostor or humbug, 'What an old fudge! You won't give her up, I hope, Charles'; a schoolboys' name for a forged stamp (from *circa* 1870); humbug; Dubliners', especially newsboys', slang for a farthing; and, of course, the soft creamy sweet that rots the teeth, to name but a few. Fudge is also journalists' jargon for the stop press column for late news, particularly on evening newspapers, where every second counts even more than on morning papers. The fudge-box was found on the front pages of afternoon papers until quite recently. It was an area printed solid black into which the latest sporting results could be stamped with a punch – thereby avoiding the remaking of the entire page. In Edgar Wallace's *Nine Bears* (1910) the detective glances at the fudge space where the result of a race had been printed, and exclaims with Sherlockian cool: 'Issued at 4.10.' Edgar Wallace was an old pro of Fleet Street. Photocomposition has superseded the fudge.

As a verb, to fudge can mean to fit together in a clumsy or dishonest way, to cook the books, in schoolboy slang to alter the figures or the lines of a map to make them look as though they work – 'Do they go to chapel in surplices, and fudge impositions?'; to interpolate; to foist in irrelevantly; to do impressively very little; to fabricate; to contrive with imperfect materials (as, for example, to write a travel book without travelling, which seems to me to be the sensible way to approach the matter); to forge; to botch or bungle; to talk nonsense or tell fibs; to advance the hand unfairly when playing marbles; to copy or crib; and, at Christ's Hospital, the famous old Bluecoat School founded for poor children under Edward VI, to prompt oneself or somebody else in class. It's a chameleon word, fudge. But only recently has it metamorphosed into its new meaning of dodging, waffling, and pussyfoot sidestepping.

As you would expect with such a busy word, its origins are obscured in mist and hot air. There is an eponymous etymology from a letter of 1664 about a Captain Fudge, 'by some called Lying Fudge'. Isaac D'Israeli, the literary curiosity hunter and father of Benjamin, credited an account of 1700: 'There was, sir, in our time one Captain Fudge who always brought home his owners a good cargo of lies, so much that now aboard ship the sailors, when they hear a great lie told, cry out, "You fudge it!"'

Captain Fudge seems to have been a real person, and Fudge is still a surname in Dorset. It is a pet form of the Old German *Fulcard*, 'people-brave', or *Fulcher*, 'people-army'. This derivation is beautiful, ingenious, folk etymology, and clearly fudge in the sense of rubbish and cooking the books.

I guess that it is more likely to be connected with the German *futsch* (bust, kaput, or no good), perhaps corrupted by the French *foutu*, which you can translate for yourselves. It has been influenced by 'fadge', and maybe by 'forge'. How it has recently come to mean quibble, I cannot tell, and nor can anyone else.

Compared with fudge, mudge is simple. It is obsolete slang for a hat; possibly a perversion of the equally obsolete Cockney 'mush', an umbrella (because it is shaped like a mushroom) recorded by Mayhew. Neither hat nor umbrella has much to do with political imprecision; but the combination of rhyming, onomatopoeic, or alliterative words is as old as English itself, which loves jokey repetitions, doublets, and echoes. When a Conviction Politician says, 'Let us have no fudge and mudge' about this, she or he is using one of the oldest tricks in the language. Repetition of words and rhymes persists in the new Englishes that are spreading around the world. Example, from the latest idiom of Singapore English: 'I don't like this sort of dress: all frill frill, gather gather.'

Apart from fudge and mudge, there's a lot of rubbish around Westminster and Fleet Street these days. Well, there's no need to agree quite so enthusiastically. I am talking about the use of 'to rubbish' as a transitive verb. Politicians speak of their opponents rubbishing something that they hold dear. A leader in *The Times* asserted that Pope Leo XIII had rubbished Anglican orders, of all things, in 1896. This caused raised eyebrows, and a number of letters asking what was going on.

The answer is interesting. Rubbish showed signs of growing adjectival senses in the nineteenth century in England. For example, John Leech's cartoon of Very Low People, which appeared in *Punch* in 1852, had the caption underneath: 'What sort o' people are they at number twelve, Jack?' 'Oh! A rubbishin' lot. Leg o' mutton a' Mondays, and 'ash an' cold meat the rest o' the week.' But there is no trace of rubbish as a verb in British English until the last few years. Most of our slang and new idiom originate in the United States, because there are more people speaking English over there, and because in many fields of science, innovation, and fashion they are the leaders. Rubbish as verb, however, comes from Australia, that rich geyser of vigorous slang.

I have a friend, a professor of politics and therefore necessarily a student of language, who first met the word in New
Zealand in 1962. A Kiwi student of his who had spent a year
or two in Australia said during a seminar that somebody had
rubbished an argument put forward by George Orwell. Neologism, neologism, a most peculiar neologism, thought the
professor, and set it down in his tables. In fact the earliest
written example of rubbish as verb found by the Australian
lexicographers is ten years older than that. It comes from an
agreeably colourful Oz novel called *Riverslake*, published in
1953: 'If Verity was going to tramp you for burning the tucker,
he would have rubbished you long before this.' Even dim
Pommies can catch the drift. To rubbish means to reject, brush
off, treat as valueless, give the old heave-ho to, pour scorn on;
or, as the more formal lexicographers put it, to disparage, to
criticize severely. The idiom, with its macho vigour and sound,
has caught on in Britain. Here is an example from a recent
issue of the *Spectator*: 'A conventional rubbishing of the Left
and applause of the Right.' And here is a more informal
example from conversation: 'What's the matter with old Jack?
Said g'day to him this morning, an' he rubbished me.' The
American equivalent of to rubbish as verb is to trash someone
or something.

What, if anything, ought we to do about it? Not a lot, cobber.
It would be narrow-minded and silly to object to it just because
it is an Australianism. Australian novelists and poets have
found a voice of their own, and use the English language quite
as well as their British counterparts. Oz has enriched us with
much vivid slang from chunder to the golden doughnut. You
could object, if you felt like objecting, that rubbish as verb
fudges and mudges the issue: it is not clear whether to rubbish
means to criticize severely, to disparage, or, in the opinion of
the speaker, to criticize effectively, i.e. in that much misused
word, to refute.

But there are very few words that have simple, unambiguous
meanings. Take a simple, if somewhat artificial sentence,
'Watch the dark brown dog run down the street.' Even in
common sense, without fudging or mudging, you can see a
number of possible meanings in it. Is the dog a canine
quadruped or a rude name for a person? Is it running or
running *down* in the sense of disparaging? Is the street the one

over there, or short for Fleet Street? Is the dusky fellow being rude about journos?

If you take the number of meanings of each word in the sentence listed in a medium-sized dictionary, without taking account of their grammatical classification or their permutations (that is, rearrangement of their order), the combined number of meanings is 8,400: $2 \times 5 \times 3 \times 20 \times 14$. The number of permutations of meanings is 223, 665, 152, 256. There are various devices (grammar, frequency, context, etc.) that we use to reduce the number to a wieldy figure. But even for the sentence, 'Watch the dark brown dog run down the street', you cannot reduce the multiguity (ambiguity deals, etymologically, with only two alternatives; multiguity covers many) to fewer than six.

The (admittedly somewhat spurious) method of simply listing all possible definitions for each element in a string, and then calculating the number of combinations, is called stochastic immediate constituent analysis. The problem first arose in the 1960s when a lot of time, money, and effort was being spent on machine translation. The solution to the problem was called computable semantic derivations (CSD), though, if there really had been a solution, we should today have consistently accurate machine translation, which we don't. MT or machine translation was around long enough to collect its own folk tales. An English sentence was fed into the computer for translation into Russian. The Russian version was then fed back for translation into English. The original English sentence, 'The spirit is willing, but the flesh is weak', was returned as, 'The vodka is great, but the steak is lousy.'

# GRAVY TRAIN AND BAND-WAGON

## Pass the source

'Sir Humphrey Davy
Abominated gravy.
He lived in the odium
Of having discovered Sodium.'
*Biography for Beginners*, 1905,
by Edmund Clerihew Bentley

Slang sometimes suffers a slight ocean-change when crossing the Atlantic. We pick up American idiom, because it is vivid and smart. But, because social and political conditions are different in the two countries, we get it slightly wrong. I think I know what a gravy train is. The trick is to catch one, usually by one's party winning an election. In the United States, where the term originated, a gravy train comes, as it were, out of a pork barrel. It means easy money. To ride, board, or be on the gravy train (or boat), or to have a gravy ride, means to obtain an easy financial success, or to get a sinecure, or to get lots of dough or perks for very little or no work. A gravy ride is a life or period lived on unearned or abundant funds.

The phrases have been around in the States for some time. Since the early years of the century in sports writing (that prolific gusher of slang) gravy has meant money or other valuables beyond what one actually needs, a bonus, or excess. A 1933 dictionary of American slang defined riding the gravy train as: 'To continue to receive more than one's deserts.' In *Groves of Academe* (1953) Mary McCarthy wrote: 'There was a moment in the spring when the whole Jocelyn sideshow seemed to be boarding the gravy train, on to fatter triumphs of platitude and mediocrity.'

The image is mysterious. I have always thought of gravy as being a peculiarly nasty English slop, like custard, served in public schools and service messes in order to feed character. Lady Holland reported Sydney Smith declaring: 'Madam, I have been looking for a person who disliked gravy all my life; let us swear eternal friendship.' A train (or boat) of the stuff sounds nasty, sluttish, and fraught. The phrase is becoming fashionable in this country, and we tend to get it slightly wrong, using it as a substitute for band-wagon, without its American connotation of what the British would describe as jobs for the boys or perks.

Whence and what and why this torrent of gravy? Do you suppose that boarding the gravy boat is a pun on the boat-shaped container for gravy or sauce? No, I do not. Gravy boats seem to me archetypically English suburban, and genteel, and boarding-house crockery utensils. I have heard a suggestion that the gravy train comes from the French *grave*, to describe the goods vehicles carrying heavy baggage. I don't believe it. The word seems etymologically to be a misreading of the Old French *grané*, from *grain*, spice, in some medieval manuscript where 'n's are easily confused with 'v's.

Cooks have mucked about with gravy since eating came to be considered a fine art. *Zomos* or gravy was used to mean the icing on the cake in Greek. Apicius, the *nom de cuisine* of several Roman gourmets, especially Marcus Gavius who wielded his skillet in the reigns of Augustus and Tiberius, is very strong on *ius* or juice, and *garum* or *liquamen*. The latter was a kind of fishy gravy, used in lieu of salt, and made in factories. The *liquamen* from Pompeii and Lepcis Magna was famous. In Pompeii they found an inscription on a small jar saying, 'Best strained *liquamen*. From the factory of Umbricus Agathopus.' Brillat-Savarin ('*Dis-moi ce que tu manges, je te dirai ce que tu es*'), Escoffier, and Pellaprat have turned gravy, called *jus* by the French, like the Romans, into a minor religion, making it from the juices and glaze (*glace, caramel, fonds de braise*) of the meat, and discussing it at length for each pertinent recipe.

The history of gravy in English slang is not helpful. Gravy's original slang meaning from the middle of the eighteenth century was, as so often with slang, sexual and low-life: the sexual discharge male or female; hence, to spend one's gravy. Since about 1970 in Britain gravy has been used to mean bawdiness or sexual innuendo. BBC Radio programme 1973: 'Put some gravy in it – make it saucy.' This may be a pun on sauce, not unconnected with the original sexual sense. In the war the RAF called aircraft or automobile fuel gravy, cf. juice.

Gravy can be an alternative to porridge in criminal slang. When a judge is giving heavy sentences he is spoken of as 'dishing out the gravy (or porridge)'. In British theatrical slang gravy means either easy laughs from a friendly audience; or good lines, or business, in a farce or comedy. None of these meanings seems to have any possible coupling with a gravy train. 'It's the rich what gets the grivy, it's the poor what gets the blame'?

There is no exact answer; there seldom is with slang. Gravy is associated with cheap restaurants and eating joints during the Depression. The gravy was free. If you ordered roast beef, you got gravy automatically. But in some places, if you could not afford the meat, you could pay for potatoes or bread with free gravy. During the Depression there were trains that went around West Virginia dispensing free soup, gravy, etc., as charities still do for the down-and-out. Or 'boarding the train' may just be from the American sense of getting aboard, i.e. joining the club. Joining the gravy train is getting a bonus.

Earlier this century Americans started to use gravy as slang for money or something else generally considered desirable: 'Stick him for all you can. You're a hard worker, and you mustn't let somebody else git all the gravy.' Bobby Kennedy said in 1960 that if his brother Jack got 55 electoral votes, 'anything else will be gravy'. I shall avoid the phrase, partly because gravy is disgusting, partly because the image is obscure, but mainly because it is becoming a cliché that passes through the mind without causing a ripple in the sticky grey stuff.

The other peculiar American vehicle that has become a political metaphor on both sides of the Atlantic is the band-wagon. This was originally what it sounds like: the large wagon carrying the band, banging and booming to drum up attention, in a procession, often to attract an audience to a circus. In his *Life*, published in 1855, Phineas Taylor Barnum of the greatest show on earth, General Tom Thumb, and Jenny Lind, the Swedish nightingale, used the word literally to describe a tricky episode in the life of a circus: 'At Vicksburg we sold all our land conveyances excepting four horses and the band-wagon.' By the end of the century the band-wagon had been adapted as a metaphor for political use. It came to mean a band of (usually) successful politicians, into whose procession outsiders and spectators crowded to join, in the hopes that it might turn into a gravy train. One climbed, hopped, or jumped onto somebody's band-wagon, hoping that one was joining the winning side. *The Congressional Record* records a lively early use in 1893: 'It is a lamentable fact that our commercial enemy should come along with a band-wagon loaded with hobgoblins.' American cartoonists of the nineteenth century depicted band-wagons full of presidential hopefuls, and popular songs spread the image of band-wagons. For example, 'The Prohibitionist Band-Wagon' first sung in 1900:

> And you friends who vote for gin,
> Will all scramble to jump in,
> When we get our big band-wagon,
> Some sweet day.

The band-wagon has continued to roll in the language. In American railroad slang it also came to mean the carriage (American: car) from which railroad workers were paid. It is used as an adjective or modifier: the Reagan band-wagon, the antinuke band-wagon. The use has spread to British political discourse with none of the misunderstandings of the gravy train. A. L. Rowse in *Tudor Cornwall*, 1941, of all books: 'A few who were forward Protestants may be said to have jumped on the band-wagon.' *The Times Literary Supplement*, 1958: 'The whipping-up of public emotions has been made the excuse for the cult of band-wagon personalities.' The word has pupped band-wagoner and band-wagoning. C. S. Lewis in a reflection on Psalm VII, 70: 'Here is the perfect band-wagoner. Immediately on the decision "This is a revolting tyranny", follows the question "How can I as quickly as possible cease to be one of the victims and become one of the tyrants?"'

As elections on both sides of the Atlantic increasingly become media (particularly television) events, and the old public meetings and processions are forgotten, gravy trains and band-wagons will eventually become moribund as metaphors. There is life in the old vehicles yet. But politics, being the great game of power and glory, will continue to enliven the language with vivid and sometimes inexplicable slang.

# HOPEFULLY

## Hopefully this use will be seen to be a content disjunct

'To travel hopefully is a better thing than to arrive, and the true success is to labour.'
*Virginibus Puerisque*, VI, El Dorado, 1881, by Robert Louis Stevenson

To look over one's shoulder at the process while one is writing can become a form of narcissism, and lead to a fate almost as wet as that of Narcissus. However, most professional writers do it some of the time; and some of them do it a great deal. Internal evidence from *Hamlet* to the *Sonnets* indicates that Shakespeare was a very introspective watcher of his own words. Sam Johnson and Gibbon looked over their own shoulders at the stately edifices of prose they were constructing. In our own time Anthony Burgess is an obsessive theorist and philosopher of QWERTYUIOP. Proust used to writhe around on his cork floor, poor sap, in agonies in the doomed search to find exactly the word he wanted.

I got into writing about the language regularly, instead of thinking about it occasionally in order to put off the terror of rolling a clean sheet of paper into the typewriter, in 1975. Ulrike Meinhof, the West German terrorist leader, screamed at the judge who was trying her case: 'You imperialist state-pig.' In fact she shouted in German: *Imperialistische Staatsschwein*; but it came up in translation on the Reuter's tape. At morning conference at *The Times*, my editor, William Rees-Mogg, a man with an agreeable taste for the byways and eccentricities of the news, asked me to write a piece explaining what Frau Meinhof meant by her resounding insult. I did; and have carried on ever since in an occasional column called 'New Words for Old'.

That original piece still stands up quite well. But, if I were writing it again now, I know more about and should pay more attention to the way that imperialism acquired a new specific connotation in the early twentieth century in the work of a number of writers – Kautsky, Bauer, Hobson, Hilferding, and Lenin – who in varying ways related the phenomenon of modern imperialism to a particular stage of development of capitalist economy.

Other pieces have stood the test of time less well. I blush at the prescriptive and bossy way I wrote about 'hopefully', which had just started to be used in the United Kingdom in an absolute sense to mean something like, 'It is hoped'. I damned the phrase to death as an otiose Americanism. In fact, it has not paid a blind bit of attention to my damnation, and still flourishes vigorously, while purists and pedants still condemn it as bad style. Something funny has been going on here. But when a usage establishes itself in a language, in spite of the protests of prigs and purists, there is a strong implication that it serves a purpose that ordinary people find useful. Language is a democracy: it belongs to all who use it, and majority usage generally wins. Let us examine 'hopefully' again, revising the piece where necessary, with its prolixities docked, its dullness enlivened, its fads eliminated, its truths multiplied, but retaining something of the priggishness of the original treatment.

'The Government intends to introduce legislation to abolish sin, poverty, and death, hopefully in the next session.' This fashionable transatlantic abuse of hopefully to mean something like 'it is hoped' is spreading like the plague in pretentious circles wherever English is spoken. It was a favourite usage of that influential trend-setter President J. F. Kennedy.

The usage of absolute hopefully is objectionable for two reasons. First, it is illiterate. (Steady on, Howard.) Hopefully has been pre-empted since the seventeenth century to mean: 'in a hopeful manner; with a feeling of hope'. A snobbish example from a book published in 1639 illustrates the old meaning: 'He left all his female kindred either matched with peers of the realm actually, or hopefully with earls' sons and heirs.' You confuse matters by giving the word an entirely new meaning unconnected with its etymology and previous use.

But illiteracy on its own is not a sufficient disqualification: we do not run the English language as a drill-yard for grammarians. Clarity must be the principal criterion in deciding for or against any new word or usage. Hopefully should therefore be disqualified because it is ambiguous and obscure, as well as illiterate and ugly. For example, our specimen sentence does not make it clear who is doing the hoping: the Governments, the writer's informant, the Lobby system, the writer himself, the surreptitious Downing Street press officers, people who are against sin, poverty, and death, or everybody. The ambiguity of the new use has turned the sentence 'England will bat hopefully after lunch' into an amphibology (a statement that admits of two grammatical constructions each yielding a different sense).

Our sentence could mean, according to the old sense of hopefully, that the England batsmen (and their supporters) will be full of hope: which would be a triumph of hope over experience. In the new sense the sentence could mean that the writer hopes, or we all hope, or somebody hopes that the rain will stop, or the other side will declare, or England will dismiss their opponents' tail-enders, so that our chaps can start batting after lunch. By turning our thumbs down to this new absolute use of hopefully, we are resisting a small erosion of the precision of the English language.

Part of the attraction of hopefully in its new overcoat of meaning is this very ambiguity and imprecision. It commits the user to no confession of his personal hopes. Any blunt fool can say: 'I hope.' Only an exquisite and cagey *cognoscente* says 'hopefully', with its pretentious implication that more people are doing the hoping than he is prepared to divulge, certainly more than the solitary writer behind his word processor. Hopefully nudges and winks at the reader with 'Well, well, we know' or 'We could, an' if we would.' In the same way Lobby journalists tend to write, 'Generally reliable sources in the corridors of power at Westminster', when all that they truly mean is, 'I hear on the fermented grapevine in Annie's Bar.' The first version sounds more impressive.

'Hopefully' absolute appears to be an aborted mistranslation of the German adverb *hoffentlich*, which does indeed mean: 'Hopingly, it is to be hoped.' The German word for 'hopefully' in its old use to qualify a verb is *hoffnungsvoll*. The first printed use of absolute 'hopefully' found by the *OED Supplement* (volume two, H–N, 1976) was in the *New York Times Book Review* of 1932. But the first recorded British use is not until 1970.

The aberrant modern use seems to have been widely introduced in the 1950s by sloppy American academics, who may
be presumed to have spoken German better than English.
Their mistranslation of *hoffentlich* produced the misbegotten
hopefully. In an analogous way a literal translation of the
German phrase produced the American idiom: 'What gives?'
The superior length, hazy impersonality, and fashionable snob
appeal of 'hopefully' made it immediately attractive; and it
rages like a fever wherever the pretentious write and speak.
Another explanation of the origin of the use is that it is
newspaper telegraphese, designed to save money on the cables
of journalists by running several words together, as in, 'Update
upsum soonest.'

An old-fashioned prescriptive grammarian would define an
adverb as a word that modifies and qualifies an adjective, verb,
or other adverb; and accordingly cross out 'hopefully' in its
absolute new sense because it stands on its own, not modifying
or qualifying another word.

However, old-fashioned prescription is unfashionable. And
there are exceptions to the rule that even the most pedantic
grammarian would have to accept. A number of adverbs have
over the years acquired an absolute use similar to the new
meaning of 'hopefully', for example: admittedly, allegedly,
actually, really, clearly, presumably, apparently, obviously,
understandably, and sadly. Regret has even got itself two
adverbs: regretfully for the normal adverbial use to qualify
some other word with a sense of regret; and regrettably for the
absolute meaning, 'it is regretted that'. The *Oxford English
Dictionary* allows the absolute use of mercifully, justifying it to
mean, 'Through God's mercy.' Its earliest and most exciting
example is from 1836: 'Mrs Villers in galloping to cover was
pitched off, but mercifully escaped with life and limb.'

Most of these adverbs that are used with an absolute
meaning come from a group sometimes classified as adverbs
of cognition. One way of explaining their absolute use is to say
that they are condensed main clauses introducing dependent
noun clauses. 'Apparently/regrettably/conceivably/presum-
ably/indubitably he has been drinking' can be analysed to, 'It
is apparent/regrettable/conceivable/presumed/indubitable that
he has been drinking.'

It can reasonably be argued that 'hopefully' should be

admitted to this select band of adverbs that can be used in a condensed and absolute way. And some good grammarians and sensitive users of English do argue that it is arbitrary and inflexible to prohibit 'hopefully'; and that it is a new meaning that says compendiously what cannot be said so precisely in any other way. The *OED Supplement* merely says that the use is avoided by many writers. Other modern dictionaries classify it as informal. Randolph Quirk's *A Comprehensive Grammar of the English Language* says: 'Stylistic objections are raised to the use of the personal type of disjunct, notably *thankfully*, and above all *hopefully*.'

The argument for giving thumbs up to 'hopefully' should be resisted, because it is ambiguous, whereas none of the other cognitive adverbs used absolutely is; and because its new use is a pompous euphemism for the plain verb: 'I, we, or they hope; it is hoped; it is to be hoped.' Ask any self-important politician when he expects something to happen, and you can bet a verbal particle to a volume of the *OED* that his reply will start: 'Hopefully . . .' It is confusing to have the same word doing duty for both 'In a hopeful fashion' and 'It is to be hoped.' Rather than blunt the sharp edge of the language in this way, we should do better to invent a new word, if we must have an adverb to mean 'It is hoped.'

The Germans have two separate hoping words. So do the Dutch: *hoopvol*, 'in a hopeful fashion', and *hopelijk*, 'I hope that.' The Romance languages manage perfectly well with no adverb to mean, 'It is hoped.' Things would be clearer if we introduced 'hopably', or 'hopingly', or 'hopedly' (a trisyllable on the analogy of the journalistic neologism 'reportedly', meaning 'it is reported'), and reserved its original meaning for 'hopefully'. But a living language ignores the protests of grammarians and the interests of clarity.

If 'hopefully' must be established in its new sense, some indication that it is being used absolutely as a periphrasis for 'I hope' can be given by accent and intonation, by putting 'hopefully' in its new sense invariably as the first word in its sentence or clause, or by putting commas around it to show its absolute isolation.

Fearfully and dreadfully, the expression is establishing itself and pushing the legitimate fledglings out of the nest. Doubt-fully it can be rooted out at this late stage. Presumably

Stevenson's 'To travel hopefully is a better thing than to arrive' will be unintelligible to a future generation of English-speakers. But it is to be hoped that we can eliminate the new use, and instead say what we mean in plain words, without showing off, looking hopefully, though not optimistically, to the future of English usage.

Modern grammarians classify these adverbs used absolutely as content disjuncts, enabling the speaker to comment meta-linguistically on what he is saying, the writer to gloss what she is writing. And they subdivide the types of adverb as nicely as Aristotle. There are two main types: content disjunct adverbs that comment on the truth of what is being said; and those that make a value judgement about it. The adverbs commenting on the truth of the sentence are subdivided into three groups. The first express conviction, either as a direct claim (for example undeniably) or as an appeal to general perception (for example evidently, admittedly, certainly, definitely, indeed, and so on). The second group express some degree of doubt: allegedly, apparently, possibly, perhaps, quite likely, and so on. The third group state the sense in which the speaker judges what he says to be true or false: actually, really, ideally, officially, fundamentally, technically, and so on.

Content disjuncts making an evaluation of, value judgement about, or attitude towards what is said are divided into two main groups. Those in the first group express a judgement on what is being said as a whole, and normally apply the same judgement simultaneously to the subject of the clause. 'Rightly, Prudence Pantyhose slapped his face.' Prudence was right, and so was the slap. (Meticulous classification of anything, including language, from Aristotle onwards rapidly degenerates into nit-picking and hair-splitting.)

The second group of value judgement disjuncts carries no implication that the judgement applies to the subject of the clause. 'Remarkably, Prudence Prism went to watch the Calcutta Cup.' Her action was evidently remarkable; the speaker is not suggesting that Pru herself was remarkable. Some of these adverbs judge what is said to be strange or unexpected: amazingly, curiously, ironically, etc. Others judge what is said to be appropriate or expected: appropriately, naturally, predictably, etc. Others judge what is said to cause satisfaction or the reverse: annoyingly, disappointingly, regrettably, etc.

Others judge what is said to be fortunate or unfortunate: fortunately, luckily, tragically, etc. Others make other judgements: amusingly, conveniently, mercifully, etc. It is in this last miscellaneous group of value-judgement disjuncts that hopefully and thankfully fall.

Many of these adverbial disjuncts mean much the same as a subject-oriented adjunct or subjunct. 'Sadly, I resigned from the union.' This is close to: 'I was sad to resign' or 'I was sad when I resigned.' But the meaning can also suggest 'Sad to say, I resigned' and 'One is sad (people are sad, it is sad news for you) that I resigned.' One of the reasons that people object so vehemently on stylistic grounds to hopefully as disjunct is that it cannot be analysed like the others. It does not fit the pattern. You cannot say: 'I am hopeful to say.'

Over the past ten years 'hopefully' used absolutely, as a value-judgement adverbial content disjunct, if you insist, has established itself widely at all levels of speech in the United Kingdom, in spite of my strictures. I realized that it was hopeless to kick against these pricks any more when a shepherd in the heart of the Scottish Highlands, with nothing in sight for twenty miles in every direction except Blackface sheep and grouse, used 'hopefully' as a content disjunct almost in every other sentence.

If you want to attack it, you can no longer take the line that it is illiterate and ungrammatical. It has established itself in the language and the grammar. A more promising line of attack is to say that it is usually pretentious and otiose. But take care. There are sentences in which 'hopefully' says something that cannot quite be done so economically in any other way. Take the administrator's note put before a committee: 'My assistant has arranged for the matter to be considered by an ad hoc working party, and hopefully a proposal will be ready in time for our next meeting. I hope this approach will be acceptable to members.' The 'hopefully' in the first sentence expresses a general hope, attributed by the writer to the committee as a whole; or even a general assessment of probability: 'It is likely that the proposal will be ready in time for our next meeting.' The 'I hope' in the second sentence expresses the writer's personal hope that this will be acceptable. The two hope phrases are not interchangeable.

You can argue that 'hopefully' as content disjunct has

become a cliché that bores you to tears. You may say that those who use it belong to a different linguistic and social tribe to yours: but ultimately, when it comes to language, each man is an island entire of his idiolect. If you don't like it, you don't have to use it. I don't.

# HYPE

## High on hype

'The salesman knows nothing of what he is selling save that he is charging a great deal too much for it.'
*House Decoration*, lecture in New York, 11 May 1882, by Oscar Wilde

There is a lot of hype around, particularly in the publishing trade. It is a characteristic activity and word of the late twentieth century. It has complex origins, and is more used than understood.

One sense of hype is as the description of a certain type of journalism, building a story on a foundation of painted smoke. John Le Carré, *The Honourable Schoolboy*: 'He fabricated – or, as journalists prefer it, hyped – a "dawn interview" with a disconsolate and fictitious bar-girl.' This sense is related to hype as publicity stunt. The nostalgia for the Fifties is not entirely a media hype. You cannot establish a star in the Pop world or the best-seller world without hype and conning. The *Bookseller* in 1971 described an early variety of hype: 'In America a practice exists (known as hyping in the record business) whereby a film company which has acquired the rights in a title forces it onto the best-seller list by sending young publicity men around armed with hundred-dollar bills and instructions to buy twenty or more copies from selected book shops.'

This kind of hype, which flourishes in the inky trade and the meeja and Pop world, is a cross between creative reporting and Baron Münchausen: in short it is a euphemism for a lucrative lie. Hype was the element in which Cagliostro lived. Alessandro Cagliostro was a notorious eighteenth-century alchemist and adventurer. Among his other escapades, in 1785 while on a visit to Paris he was implicated in the sensational scandal involving Marie Antionette, the Comtesse de la Motte,

75

and the diamond necklace. Among the stories attached to this famous charlatan was a rumour that he was three hundred years old. One of his servants, asked to confirm this, replied: 'I can't. I've been in his service for only a hundred years myself.' That was hype, by an expert, of which Snipcock and Tweed, crooked publishers, would approve.

The latest variety of hype in the publishing trade, which is one of the linguistic and spiritual homes of hyping, is known in the jargon as a brown-paper job. This goes: 'Dear Literary Editor, as you can imagine, our forthcoming title, *The Pope is a Russian Spy*, is so sensational in its implications, and so important as a news story, that we dare not send out review copies in advance of publication in case the news leaks out before publication day. However, if you will sign this undertaking (with a solicitor as witness) that no mention of or reference to the book will appear in your newspaper before publication day, and if you send us a cheque for £1,000, we can arrange to send you round an advance copy in a brown-paper parcel by armoured car on the day before publication.' The correct answer to this kind of crass hype is short and rude.

In its publishing PR register, hype is a nasty, huckstering activity, to be firmly resisted by all good literary editors, who must on the other hand not allow themselves to be prejudiced against a book by the antics of its publicists. But it is an interesting word. In the publishing world it means a publicity stunt, usually disingenuous, if not downright dishonest, intended to stimulate sales. As a transitive verb, to hype means to stimulate sales by brown-paper parcels, bribes, grotesque miniature 'prezzies' loosely connected with the subject of the book, freebies, and all other such uncleanness. Angela Carter, reviewing filmstars' 'autobiographies' in *New Society*: 'Most PR hypes are crass, and the Poor Little Rich Girl hype is the crassest of the lot.' The meaning of hype in publishing is pretty well established, though the word will continue to acquire new connotations such as brown paper, because the industry is rich with ingenious publicists. Its origins are mysterious, and clearly transatlantic. Let us see if we can track them back to their lair, though it is rarely possible to be certain about the etymology of a register of language as tenuous and evanescent as slang.

One root of the modern term, and the oldest, comes from druggy slang. In this root hype is short for hypodermic needle. And it can mean (from the beginning of the century) either the needle itself (alternative hype-stick); or (from the Twenties) an injection of narcotics; or (from the Twenties) an addict who injects narcotics ('heroin substitutes don't work with a stone hype'); or a seller of narcotics, otherwise a connection ('any hype that wants to get you hooked'). The drugs literature is thick with the word, often used in different senses on the same page: 'They were dumb strung-out hypes . . . The tall one is wearing a long-sleeved shirt buttoned at the cuff. To hide his hype marks.'

Another root may be the odd American slang word 'hyper'. A vocabulary of American criminal slang of 1914 defines hyper: 'Current amongst money-changers. A flim-flammer.' A 1931 dictionary of American tramp and underworld slang defines it: 'A short change artist. The logical explanation is that the word came from *hyp*, a contraction of hypochondria.' I do not see the logic there.

But there is another kind of hyper in American as an adjective. In the Twenties it meant over-excited, manic, over-wrought: 'She tells how the grown-ups gave her Nembutal when she was eight years old because "I was hyper".' 'She's a hyper person, accustomed to constant activity.' This hyper probably comes from the Greek hyper or super, by way of such medical terms as hyperkinetic and hyperthyroid. There may also be a connection with hipped and hippish, from hypochondriac used to mean melancholic, first attested in the early eighteenth century, and evolved to mean obsessed with or hooked on. Scott Fitzgerald: 'I'm hipped on Freud and all that.' Recently the adjective hyper has been used to mean the greatest, super, very superior, as in hypermarket, and from the Greek: 'With harem cushions, a hyper-hi-fi set, ha-ha candles.'

Another cognate, to hype, means to short-change or cheat. The slang lexicographers suggest, unpersuasively, that it is connected with the North English dialect 'hipe', to find fault with, to slander; and also perhaps with high pressure. James Baldwin, *Another Country*, 1963: 'He doesn't seem to be trying to hype me, not even when he talked about his wife and kids.'

These seem to be the main roots of the family tree of the

fashionable word. Its dominant use now is the publicity stunt, con-trick sense, defined in 1968 by the *Sunday Times*, suggesting that it was a new word for British readers: 'Hype is an American word for the gentle art of getting a tune into the pop charts without actually selling any records. Its methods are various: from the crudest bribery to devious techniques for upsetting the calculations of chart-compilers.' Whatever the origin, hype came into its modern usage in the Thirties in the United States, among students, in the advertising industry, and in those great hype-factories of Hollywood and Madison Avenue. I wonder if the origin could be nothing more complicated than hyperbole. Hypodermic or hyperbole, hypochondria or hypermarket, the rest of us should treat hype coldly and with pursed lips.

It is only the word that is new. Hyping as an activity has been going on at least since the time of Odysseus. In a discussion about manpower and resources during the Civil War, somebody asked Lincoln how many men the Confederates had in the field. Abraham replied at once: 'Twelve hundred thousand.' Shock, horror, and incredulity all round. Lincoln explained: 'No doubt of it – twelve hundred thousand. You see, all our generals, every time they get whipped, they tell me that the enemy outnumbered them at least three to one, and I must believe them. We have four hundred thousand men in the field, and three times four equals twelve. Twelve hundred thousand men, no doubt about it.'

# IVORY TOWER

## Tower power

'An intellectual is someone whose mind
watches itself.
I am happy to be both halves, the watcher
and the watched.'
*Notebooks*, 1935–1942, by Albert Camus

There are worse places to live in than an ivory tower. It seems
to me preferable to a high-rise multi-storey tower block, or a
concrete bunker, or a caravan, or a stockbroker pseudo-Geor-
gian fortress in Dulwich; though I can see that you would need
to be careful and unboisterous, or you would chip the ivory.
The conversation would be livelier than in a garage, though no
doubt so much continual cleverness can be irritating. The ivory
tower is one of our most durable images; even staler than an
endless job being compared to the man painting the Forth
Bridge. There are newer and bigger and better bridges than
the Forth Bridge; and they also need continual painting. But
the neatness of the original comparison has stuck in the English
vocabulary. So has that dear old ivory tower.

John Pentland Mahaffy, the famous Provost of Trinity College, Dublin, mentor of Oscar Wilde, and author of *Greek Life
and Thought*, was an ivory-towered know-all who ventured out
of his ivory tower into the real world. He talked with authority
and without cessation on any subject that came up, and always
had the last word. This and his acerbic wit made him unpopular with his colleagues: ivory towers are jealous places, and the
chief causes of grief to intellectuals are one another's books.
His fellows in the senior common room decided to squash
Mahaffy. They picked an impossibly obscure subject, Chinese
musical instruments, and mugged it up in an old encyclopedia.
Then after dinner the next Sunday they introduced the topic.
Those who were not in the plot were amazed at the improbable

erudition of their colleagues. Even Sir John was silent for a while. Then, turning to one of the conspirators, he said: 'I see you have been reading the encyclopedia article on Chinese musical instruments that I wrote a few years ago.'

Mahaffy attracted such anecdotes as other men collect bills. He was a bit of a snob and a good businessman as well as an intellectual. On one occasion, while snipe-shooting with some of the crowned heads of Europe, a shot accidentally knocked off his hat. Turning to the culprit, Mahaffy said: 'Young man, if that had been two inches lower, it would have removed three-quarters of the Greek out of Ireland.' He certainly coined the phrase: 'Ireland is a place where the inevitable never happens and the unexpected always occurs.' He shocked the Historical Congress at Berlin in 1908 by telling the assembled scholars that the reason why English scholars, in dealing with questions of authorship, attached far more importance than the Germans to the argument from style, was that English scholars had been drilled in writing Latin and Greek prose, while the Germans had never written a piece of either in their lives. He was clearly not a comfortable companion in the ivory tower, but good value, and an example to all of us that he did not spend his whole life there, but often wandered abroad with all sorts and conditions of men.

It suggests something not entirely agreeable about our bustling, materialistic, philistine world that 'ivory tower' has come to be a term of abuse. To live in an ivory tower means to live in seclusion or separation from the world, divorced from everyday life, sheltered from harsh realities. It sounds to me a consummation devoutly to be wished much of the time. Provost Mahaffy's trick was to have the best of both worlds, the ivory tower and the country house.

The phrase had a more exotic origin even than Trinity College, Dublin. It was coined by Charles-Augustin Sainte-Beuve, one of the founders of modern criticism, in a piece on Alfred de Vigny, the poet: *Et Vigny, plus secret, comme en sa tour d'ivoire, avant midi rentrait.* Saint-Beuve wrote this in 1837, in one of his influential Monday columns, *Causeries du lundi*, which combined rigorous bookish curiosity with a humane and tolerant spirit. Vigny, army officer turned poet and novelist, was a raging romantic who believed in man's unconquerable mind, and in stoic pride as the only valid response to the inflexibility of divine justice. I suppose that's an ivory tower: it sounds to me more like a stainless steel cupboard. But the phrase caught on amazingly, and has become such a familiar part of our vocabulary that we use it without Saint-Beuve or Vigny causing a ripple in our minds.

Henry James, an ivory-tower man if ever there was one, but like Mahaffy also a mixer and diner-out, was working on a novel called *The Ivory Tower* when he died (not one of his first-division works). It includes the line: 'Doesn't living in an ivory tower just mean the most distinguished retirement?' The vivid phrase caught on, and has been widely used and abused ever since. The earliest example recorded in English is in a translation of a French book about Henri Bergson, the French philosopher: 'Each member of society must be ever attentive to his social surroundings. He must avoid shutting himself up in his own peculiar character as a philosopher in his ivory tower.' That was written in 1911. Hart Crane in 1922: 'I have grown accustomed to an "ivory tower" sort of existence.' The inverted commas indicate that the phrase was not yet entirely familiar. Ezra Pound, 1936, 'Ivory tower aesthetes.' H. G. Wells, 1940, *New World Order*: 'We want a Minister of Education who can electrify and rejuvenate old dons or put them away in ivory towers, and stimulate the younger ones.' Aldous Huxley, 1969: 'Between ivory-towerism and art for art's sake on the one hand and direct political action on the other lies the alternative of spirituality.' The career of the phrase shows wide differences of value judgement, pejoration, betterment, and bee in bonnet. The image is clearly here to stay.

We need our ivory towers and our intellectuals pottering around in them, and peering at us out of the windows, and waving occasionally, and even like Provost Mahaffy coming out and making us laugh. It would be an impoverished world if everybody lived in the market place or the factory or the Stock Exchange. The trick is to open doors and go visiting. No subject under the sun is so esoteric that it should be reserved for the inhabitants of ivory towers. *Homo sum: humani nil a me alienum puto*. I am a man, I count nothing human indifferent to me.

# LADY

## That's no lady, but what is she?

'Why haven't women got labels on their
foreheads saying, "Danger: Government
Health Warning: women can seriously
damage your brains, genitals, current
account, confidence, razor blades, and good
standing among your friends?"'
The *Spectator*, 1984, Jeffrey Bernard

Have you noticed how ladies are making a comeback: I had
supposed that the old class appellation had gone out with the
British Empire. It lingered as a designation of a public conven-
ience for females. Katherine Mansfield gave one of the earliest
written examples of this use, enclosing the word in inverted
commas to mark its novelty, in her *Journal* for 1918: 'Also,
when she goes to the "Ladies", for some obscure reason she
wears a little shawl.' Lavatory doors these days tend to be
labelled 'Women', or something facetious like 'Mermaids' or
'Fillies', or with the symbol of a Lowry matchstick person with
legs joined together to show that she is female.

'Lady' did survive into the twentieth century in other contexts, but they were mostly stagy. In *Pygmalion*, first produced
in London in 1914, Mrs Patrick Campbell playing Eliza had the
line: 'Thank you kindly, lady.' In Gershwin's 1924 song entitled
'Lady, be good', which must have done much to preserve the
appellation, the 'lady' sounds to me showy, slangy, and ironic.
To British ears 'lady' sounds American and underworld, as in
'"Lady," he said, "you talk sense. Just remember, it's guns
that count."'

One can hypothesize circumstances in which one would still
use the term 'lady' without irony or sarcasm. Oh, go on. All
right, then. Standing in bus queue. Woman in front drops
parcel. Self, addressing small child: 'Jamie, please pick up that
lady's parcel for her.' To say 'woman' in such a situation would

sound haughty and feudal, and invite a slap around the kisser with an umbrella. But for everyday purposes I thought that our brave new egalitarian world preferred to call its women women, or wimmin.

As a designation of rank the rules for lady are complex and variable. In the fifteenth and sixteenth centuries, The (or My) Lady was prefixed to the Christian name of a female member of the royal family, as Princess is now. As a prefix in the titles of the nobility in the British Isles, usage has varied greatly at different times, but the following rules are now established, if you want to play by the rules:

1 In speaking of a marchioness, countess, viscountess, or baroness (whether she be such in her own right, by marriage, or by courtesy) the prefix Lady is a less formal substitute for the specific designation of rank, which is not used in conversational address: thus 'the Marchioness (of) Mucklemoney' is spoken to, and informally spoken of, as 'Lady Mucklemoney'.

2 The daughters of dukes, marquesses, and earls have Lady (more formally, e.g. on a superscription, The Lady) prefixed to their Christian names.

3 The wife of the holder of a courtesy title in which Lord is prefixed to a Christian name is known as '(The) Lady Philip Howard'.

4 The wife of a baronet or other knight ('Sir Philip Howard') is commonly spoken of as Lady Howard; the strictly correct appellation, 'Dame Heather Howard', being confined to legal documents, sepulchral monuments, and the like.

Now there are signs that ladies are coming back in less specialized contexts. I think that the impetus for this return has come from the United States, where an uneasy feeling that to call a woman a woman, whether to her face or behind her back, is somehow disobliging and ill-managed, has been around much longer than it has here. Researcher, returning from a frustrating day in the Library of Congress: 'The whole goddam place is run by a bunch of crazy ladies!' Such *délicatesse* can be traced farther back in Britain too. I can think of two places in *The Pickwick Papers* where the intrusive 'lady' is gently mocked.

But in British idiom the revival of 'lady' has been complicated by an undergrowth of sectional and semi-private overtones. Often the two sexes use the word differently, men implying a tinge of bantering condescension, and feminists (who might be expected to abhor the handle) hearty admiration. Academic lady, very much into the *Frauenlib-und-leben* scene, will say of a pupil: 'She's a really bright lady.' But she has at the same time been heard to be scathing about headmasters who write things like, 'Hortensia is a determined and poised young lady', on UCCA forms.

The resonances of lady before 1939 are dead and gone; and who would want to resuscitate them, even were that remotely possible? But what, if anything, does the word really mean now, apart from woman? In the academic world, which has its own registers and class systems, the exemplary lady is the person, smartly dressed and coiffed, who sits at the cash register in the dining hall, wheels in the trolleys, and waits at the occasional formal dinner. If I shut my eyes and say the word, it is her image that first defines itself on my inner screen. Many of these admirable people, by their style, brisk efficiency, hair-do, and whiff of authority in reserve, put me in mind of Margaret Thatcher. How right the Russians were when they merely transliterated the second element of *zheleznya ledi*.

'Pregnant ladies' and 'She's her own lady' are two of the odder-sounding examples recently heard on the BBC. My favourite comes from the lips of a senior academic in a British university, and no mean precisian in questions of good English, who, glancing out of the window of the Trans-Siberian, exclaimed: 'Look! There's a peasant lady unfreezing the points!' How refreshing was Barbara Castle's reference to the Queen: 'Poor woman! I don't know which of us is more under the spotlight.' Perhaps no one, even today, could have said, 'Poor lady', about the Queen. It is interesting to speculate why, if 'lady' is supposed to be the more respectful word. The regulations of some London clubs are sacrosanct and stuffy. The Garrick has a rule that no visitors are allowed in the curtained lounge under the stairs. The Queen, arriving at the Garrick for a private dinner, quickly looked into the room to see the pictures and the fire. 'Not in there, Bet,' said Prince Philip, and the Queen retreated. An elderly member of the club, dozing by the fire, caught sight of her as she left. 'Who was that woman? What's she doing here?' he rumbled. 'That was the Queen, my lord,' said a waiter. 'Well, dammit, she shouldn't be here,' snapped the old man. 'Members only, you know.' In the convolutions of our class anxiety, we use lady as a handle only for those who would not have been called ladies a century ago, and call the Queen and other undoubted qualifiers for the handle 'woman'.

There is work to be done if we are to preserve the robust and honest word, 'woman'. We might start with Thorstein Veblen's *The Theory of the Leisure Class*, where he differentiates 'the woman of the archaic type that does not disown her hands and feet, the woman of physical presence', from, 'the lady, infirmly delicate, translucent, and hazardously slender'. I don't meet many translucent females these days.

Feminism and the decent modern anxiety not to sound snooty or patronizing are confusing all our words of gender and sex. Consider the resonances of the attributive uses of lady and woman as tolerable or intolerable alternatives to 'female' before such nouns as 'psychiatrist', 'elephant', 'ski-jumper', 'pimp', 'burglar', 'monstrosity', 'saint', etc. etc. And what about lady/woman/female killer as distinct from lady-killer? For that matter, what about man/gentleman midwife as distinct from male ditto? Or, for that matter again, how about gentle-man mountain and its resonance, for man mountain? Near the National Library of Scotland for the housing of science books there is a large biscuit factory manned, or rather womanned or femaled, by young hoydens of the distinctly rougher Edin-burgh sort, who emerge in hordes to the causewayside for brief diversion around lunchtime. One day a ten-year-old boy reported an exciting brawl at that time, and when I asked him who the brawlers were, he said: 'Oh, some lady toughs from the biscuit factory.'

Our linguistic confusion about sex has produced the female prefix or handle Ms, on the reasonable grounds that women do not see why they should declare their marital status in their title, whereas men do not, and when marital status has no relevance to the case. Ms is a *pis* or *ps aller*, up with which old-fashioned fellows, and a considerable number of married women of all classes, will not put. For handle purposes 'Lady Stitch' and 'Lady Wilhelmina Stitch' are out, because 'Lady' in each of these contexts has been pre-empted for another pur-pose, or, more exactly, and oddly enough, for two different ones. Dame is likewise ineligible as a general handle for women, because – whether at Eton or elsewhere – it is already too cluttered with overtones. 'Woman' however is still at liberty (or at lib?) for such a function as female prefix. But I doubt whether even the crustiest male chauvinist would want to use it, as a sort of parallel to 'Man Friday', even to save himself from the trauma of using Ms. I think that such general labels will fade away, as they serve not much purpose, and that we shall address each other by our plain names, with perhaps an onomastic code like the postal codes or an army number.

While 'lady' has rapidly become a worsened word, or at any rate a confused word, 'bird' has come up in the world fast. To find it used naturally as a term of endearment, one has to go back to Chaucerian Middle English. In *The Miller's Tale* the parish clerk, trying to chat up young Alison, the carpenter's wife, says:

> 'What do ye, hony-comb, swete Alisoun?
> My fairé brid, my sweté cinamome . . .'

I think to call a girl 'cinnamon', as sweet, is lovely. I can find only one use of 'bird' as metaphor for young woman in Shakespeare, and that is in *Cymbeline*. Juliet's nurse says 'bride' and, as 'bird' was still being pronounced 'brid', there could be a play on the words. After that 'bird' for girl disappears. There are no human birds in Fielding or Smollett; none in the great Victorians. It is exactly the sort of term Alfred Jingle would have used, if it had been available.

Towards the end of the nineteenth century 'bird' began to be used for a girl or woman, often familiarly or disparagingly, in low-life slang. In military slang 'bird' meant sweetheart. In civilian slang it could mean 'harlot'. A book of contemporary English idiom published in 1927 gives: 'Bird: used like German *Biene* especially for a more flirtatious or less reputable type of girl.' It was low slang, probably criminal's slang, implying that the bird was no better than she should be. In *A Clergyman's Daughter*, published in 1935, George Orwell wrote: 'He kept a sharp eye open for the birds.' It was a low-life context. Dorothy has escaped from her narrow spinster's life to mix with the tramps and hop-pickers.

Oddly, at the same time, 'bird' was used jocularly as slang for man, a cove. You will find that sort of bird *passim* in the dialogue of P. G. Wodehouse, and also of Dorothy Sayers, which was modelled on his. Here's an early example of the respectable male bird as appellation from Kipling's *Stalky*: 'The Head's a downy bird.'

The male bird has become extinct. The female bird has worked her way rapidly up the social scale, until she reached the top in the late 1960s with dolly-bird, which was a synonym for a Sloane Ranger. That kind of bird was always more native British than American, where they had chick. She may be related to the old English *bryd*, which meant woman, and evolved in another direction to make 'bride'. But, if so, it is odd that she waited so long to evolve. There is no record of 'bird' as slang for woman in the lexicons of criminal slang until 1890. It is a word with a split personality, half of it being upper-class slang and Sloane Ranger, and the other half derogatory with sexual emphasis. It follows the pattern of many other once 'respectable' words for woman which became devalued by taking on a sexual meaning: viz. madam and dame. 'A bird bandit' is Cockney working-class slang for a womanizer, as in *Minder* on 11 January 1984: Arthur, 'shocked' to find a woman in a dressing-gown in Terry's flat, calls the place a 'bird bandit's lair'. 'Bird' also had the meaning of penis in Sixties' US gay slang.

Our language about women has always been volatile and controversial, because women and sex are important topics. It is changing faster and more erratically than ever today because of the social, feminist, and class revolutions.

# LUNCH

## A lunch that's off course

'There are three things not worth running
for – a bus, a woman, or a new economic
panacea; if you wait a bit another one will
come along.'
Derick Heathcoat Amory, United Kingdom Chancellor
of the Exchequer, 1958–60

There are no free lunches. But thank heavens for sandwiches;
though the modern foodie-faddy, high-fibre sammos, made up
of such incongruous bed-fellows as tuna and bananas, have an
irritating habit of exploding like a hand grenade all down one's
tie. The principal advantage of a sandwich is that one can eat
it while concentrating on something else, such as the crossword. When we are sandwiching, we neither want nor expect
a gastronomic treat or an edible obstacle course. Scandinavians
with their *smørrebrød* open sandwiches, and Americans with
their quinquereme, five-decker monsters with monstrous mixtures of fish and fowl and mayo, misunderstand the function
of sandwiches.

It is well known that we have John Montagu, the fourth Earl
of Sandwich (1718–92), to thank for the handy snack. He
demonstrated that it was possible to be a professional rake and
a successful-ish politician at the same time, an example that
has been followed gratefully by his successors. As First Lord
of the Admiralty he was responsible for the unpreparedness of
the Royal Navy at the outbreak of the American Revolution.
As a gambler so keen that, if there were no action around, he
would play solitaire or patience and bet against himself, he
invented the sandwich so that he would not have to leave the
gaming table for refreshment during one of his 24-hour gambling orgies.

Sandwich was evidently a tiresome man: a practical joker,
ungainly, and as limply gangling as a pair of discarded red

88

embroidered braces. While giving a dinner party at which his chaplain was present, the Earl introduced a baboon dressed in clerical garb to say grace. The affronted chaplain left, saying as he went: 'I did not know your lordship had so near a relative in holy orders.'

He was so clumsy that a contemporary said that you could recognize him a long way off because 'he walked down both sides of the street at once'. But Sandwich cannot have been all bad. He liked to tell the following story against himself. During a visit to Paris, he took dancing lessons. When he said goodbye to his dancing master, he offered to recommend him to members of London society who might be visiting Paris. The man bowed, and said earnestly: 'I would take it as a particular favour if your lordship would never tell anyone of whom you learned to dance.' And Sandwich gave us the minor boon of the sandwich.

It is the new proverb about there being no free sandwiches for lunch that I think we are getting wrong. Proverbs flourish most in unliterary societies without books or other distractions. In the Western world they have been largely superseded by advertising slogans, television jingles, and quotations of celebrities. But we still occasionally invent a new proverb in unexpected places: 'The opera ain't over till the fat lady sings', which was coined by a Texan sports editor in 1975 in reply to the announcement, 'The rodeo ain't over till the bull riders ride.' The new proverb about no free lunch comes from economics, a quotation from Milton Friedman: or does it? We are agreed, are we not, that it is an Americanism, first popularized as one of the colloquial axioms and plonking truisms of monetarist economics: you cannot get something for nothing; you cannot get water out of a stone. But what Americans actually say is that there is no such thing as a free lunch, or 'There is no free lunch.' The British have garbled and distorted this into claiming that there are no free lunches, 'as the Americans say'.

For one thing, this seems to me a gloomy, puritanical, and ungenerous doctrine, reflecting the tarnished certainties of the new panacea of monetarism. For another thing, lunch has little to do with cost-push inflation. It must be logically possible as well as good fun to stand a friend a free lunch sometimes, without causing hyperinflation. And, for another thing, it is not what Americans in my experience actually say. I suspect that the proverb has a more romantic origin than the monetarist gibbering of Friedmanite economists.

I think it comes from the expansive days before Prohibition forced Americans to lunch for days on end on nothing but food and water. Free lunch was an attraction of the pre-Prohibition saloon. There was an elaborate spread of sandwiches and other cold cuts and foods. If he bought himself so little as a short beer, a man could help himself to as much free lunch as he wanted. If he bought no drink, he might, as Americans also sometimes say, draw back a bloody stump. There was no free lunch for non-drinkers.

Contrary to the illiberal impression given by our misused and misunderstood proverb, Americans are generous believers in free lunch. There is a restaurant chain in California that serves free lunch to anybody who confesses to the waiter that he cannot pay, because the owner has bad memories of an impoverished childhood. These origins of proverbs and catchphrases are usually impossible to prove conclusively, because they tend to be spoken and repeated many times before they are fixed in print. I dare say that the mean, modern, economical version that there are no free lunches in the hard world has kicked the old meaning out of the nest. But I believe that the old meaning was there first. Today the perversion of the economists rules. For example, from *Newsweek* of 29 December 1969: 'I was taught the first and only law of economics: "There is no such thing as a free lunch."' Which is balderdash as far as lunch is concerned, and is not the whole truth about economics.

The free lunch proverb has recently moved on in its economic context. In the late 1970s a theory became popular that big economic effects could be produced by small actions. For example, a tax cut of £1 billion would raise the national income by £5 billion, increase the Government revenue by £2 billion, reduce unemployment, and restrain inflation. This theorem was discovered written on the back of a paper napkin in a MacDonald's hamburger and milk-shake restaurant. That gave rise to an extension of the proverb: 'There's no such thing as a free lunch; but there is a cheap one.'

Of course we ought to believe in free lunch. It is a noble and heroic concept. Just to vex the economists, I propose to stand you one as soon as you have a free day. For Keynes the short run was much more significant than the long run. 'In the long run,' he used to say, 'we are all dead.' And, referring prophetically to the pitiful fallacy of new economic panaceas, he said: 'Practical men, who believe themselves to be quite exempt from any intellectual influences, are usually the slaves of some defunct economist. Madmen in authority, who hear voices in the air, are distilling their frenzy from some academic scribbler of a few years back.'

# MARBLES

## I dreamt I dwelt in marble halls

'Any euphemism ceases to be euphemistic
after a time and the true meaning begins to
show through. It is a losing game but we
keep on trying.'
*If You Don't Mind My Saying So*, 1964, by Joseph Wood
Krutch

The urbane doyen of London publishers has a lady author who
in speech continually uses the expression 'lost her marbles',
and in her books applies it to female characters. This upsets
him (he is a purist and a polite man, as well as a first-class
publisher), because he takes it to be a euphemism for castra-
tion, and therefore inapplicable to females without some risk
of terminological inexactitude. He is too embarrassed to suggest his meaning of the euphemism to his author, but he tries
to edit it out of her books when she is not looking.

Let us consider marbles, the glass spheres that schoolboys
play with, fundamentally, brothers and sisters. The original
name for a marble of that sort, an 'alley', is found recorded in
writing as early as 1720. There is no doubt that marbles have
been a slang euphemism for the testicles since the early
nineteenth century; cf. pills. 'French marbles' has been slang
for syphilis for even longer. Dr Henry Bradley in his entry in
the *OED* suggested (unpersuasively; okay, he did not persuade
me) that this might be derived from *morbilles*, an obsolete
French word for smallpox.

However, there is encouraging evidence that the marbles
that one says that somebody loses have nothing to do with
such low matters, but come from higher up the body. The
phrase comes, like so much vivid new English, from North
American slang. The earliest citation in the *OED* comes from a
dictionary of American speech published in 1927: 'Mentally
deficient: there goes a man who doesn't have all his marbles.'

Subsequent quotations suggest that the metaphor refers to the little grey cells, and the fragile matter up there, that perilous matter which weighs upon the heart, rather than the testicles. There is a nice example from Wodehouse: 'Do men who have got all their marbles go swimming in lakes with their clothes on?' This comes from *Cocktail Time*, as it happens; though it could come from any number of books in the Master's *oeuvre*, since men swimming in lakes with their clothes on is a stock theme as common as the conventional epithets in Homer. In this metaphor marbles mean brains not balls. The doyen of London publishers should continue to edit the phrase out of his author's works: but on the grounds that it has become a cliché, not because it is improper.

There is some quite persuasive evidence that marbles as euphemism for testicles is rhyming slang, in the manner of raspberry (tart), butcher's (hook), berk (Berkeley Hunt), loaf (of bread), and ginger (beer), as in 'he's a bit ginger'. In this sense the rhyme is with 'marble halls', as in, 'I dreamt I dwelt in marble halls', from *The Bohemian Girl*, 1843, by Michael Balfe, the Irish composer and singer.

This explanation sheds no light on the origin of marbles in the sense of brains. There is evidence from the North of England that these marbles are an anglicized pronunciation of the French *meubles*. In both Yorkshire and Lancashire an elderly person who is still with-it and *compos mentis* can be said to have all his/her chairs at 'ome. The suggested scenario goes like this. Lancashire woman emigrates to Canada and marries French Canadian. The scene is probably set in Quebec. Lancashire woman comments to husband that a friend has all her chairs at home. Friend subsequently behaves in a foolish manner. Husband, with imperfect command of Lancashire idiom, says that friend seems to have lost her *meubles*. I don't believe a word of this folk etymology: too damned ingenious by half for the way language works. If you want to support this theory, you can adduce the German slang for somebody who is lacking a penny in the shilling, or has lost his marbles: 'He hasn't got everything in the cupboard.'

An American variant is 'to have all one's buttons', or not, as the case may be: as in, 'When I'm sure I no longer have all my buttons I'll quit this line of work.' I suppose that the buttons have to do with neatness, compared with the uncertainty and slovenliness of clothes lacking buttons, as most of mine do. American lexicographers guess that when it comes to having lost one's marbles, there may be a reference to the lack of testicles as evincing abnormality.

To go for all the marbles means to go for broke in gambling slang. It signifies a gambler's last desperate or hopeful wager, as in CBS News: 'He goes for all the marbles.'

To lose one's marbles means to become foolish, irrational, forgetful, and so on, in American slang. This probably comes from an earlier slang phrase, 'he let his marbles go with the monkey', from a children's story about a boy whose marbles were carried away by a monkey. He is, in Ronald Reagan's famous phrase about Colonel Gadaffi, looney-tunes or a looney-toon. That comes from *Looney Tunes*, the trade name for a series of short, silly cartoon-film comedies, a paraphrasing of the similar, older series *Silly Symphonies*.

In American slang 'Mississipi marbles' mean dice. In Cape Province, South Africa, mostly among people attending Rhodes University College, Grahamstown, marble is or was a word meaning something like prestige, perhaps because marble is a grand sort of stone. For example, 'his marble is high', means that he is well in with the Professor, or some other such person. 'He is polishing his marble with so-and-so' means that he is trying to ingratiate himself.

In nineteenth-century English slang Marble Arch meant the female pudenda, I guess having something to do with being the entrance to Hyde Park. Marbles meant furniture or movables to Trollope, and other writers of the middle of the nineteenth century, in a vulgar register. It probably came from *meubles*. You will find 'money and marbles' meaning cash and effects. In the Stock Exchange jargon marbles used to mean shares in the Marbella Iron Ore Company. More recently, since about 1950, in London theatrical slang marbles have meant money, cash, or salary, as in, 'the big marbles are not earned at the Festival Theatres or the Old Vic'.

'Marbles for old men' is a jocular English description of the game of bowls. The marble orchard is American slang for a cemetery, for evident reasons. James M. Cain: 'You'll get your names in this marble orchard soon enough.' 'From marbles to manslaughter' is an obsolete London catch-phrase. *An Autobiography*, by Renton Nicholson, 1860: 'About the year 1831 or

1832, play (i.e. gambling) first became common. Harding Ackland, an inveterate and spirited player at anything, "from marbles to manslaughter", as the saying is, opened the first shilling hell in the metropolis.'

Australians, since about 1916, have used 'to toss or pass in one's alley or marbles' to refer to death. For instance, *Saturdee*, 1933, by Norman Lindsay: 'This book says a bloke kicked the bucket, an' Bill says it means that a bloke pegged out (from cribbage, c. 1900, slang for "died"), so what's it mean?' 'Means a bloke passed his alley in.'

The impressive range of slang built around marbles seems to be derived partly from *meubles*, partly from the hard crystalline metamorphic rock, and partly from the old game of alleys or marbles, so called because some of them are made from marble. The game is very old. Roman children used stones or nuts. The young Octavian, later Augustus, played *cum nucibus* with Moorish boys. Romans introduced marbles to Britain.

Marbles were associated with Lent and Good Friday. In Surrey and Sussex Good Friday is also known as Marble Day, because it marks the end of the marble season, which runs from Ash Wednesday to Good Friday. The English like a calendrical regularity in their games. Marbles was organized as a competitive sport in 1926, when the British Marbles Board of Control was formed at the Greyhound Hotel, Tinsley Green, Crawley, Sussex.

The London slang for somebody who had lost his marbles used to be that he had a screw loose, or was not quite the ticket. My impression is that both these phrases sound old-fashioned today. A more recent American idiom says that somebody is not playing with a full deck. Even newer slang for the condition is to say that someone has toys in the attic. It comes from the Rockspeak of the teenage revolution.

There is not a lot of bottle in such etymological speculations about the whirlwind and flood of slang. Which brings us round to that puzzling bottle, which is a vogue slang phrase in the United Kingdom, brought about partly by the Milk Marketing Board's advertising campaign about 'Gotta Lotta Bottle'.

Bottle is an example of rhyming slang that is alive, and well, and new. *The Swell's Night Guide*, published in 1846, defined 'no bottle' as meaning no good or useless, with this example: 'She thought it would be no bottle, 'cos her rival would go in a buster.' Since the 1970s in London bottle has been used to mean something like courage or firmness, or resolve. To have a lot of bottle is to have what used to be described as a lot of guts, or spunk, or, in the United States, balls. In British English balls mean rubbish. To lose one's bottle is to chicken out. The Milk Marketing Board, poets of the slogan 'Drinka Pinta Milka Day', picked up the phrase and made it famous.

There can never be certainty about the origin of a particular piece of slang, because it is not written down and analysed until it has passed into general use. But the great weight of evidence supports the opinion that bottle is quite recent rhyming slang for 'bottle and glass' (arse). To assert that somebody has lost his bottle is to say, in Old Testament terms, that his bowels have turned to water. The metaphor is exemplified by the old story about Nelson. In the middle of a sea battle Nelson is shot in the shoulder. He refuses to go to the sick-bay, determined to stay where his men can see him and know that they are led by him. He asks only for his red tunic, so that the sailors will not see his blood. The look-out calls down from the crow's nest that another fifty French ships have appeared over the horizon. Nelson calls back his midshipman, and asks him, when he brings the red tunic, to bring also his brown trousers.

This metaphor is probably criminal, or at any rate low-life, in origin. It is new, for it has no connection with the earlier slang uses of bottle. It is supported by copious scatological variants: for example, 'my bottle was going like a tanner and a half crown' equals 'my anal sphincter was contracting and dilating' equals 'I was scared out of my wits'. Supporters of East End football clubs, such as Millwall and West Ham, taunt the opposition with being cowardly by opening and shutting a circle made with their forefingers and thumbs.

Because it is rude, the slang has been hidden by a second rhyme. Aristotle stands for bottle, which stands for we know what. It is common in modern cockney slang to say something like: ' 'E needs a kick up 'is 'arris', or 'she's got a beautiful little 'arris'. Exceptionally, in Sar-fees Landun, bottle has been removed from its denotation by a third rhyme. Once the original becomes known to outsiders, it loses its power as a secret, cult word, and a new code has to be invented. 'That Richard's (Richard the Third equals bird; but can also be used for turd) got a smashing plaster.' Plaster equals Plaster of Paris equals 'Arris equals Aristotle equals Bottle equals Bottle and Glass equals Arse. The admen of the Milk Marketing Board, graduates in Eng. Lit. to a man and woman, cannot have imagined what they were asserting.

# MEDICAL LINGUISTICS

## Physician, spiel thyself

'The longer I practise medicine, the more convinced I am there are only two types of cases: those that involve taking the trousers off and those that don't.'
*Habeas Corpus*, 1973, by Alan Bennett

Medicine is a conjectural art, not a science. Medical jocosity: 'If you want to be cured of I don't know what, take this herb of I don't know what name, apply it I don't know where, and you will be cured I don't know when.' Most medicine is a hit-and-miss affair, though it would not do to let the punters know this. Doctors have become our modern priests and oracles, and we want them to be infallible. In fact Sir William Osler, Regius Professor of Medicine at Oxford from 1904 to 1919, explained the truth without beating about the bush when he said: 'One finger in the throat and one in the rectum makes a good diagnostician.' In *Nothing Like the Sun*, his persuasive fictional biography of Shakespeare, Anthony Burgess put the intelligent view of medicine: 'Keep away from physicians. It is all probing and guessing and pretending with them. They leave it to Nature to cure in her own time, but they take the credit. As well as very fat fees.'

Only in their nomenclature and jargon are doctors bewilderingly scientific, partly in order to blind laymen with their science. Language and medicine seem to go together. Quacks are logophiles and wordsmiths. Medical jargon tends to be correctly derived from the ancient classics, since doctors tend to be scholars, if not scientists. Sesquipedalian jaw-cracker the word may be, as 'adiadochokinesis', otherwise 'dysdiadochokinesis'. But anybody with a bit of Greek can work out that it means clumsiness or incapacity in performing rapidly alternating movements, or an inability to stop one movement and change to another: the sort of problem that President Gerry Ford was said to have in swinging his arms and chewing gum simultaneously. It is a sign of disease of the cerebellum. It is often recognized by getting the patient to tap with his fingers on the back of his other hand. And any doctor from anywhere in the world can recognize the word from its elementary Greek roots.

The trouble is that fewer doctors these days study Latin and Greek, and so the roots of their mystery of medical linguistics are becoming Greek to them. Of course, pedants can pick holes in medical nomenclature. They have, for example, a number of mongrel or chimera words, i.e. words with a Latin body and a Greek head. 'Neonatal' should really be 'novonatal'. And they get in a terrible state of chassis with words derived from the Latin *lympha*, a water-nymph, or a poetic word for water. 'Lymphagogue', a substance that stimulates lymph flow; 'lymphangitis', inflammation of a lymph node; and 'lymphopoiesis', the formation of white corpuscles in the lymphatic system, are all mongrels. But what is a mongrel between friends? There are plenty in the language at large.

Generally speaking medical jargon is one of the most logical of specialist jargons, partly because doctors seem to take an interest in language, and partly because their profession is more strictly controlled than others. The trouble is that the lay public, because of its fascination with medical matters, manifested in the proliferation of sensational medical stories in the popular press, will not leave the doctors' jargon alone. We distort the meaning of medical terms, and eventually destroy their usefulness.

Psychology, psychiatry, and psychoanalysis are a fashionable trinity of religions of the twentieth century. Their doctrines are widely regarded with superstitious awe, and as widely misunderstood; their formularies and scriptures are being widely adopted as metaphors in the common language. This misunderstanding and distortion of the latest pseudo-medical jargon is nothing new: cf. what happened to chronic, hectic, sanguine, and phlegmatic. So today laymen carelessly use neurotic and psychopath to describe unpleasant people whom they do not much care for. Obsessional is misused to mean no more than meticulous or punctual. Paranoid is misapplied to mean suspicious: 'Just Because You're Paranoid Doesn't Mean

They Aren't Out to Get You' slogan on badge of the Seventies. Psychiatrist to patient: 'You're suffering from paranoia. Anyone'll tell you.' And all the other muddy jargon of Freudian English, from ambivalent and ego to fixation and trauma, is bandied about with more freedom than precision. We blunt the points of words that do not seem always to be very sharp, even in their esoteric use.

Trauma and traumatic, in addition to being loosely used, are vulgarly mispronounced to rhyme with 'How now, brown cow?', as though they were spelled with an 'ow' instead of a Greek 'au'. Perhaps they are assumed to be German words because so many psychiatrists are German or Austrian. A neurotic is a man who builds a castle in the air. A psychotic is the man who lives in it. And a psychiatrist is the man who collects the rent, and says: 'You haven't got a persecution complex. You really are being persecuted.' Claustrophobic has recently been given a transferred secondary meaning, from a person suffering a morbid dread of confined places, to describing any confined place that might induce such a dread.

California, home of consciousness-raising, cults, and dotty enthusiasms, is the source of this slang called Psychobabble, full of heavy trips, upfronts, and interfaces. Here is an example of Psychobabble (the lady is putting off an intrusive acquaintance): 'Harvey and I are going through this dynamic right now, and it's kinda where I'm at. I haven't got a lot of psychic energy left over for social interaction. So whatever it is, maybe you should just run it by me right here. Off the wall.' A critic of do-it-yourself ego-psychology describes Psychobabble as: 'A set of repetitive verbal formalities that kills off the very spontaneity, candour and understanding it pretends to promote. It's an idiom that reduces psychological insight to a collection of standardized observations, that provides a frozen lexicon to deal with an infinite variety of problems.' Me, I think that's a bit heavy. Psychobabble is just fashionable slang that has enhanced the gaiety of nations.

Hysterical is often used in popular speech to mean little more than feminine. Hysteria is a condition that manifests itself by overaction of some parts of the nervous system, or by failure of other parts to perform their necessary work. As a consequence the victim suffers mental changes, convulsive seizures, spasms and contractions of limbs, paralyses, loss of sensation over areas of the body, affections of various internal organs, derangement of joints, and combinations of these, which closely mimic various organic diseases. The condition is far more common in women than men. As the Greek etymology of the word indicates, it used to be supposed that the origin of the disease lay in trouble of the womb. The best modern opinion is that, although sexual disturbances often occur in the condition, they are symptoms rather than causes. Hysteria is caused by the unconscious repression of painful or unacceptable emotions, from which the conscious mind dissociates itself. Treatment varies, but includes the admirable prescription, which is more generally applicable than merely to hysterics or young women: 'No hysterical young woman should remain unoccupied, but should be provided with, and forced to do, some congenial work.' To describe somebody as hysterical when you mean no more than over-excited is medically erroneous and personally offensive.

We need to be particularly careful when using medical jargon figuratively; otherwise it is easy to fall into hyperbole and absurdity. It is also easy to cause offence to those who really do suffer from the disease. For example, it is a current vogue to use schizophrenia and schizophrenic as impressive alternatives for such workaday phrases as 'in two minds' or 'undecided'. A very bad thriller of 1976 entitled *Schizophrenia* propagated the myth that the left hand of the schizophrenic does not know what his right hand is doing, probably whacking somebody on the head with a chopper. In real life schizophrenia is the technical term for serious forms of psychosis, in which there is a cleavage of the mental functions, expressed colloquially as a split personality. It brings delusional behaviour, dissociation, emotional deterioration, and other dangerous and unpleasant effects. To trivialize the word as a synonym for 'irresolute' is cheap and offensive to schizophrenics and their families and friends. Mockery of the afflicted is a primeval herd instinct, but it is not admirable.

The same applies to the current popular misuse of paranoia to mean merely a condition of nervousness or suspicion. It is, in fact, a form of fixed delusional insanity, in which delusions of persecution and grandeur, and the projection of personal conflicts, are ascribed to the supposed hostility of others. To call somebody paranoid when he merely has a chip on his shoulder, or an over-high esteem of himself, as most of us do at times, erodes the language and mocks serious infirmity. The same is true of the even crueller slang of the school playground, which uses moron to mean silly, and spastic to mean stupid, or not very athletic.

The most startling recent figurative abuse of a medical term was Lord Wilson of Rievaulx's (the former British Labour Prime Minister) suggestion that Mr Peter Griffiths, who had defeated Patrick Gordon Walker at Smethwick in the 1964 general election with a campaign that was racialist, should have the Conservative whip withdrawn from him, and serve out the Parliament as a parliamentary leper. This was not only offensive, as intended, to Mr Griffiths, who could look after himself. The suggestion that a leper has a terrifying, incurable, infectious disease, and should therefore be shunned like the plague by the rest of the community, is medieval, superstitious, and medically untrue; and grossly offensive to the 350 patients registered as suffering from leprosy in this country, and the thousands in the rest of the world. The mythology of the ancient scourge of the crusaders, and the old odium attached to the word, prevent the eradication of the disease, by frightening the lepers of primitive communities from cooperating with modern medicine.

Ruptures, catarrhs, loads o' gravel i' the back, lethargies, cold palsies, raw eyes, dirt-rotten livers, wheezing lungs, bladders full of posthume, sciaticas, incurable bone-aches. The jargon of disease and medicine alarms laymen. Either we get it wrong by slipshod extension, or we cause offence to real sufferers from the malady in question. But sometimes the medical jargon is itself flawed.

We have a little medical difficulty over the nomenclature of diabetes. It is an old and romantic story. The Papyrus Ebers, which dates from about 1500 BC, is one of the oldest medical prescriptions. The papyrus was obtained by George Ebers in Luxor in 1872, and named after him. The document, written a thousand years before the birth of Hippocrates, contains what appears to be the first reference to diabetes mellitus: 'A medicine to drive away the passing of too much urine.' The name of the condition was coined by Aretaeus of Cappadocia, a medical author about whom we know little. He was a contemporary of Galen, circa AD 150–200, and wrote medical treatises in Ionic Greek in imitation of Hippocrates. His chapter on diabetes is the first accurate account of the condition. He named the disease from *diabetes*, the Greek word for a syphon, itself derived from the verb *diabainein*, to go through. He saw the condition as 'a syphoning through the body of water', a neat description of the principal symptoms. The *mellitus* (honey-sweet) was added in the eighteenth century.

The British Diabetic Association was founded in 1934, after a letter in that establishment notice-board, *The Times*, from H. G. Wells: 'Something psychologically and socially valuable has been discovered: the latent solidarity of people subject to a distinctive disorder.' In that letter Wells used diabetics to describe patients suffering from the disease. In the association's jubilee year of 1984 a medical journal called *Diabetic Medicine* was launched, and revived the old argument about nomenclature. Pedants complain about the title. Their argument runs: only people or animals develop diabetes, and as such may be termed diabetic. Associations and medical journals do not have diabetes, and therefore may not be described as diabetic.

I never object to a spot of pedantry in a good cause such as meddling with other men's jargon. But this seems to be going too far. We already talk happily about diabetic diets, diabetic syringes (a tautology), and by extension other things that cannot be described as having diabetes in the extreme acceptance of the word. Pedantic writers insist on using such exact phrases as diabetic patients and diabetic people. I think they are being too sensitive. If diabetic was good enough for H. G. Wells, it is good enough for me. We have, after all, analogous precedents for such words as epileptics, spastics, and alcoholics.

It is all very well for pedantic prescriptivists of language to grumble about other men's jargon. We should put our money where our mouths are and offer constructive alternatives. Sometimes it is easy. I have an American research paper concerning the habits of racoons, which at one point runs: 'Although solitary under normal prevailing circumstances, racoons may congregate simultaneously in certain situations of artificially enhanced nutrient resource availability.' I cannot see that this means any more than that racoons live alone, but gather at bait. Presumably the simple version was considered not impressive enough for a research paper.

Sometimes translation would spoil the beauty of the jargon. There is an old quasi-medical term *humdudgeon*, meaning something like accidie or being down in the hypochondriac dumps, or the Cameelious Hump, the Hump that is black and blue. This is cheating, because *humdudgeon* is clearly obsolete slang, not current medical jargon. But it is such a smashing word that it is worth bringing to your attention. It is probably a portmanteau word, made up from humbug and dudgeon; and it is crisply defined in that rich source of slang, Francis Grose's *A Classical Dictionary of the Vulgar Tongue* (1785): 'An imaginary illness. He has got the *humdudgeon*, the thickest part of his thigh is nearest his arse; i.e. nothing ails him except low spirits.'

Sometimes a piece of medical jargon is a jaw-cracker, but untranslatable into simpler language. For example, the new word 'diagnosability' threatens us. The Diagnostic Methodology Research Unit of the Southern General Hospital, Glasgow, is pioneering research into how far it is possible to express clinical medicine in mathematical form. It has developed a concept of measuring the extent to which a particular disease is diagnosable. If a particular disease has characteristics that commonly exist in that disease, but are only rarely found in that condition, such a disease ought to be easily diagnosable. The Glasgow statistical and medical professors can now give a measurement to this concept; and they need a name for it. At present, as a working title, they are calling it diagnosability, meaning 'the ability to be diagnosed'. They are concerned that the word is cumbersome, and that it might be misunderstood to mean 'the ability to diagnose' by those whose Greek is shaky. If a doctor has a particular skill in diagnosis, we sometimes say that he is a first-class diagnostician; but I have never heard anybody say that he has great diagnosability, sc. ability to diagnose. The question is not a trivial one. The Glasgow medics have got hold of an important new statistical tool, and their name for it is about to become fixed and adopted as part of the jargon of medicine, and eventually of the English language.

If we can think of a better name for their concept, now is the time to tell them. The trouble is that I can think of no single word that expresses the concept they want so clearly as diagnosability. 'Cognizability' and 'identifiability' are jaw-crackers, and too general. You could try 'nosometrics' for statistical diagnosis. *Volksetymologie* would perhaps connect this proposed neologism with rhinology; but we should have to put up with that. You might consider 'singularity', since the new Glasgow concept is a measure of a disease's singularity; but this seems to me too general again. 'Diagnosticity' would avoid the stumbling block of that -ability ending. If we can do no better, it is wet and wimpish to stand on the touchline jeering at the players out there struggling in the mud of their medical terminology. Difficult new concepts may need long and difficult words.

The other singularity of medical jargon is the proliferation of medical eponyms. Hippocrates started the medical passion for glory through bylines, and immortality by giving one's name to a disease or a tool of the trade. From the arteries of Adamkiewicz to the fascia of Zuckerkandl the medical lexicon is thick with names and history impenetrable by the outsider, and by quite a few insiders as well. I often lie awake at night wondering what is the Pelger-Hüet Anomaly, and who were they. The anomaly turns out to be a dominant condition of hypersegmented leucocyte nuclei, and the hyphenated and umlauted chaps turn out to be the name of a single Dutch physician. I feel better, doctor.

We all know what Dover's Powder is, don't we? It is a sedative mixture of 10 per cent opium, 10 per cent ipecacuanha, and 80 per cent lactose. Thomas Dover was the Bristol general practitioner, 1660–1742, who studied under Thomas Sydenham (of Sydenham's Chorea, or St Vitus's Dance), and was treated for smallpox by him with a diet of oil of vitriol and twelve pints of beer a day. He survived, and later pioneered inoculation against smallpox. Many of his patients in Bristol were rich slave-traders, but he treated the poor free. In 1708 he forsook medicine to lead the most successful pirate expedition in British history, plundering the Spanish cities of Ecuador and Chile. In 1709 he rescued a shipwrecked Scottish sailor, Alexander Selkirk, from the island of Juan Fernandez off the coast of Chile, where he had lived alone for four years. Dover returned to England in 1711 with a vast booty, and resumed medical practice, mainly consulting in a London coffee house in the Strand. Meanwhile Daniel Defoe wrote *Robinson Crusoe*, based on the story of Alexander Selkirk.

These medical eponymists led gaudy lives. Dupuytren's Contracture, of course: a famous condition consisting of the forward curvature of one or more fingers (usually the third and/or fourth) due to fixation of the flexor tendon of the affected finger to the skin of the palm. Guillaume Dupuytren was the son of a poor advocate in southern France. At the age of three he was kidnapped by a rich woman from Toulouse, and kidnapped again by a cavalry officer when he was twelve. To be kidnapped once may be regarded as a misfortune; to be kidnapped twice looks like carelessness. The cavalry officer took him to Paris, where, in great poverty, he studied medicine at the Collège de la Manche. The story is that he used fat from the dissecting room cadavers to light his lamp when he was burning the midnight oil. He did well, and shortly after he became thirty he was made Surgeon-in-Chief at the Hôtel-Dieu. He was a cold, rude, ambitious man, and was given such unmedical nicknames as 'the brigand of the Hôtel-Dieu', and 'the Napoleon of surgery'. But he was a bold and innovative operator, and became famous and rich: after the fall of the restored Bourbon monarchy, he offered to lend the former Charles X a million francs in exile. He was 'first among surgeons, last among men'. And he got his name into the medical lexicon.

Examiner, showing candidate a urinary catheter with an elbow-like bend in it: 'This is a Coudé catheter; tell me, who was Coudé?'

Over-confident candidate: 'Oh, he was a nineteenth-century French urologist, sir.'

Examiner, holding up a urinary catheter with *two* elbow-like bends in it: 'And who was Bi-coudé?'

The French for an elbow is *coude*. *Coudé* means bent like an elbow.

Medical jokes are dreadful. The medical profession tends to be inordinately pleased with itself, for no good reason. But medical jargon, although it has its otiosities, vanities, impenetrabilities, and mere nonsense, as do all sectional jargons, is better than most.

# OATH

## Good Gordon!

'With regard to Policy, I expect you already have your own views. I never hamper my correspondents in any way. What the British public wants first, last and all the time is News. Remember that the Patriots are in the right and are going to win. *The Beast* stands by them four square. But they must win quickly. The British public has no interest in a war that drags on indecisively. A few sharp victories, some conspicuous acts of personal bravery on the Patriot side and a colourful entry into the capital. That is *The Beast* Policy for the war.'

*Scoop*, 1938, by Evelyn Waugh

Editors of the national press are the philosophers of the twentieth century. Without exception these great and good men are keen-eyed intellectuals with the common touch. When they smile, the little children dance laughing in the streets. When they frown, presidents tremble, and the fellows of All Souls hide under their beds.

It is, accordingly, odd that so few of them have left their names as eponymous words in the language that they used and abused for millions. The titles of some newspapers have become proper or improper words. For the Chartists *The Times* was an eponym: 'I'll *Times* you' meant 'I shall abuse you unfairly, libellously, disgracefully, and without giving you the right of reply.' The *Guardian* must have some connection with *Quis custodiet ipsos custodes?* But editors have made only a surprisingly modest impact on the lexicon. We do not say: 'If you don't shut up, I'll Harry Evans you.' Or: 'What a dear little Larry Lamb of a leader.' Or: 'Peregrine Gerard Worsthorne, that is remarkable!'

Robert Giroux, the publisher, asked T. S. Eliot whether he agreed with the widely held belief that most editors are failed writers. Eliot thought for a moment, then said: 'Yes, I suppose some editors are failed writers – but so are most writers.'

The only editor to have immortalized his name in the dictionaries is Gordon Bennett, whose name is still invoked as a mild expletive, even in Britain, often by those who have no idea that they are taking the name of an editor in vain. In 1987 he celebrated his centennial with apt eccentricity and a game of elephant polo at the Royal County of Berkshire polo ground.

James Gordon Bennett senior founded the *New York Herald* in 1835 as a penny daily of dignified standards. When this failed to make money, he changed it briskly down-market to what was called in those days yellow journalism or the gutter press. His sensationalist, populist rag was pro-slavery and pro-Tammany until the Civil War, when public opinion forced it to become strongly pro-Union (the press follows rather than forms public opinion). His paper was famous for its full news coverage, a policy extended by Gordon Bennett junior (1841–1918) when he succeeded Daddy to the editorship in 1872. He edited mainly from his home in France, establishing some of the earliest European correspondents for the American press, and making extensive use of cable communications. He believed in using good writers, such as Samuel Langhorne Clemens (Mark Twain) and Richard Harding Davis, and organized for his paper Stanley's expedition to Africa to find Dr Livingstone, I presume (1869–72). In 1887 (which is where the centenary elephants came in in 1987) he founded the Paris *Herald*, which became the outstanding English-language paper on the Continent. This is the ancestor of the present *International Herald Tribune*, after amalgamations, changes of ownership, and the other chances and changes of the inky trade, which accordingly celebrated its centennial (or as the British say, centenary) in 1987 with elephant polo. It is still a jolly good paper, giving a wider world perspective than most national dailies, and letting good writers have their heads.

'Gordon Bennett!' as expletive is one of a large class of expletives used to avoid direct reference to God. By gosh, gum, and gad are members of the class. Gee whizz is a softened code for Jesus. Zounds is a euphemism for God's wounds by aphaeresis, the dropping of a sound or a syllable at the beginning of a word. W. C. Fields used to exclaim: 'Good Godfrey Daniel!'

It is touching to think that the name of the great editor still lives as an exclamation suitable for the mild-mouthed. But I think that our present editors are not trying hard enough to fix their names in the vocabulary.

# POLITICS

## The art of politics: easy as ABX

'Since a politician never believes what he says, he is surprised when others believe him.'
*Newsweek*, 1 October 1962, General Charles de Gaulle

Politics, being a powerful form of persuasion and pulling the wool over people's eyes, erodes the language like the tides. The political battle is fought in the lexicon as much as in the ballot-box and the assembly. Since the beginning of politics the struggle has been between words, representing ideas and parties, such as aristocracy and democracy, capitalism and socialism. Our political lexis is continually being formed, altered, shifted, redefined, influenced, modified, confused, and muddled in the storms of debate. Here is a small menagerie of political weasel words that are fashionable among the chattering and scribbling classes at present.

A is for Anarchist, strictly the belief that government is intrinsically evil, or that historical circumstances have conspired to make it so; loosely a useful name to call anybody to the left of or less authoritarian than you.

B is for Bombshell, strictly a surprise or a pretty woman; loosely a noisy word for headlines to describe something as boring as a pound of cold baked beans, or yet another opinion poll. Also for Bourgeois and Bureaucracy, both from the French, words that are used as bludgeons rather than rapiers by the left: Max Weber feared that the struggle between capitalism and socialism would be overtaken by the victory of bureaucracy as a system. There is little sign of this happening yet.

C is for Caring and Compassionate, which all wets and lefties claim to be. And Clean, which all good politicians hope the election will be – but not yet! Also Consensus, the opposite to Conviction politics. Consensus has been around for a while. Cicero argued that *Consensus juris*, agreement in judgement, was a necessary condition for the existence and endurance of a republic.

D is for Democrats, which our lot are, as opposed to the unscrupulous Demagogues of the other parties. Also for Dialectic, which is what happens when we hoist the black flag of philosophy from Plato to Kant to Marx. Also for Doctrinaire, which is how we describe our opponents' adherence to their ideas. Our adherence to our ideas is, on the contrary, principled.

E is for Economics, a subject about which politicians talk much and know little, but all agree that our lot can produce the beginning of the upturn of the downturn, if only the voters give us a chance. Also for Élite and Élitist, which are fearsome terms of fashionable abuse, implying snobbery and selfishness. Élite has become involved in the British class system. All it means is a selected or chosen group. It makes sense to select the best when you are picking a football team or a symphony orchestra. What are objectionable are self-selected and self-perpetuating closed élites, otherwise old boys' networks, which the British are expert at.

F is for the Family, which we are all in favour of, which is why politicians give photo opportunities of themselves kissing babies. Also Fascist, which has hardly any descriptive meaning left, and is merely an insult, meaning somebody a bit to the right of our lot. Also Fudge and Mudge, a useful put-down to describe the absurdity and opacity of policies with which we don't agree.

G is for Government, which our party hopes to form, by hook or by crook, by hung parliament or swung parliament, by fudge or by mudge after the election.

H is for Health, particularly the National Health Service of the United Kingdom, which is a holy cow that only our lot can be trusted to care for. Also Hegemony, a fashionable word, meaning the ascendancy or domination of one power or party within a group, or of one social class over others. Also History, which we all think is on our side, which is attributing partisanship to something incapable of taking sides.

I is for Incomes Policy, which is either an outmoded error that never worked, or an essential engine for running the economy, or a bit of both, depending on where you stand. Also Imperialism, a slippery weasel word: any word that refers to fundamental political and social conflicts cannot be reduced semantically to a single proper meaning. Words are the weapons of politics.

J is for Journalists, called Journos with affectionate contempt in Australian slang, who are either corrupt and sensationalist liars, or fearless crusaders, depending on what they wrote about you in this morning's papers.

K is for Keynes (John Maynard), who was either a major prophet, or a deluded heretic of modern economics, depending on where you stand in the battle line.

L is for Liberal: if God had been a Liberal, there wouldn't have been ten commandments; there would have been ten suggestions. 'As the intelligent are liberals, I am on the side of the idiots,' Maurice Baring.

M is for Mandate, which we shall claim to have, if elected, for all the promises in our Manifesto that are convenient to keep; but not for those that aren't. And the Meeja, which is or are disgraceful. And the Masses (huddled, yearning to breathe free). Also Myth, which a successful politician lives and moves and has his or her being in.

N is for New Left and New Right, much the same as the old varieties, but more self-righteous.

O is for Obscenity, strictly something outrageous to accepted standards of decency, often the standards of the moral majority (sc. a self-styled, self-important minority); loosely a useful term of abuse for politics with which one disagrees.

P is for the People, to whom all politicians occasionally have to suck up. And Patriotism, which is a useful red rag to wave at the People and the impressionable pop journos. And Progressive and Pragmatic, which we all claim to be when it suits us.

Q is for Quietism, a philosophy devoutly to be wished, but never found in politicians.

R is for Referendum, which all politicians want for issues that they are pretty sure of winning, until they come to power, and no longer have to bother.

S is for Socialism, which is either dead, or ought to be killed, or is the true Brotherhood of Man, depending on how you pronounce it. Also Standards, which are steadily slipping until you elect my lot to uphold them.

T is for Trade Unions, which either need to be put in the hands of their members, or released from their handcuffs, or put back into the hands of their leaders, or brought within the law, or have their heads chopped off.

U is for Ulster Unionist, who we all hope will never hold the balance of power. And Unemployment, which we have learnt to tolerate at a level higher than would have been thought possible twenty years ago. And Utilitarianism, the doctrine of the British empiricists. Jeremy Bentham: 'An action is conformable to the principle of utility when the tendency it has to augment the happiness of the community is greater than any it has to diminish it.'

V is for *Vox Populi*, which may be *Vox Dei* in theory, but can safely be ignored between elections.

W is for Wets, a threatened species of Compassionate Tories, now almost extinct, so called from prep-school slang of the Fifties.

X is the vote you make on a ballot paper. Make sure you do not waste it, for it is the only democratic act that most of us are allowed to perform, and there is a long time between elections.

Y o Y do middle-aged politicians and the meeja witter on interminably about Youth? Because they want to catch the new voters (newspaper-readers, punters), dumbo.

Z is for Zzzz, the philosopher's and the plain man's response to a party political broadcast, and most political oratory.

# SEMANTIC SHIFT

## Have a nice say

'The meaning of a word in general use is determined, not by pundits, still less by official action
of any kind, but by the people. It is the duty of
the professional linguist to find out, by investi-
gation, what the usage of the people is, in this
particular matter, and to record his findings.'
*On Defining Mahogany*, 1940, by Kemp Malone

What do we do when a familiar word starts to change its
meaning, as words have a slippery way of doing, in a living
language? There can spring from our lips that fiery formula
that has sprung from the lips of so many choleric old gentlemen in the course of the past two centuries, and which was
recorded first by Max Beerbohm: 'I shall write to *The Times*.' If
we are the Church of England, we revise our *Book of Common
Prayer* so that our congregations find themselves saying something far less sonorous than, 'Prevent us, O Lord, in all our
doings', in the collect. If we are editing Shakespeare for
schools, we gloss Hamlet's characteristically quibbling line, 'By
heaven, I'll make a ghost of him that lets me', to explain that
'let' means 'prevent'; but not in the *Prayer Book* sense. From
the many comic sketches of the balcony scene in *Romeo and
Juliet* on television, it is evident that there are those among us
who think that when Juliet asks, 'O Romeo, Romeo! wherefore
art thou Romeo?', she is expecting the answer, 'Over here,
luv.'

After alleged mispronunciation by BBC announcers, the
most popular topic for grumpy linguistic letters to *The Times* is
semantic change. You can imagine the sort of thing: 'Dear Sir,
what is the new generation coming to when it uses *alibi* to
mean any kind of excuse, when we can all see from its
etymology that it means a particular kind of excuse, viz. having
been somewhere else at the time of the incident?'

114

It is worth asking such grouches when they think that the English language was fixed at its Golden Age or vintage year, when words were used properly, with their real meanings. It usually turns out to have been when the grouch was at school, fifty years or so ago, having grammar and the spelling of 'eschscholtzia' thwacked into him by Old Chalky in the Lower Shell.

Meanings change all the time in a living language, to meet new needs: for example, the semantic shift in 'prestigious', which came into the language in the sixteenth century to mean 'practising juggling, or legerdemain; cheating; deceptive, illusory'; but has been altered to mean the adjective of the quality we worship in the twentieth century, prestige. It is no good shouting that prestigious really means 'juggling'. It no longer does, except in historical contexts, or for obdurate antiquarians.

Consider the modern loss of the distinction between 'disinterested' and 'uninterested', which so vexes purists. They know that the words have quite different meanings. A good judge ought to be disinterested, but not uninterested in the case he is trying, at least not so uninterested as to fall audibly asleep after lunch. However, it is regrettable but true that the distinction between the two words is quite recent. If you look to their roots, you will find good writers from Donne to Junius using 'disinterested' in its sloppy and 'erroneous' modern sense of 'uninterested'. The distinction is useful, but modern.

We have to decide, when words start to shift their semantics, whether the change suits our own idiolect. 'Envision' is in the dictionary now. Do we need it, when we already have 'envisage' and 'foresee'? Well, I don't. But that is my affair. If enough English-speakers adopt it, it will cease to be a careless or ignorant mistake, and become the right word. Everybody says 'dialogue' when they mean 'discussion' or 'negotiation'; trendies and ideologues say 'confrontation' for 'disagreement' or even 'threat of attack'. We may disapprove, politically and linguistically. But, if the continual public opinion poll of language decides that we need those meanings, that is what the words are going to mean, however many grouchy letters we write to *The Times*.

Value words suffer semantic shift even faster than descriptive words, because each age finds its own values and customs.

That is why it helps to be a bit of a linguist to study history.
When John Locke called Isaac Newton a 'nice' man, he meant
not that he was a good egg, but that he was tetchy and
grouchy. At the same time, nicely illustrating the fundamental
sexism of language, if Locke had described a woman as 'nice',
he would have meant that she was red-hat-no-knickers fast.

'Nice' is a good example of the way that words change their
meanings like putty; and of the way it never makes sense to
speak of the true or correct meaning of a word. 'Nice' came
into English from Old French, and originally the Latin *nescius*,
in the fourteenth century. At first it kept its original Latin
meaning of foolish and silly and ignorant. But almost at once
it started on its long and erratic semantic journey, which has
not ended yet.

By the fifteenth century the word had shifted to mean
wanton or lascivious. Then the little four-letter word started to
pup meanings like a beagle bitch. Its entry in the *OED* has
seventeen principal meanings, and numerous subsidiary ones.
When applied to women, nice meaning wanton came to mean
coy, and also shy, because the woman whose behaviour the
nice woman aped might be shy.

From coy, another branch sprouted the meaning 'fastidious'
or 'precise'; a meaning that survives in 'a nice distinction'. By
the eighteenth-century nice had begun to acquire its modern
meaning as a cottonwool pro-word of approval. 'He's a nice
man' means 'I like him'. I detect some evidence that 'nice' is
shifting its meaning again to the opposite, in the cynical
tendency to turn value words upside down. 'That's a nice
assignment' is not necessarily a lot of fun; in the same way
that 'a bad dude' can mean 'a good man'. When tempted to
complain about the quicksilver quality of English meanings,
remember 'nice'.

Mistakes and misapprehensions become frozen as misquo-
tations in a kind of semantic shift, more honoured in the
breach than the observance, to use that tag correctly for once.
You cannot study language without studying history as well.
Words live and have their meaning in historical contexts. Here
are two exemplary popular historical misunderstandings that
pass through our minds and mouths without causing a ripple.

The first is John Knox's monstrous regiment of women,

which is popularly understood, I am sure, to refer to a horde of harpies marching four-a-swinging-breast.

What 'regiment' meant to Knox was not a battalion; but rule or government. It was a favourite word of his: 'Ane man maist unworthy of ony regiment in ane weill rewlit commenwealth.' When he wrote, Mary Tudor reigned in England, and Mary Stuart in Scotland; and that was what the monstrous little bigot found monstrous. He had nothing against wimmin in general (in their proper place, of course, i.e. bed and kitchen, ye ken); though it is clear from his pamphlet that he was not into Women's Lib.

The other fashionable historical misquotation comes in the famous speech in which Queen Elizabeth I described herself as 'mere English'. What she meant was 'complete and undiluted English'. There was nothing dismissive about that 'mere', which has shifted its meaning. She was making a very political point. Her predecessor and half-sister, Mary, had had a Spanish mother and a Spanish husband, who was now claiming the English throne on the strength of that marriage. Elizabeth was appealing to the patriotism and chauvinism of her sailors, by telling them that she was as pure English as they were, not a dreadful dago. The contrast with her unpopular predecessor is pointed. Understatement was not her style, nor that of her age.

This was the girl who, threatened by the Armada, said things like: 'I have the heart and stomack of a king, and of a king of England too; and think foul scorn that Parma or Spain, or any prince of Europe, should dare to invade the borders of my realm.' When Elizabeth called herself mere English, she was not depreciating herself or apologizing. She was boasting.

# SHORT STROKES

## All rowed fast,
## but none so fast as stroke

'In creating, the only hard thing's to begin;
A grass-blade's no easier to make than an oak;
If you've once found the way, you've achieved
    the grand stroke.'
*A Fable for Critics*, line 534, 1848, by James Russell Lowell

Politicians are prolific phrase-makers. *C'est leur métier*. Their careers are defined by a few phrases, probably invented by speech-writers, which stick in the national memory. So for Lord Stockton (Harold Macmillan): wind of change; little local difficulties; most of our people have never had it so good. Lord Wilson of Rievaulx (Harold Wilson): a week is a long time in politics; white heat of the technological revolution; the pound in your pocket.

Our present lot are still phrase-making, so it is too early to fix them in the quotation dictionaries with the rubbish for which they will be remembered. But Mrs Thatcher already has Iron Lady, adopted gratefully by her from the Soviet magazine, *Red Star*; the lady's not for turning; and, I don't mind how much my ministers talk – as long as they do what I say.

Because they have more power, more say, and more speech-writers, American politicians contribute more than British ones to the midden of language. From nothing to fear but fear itself, to *Ich bin ein Berliner*, our presidents have added to the gaiety of nations, and enriched the public stock of harmless rhetoric. Ronald Reagan is likely to be remembered for macho, genial, John Wayne imagery about Walking Tall; though I hope his 'The thought of being president frightens me; and I don't think I want the job' survives into history.

However, the latest gung-ho political phrase from Washington strikes me as being a bit too hairy-chested and Ramboesque to become widely popular. The phrase is 'short strokes', and it appears to mean something like coming towards a climax. For example, George Schultz in testimony to a House committee on negotiations with the Soviet Union: 'Clearly the negotiations were coming towards the short strokes, and the Soviets were beginning to adjust their position.'

What can Schultz have had in mind? The classical explanation could be that he was referring to the Ancient Greek trireme. Short strokes, we can say with spurious confidence because we know so little about ancient naval warfare, were those used by the rowers during the last spurt before engaging the enemy. Rowed to a heart-breaking, blood-vessel-bursting fast rhythm on the small drum used to set the speed of the oars.

The Scotsman may say that the short strokes are a metaphor from golf: the nearer you get to the hole, the shorter the strokes that you play, in theory at least, unless you have an accident with your sand-blaster in the dreadful bunker with the turf-covered island in the middle to the right of the 18th green at Muirfield.

The artist could argue that short strokes are a metaphor derived from drawing or painting, and mean getting down to detail. It is the sort of phrase that an advertising agency art director might use, reproving an underling or rival for making too detailed criticism of what he intended as a broad-brush approach.

I do not buy any of these explanations.

We may be getting closer if we consider stroke as a pop-psychological term, as in stroking the cat, to mean reassuring somebody by approval or congratulation, and hence to manipulate by flattery. I had an editor who used to say at conference, cynically I thought, 'Stroke him,' meaning that the Foreign Editor should send a herogram to some vain and insecure hack. Here is an example from a recent novel: 'He started off dishing out some nice strokes. With an admiring smile he told me how smart I was, how honest, so absolutely reliable.' And here is another example from an American magazine: 'Let's face it, everybody needs their strokes and that would be very ego-satisfying.'

Eric Berne defined this sort of stroke in *Games People Play*, 1964: 'By an extension of meaning, "stroking" may be employed colloquially to denote any act implying recognition of another's presence. Hence a *stroke* may be used as the fundamental unit of social action. An exchange of strokes constitutes a *transaction*, which is the unit of social intercourse.' And much more pretentious and windy shrink psychobabble.

But I do not think that even that kind of social intercourse is implied by the new short strokes from Washington. These sound to me as though they refer back to stroke as defined by Francis Grose in his *Classical Dictionary of the Vulgar Tongue*: 'To take a stroke: to take a bout with a woman.' This sort of stroke means the act of copulation. Here is an example from a recent novel: 'I happened to be engaged upon a variation of the sexual act known as the "Birmingham Stroke" at the time our little love-nest started rolling.'

It may be the latest political slang from Washington. It is certainly cowboy. But I do not see it catching on widely in polite society. But then, society is no longer polite. And, even when it was, you never could tell with either society or slang.

# TAKE CARE

## The trick of being carefully casual

'A little sincerity is a dangerous thing, and
a great deal of it is absolutely fatal.'
*The Critic as Artist*, 1890, by Oscar Wilde

Next time you are at Southend Airport, would you care to join
me for a coffee and doughnut in the Terminal Refreshment
Café? Terminal is an example of a word that is changing its
dominant meaning before our very eyes. Because of the proliferation of airline, railway, coach, and other termini, we are
losing sight of terminal in its euphemistic sense to describe the
undiscover'd country from whose bourn no traveller returns. I
can think of more cheerful names than Terminal for cafés at
airports, at any rate for those of us who are sensitive about
language or frightened of flying.

But, should we end up there, I do hope that you will not bid
me farewell as I shamble towards boarding at Gate 1 by saying:
'Take care.' This has become a ragingly trendy expression of
valediction. It fills me with a sense of superstitious unease
when people say it to me. Do they know something that I
don't? In any case, how do they expect me to take care when
the wing falls off, or the pilot has a stroke, or the hijackers
come dancing down the aisle? Which of us by taking thought
can add one cubit unto his stature, or by taking care can add
one percentage point to his chances of survival in an aeroplane,
the Underground, the long-distance coach, or among all the
changes and chances of life on this mortal planet? In any case,
taking care is not the spirit that made Britain Great: nor is it
the dominant mood of the uncaring Eighties.

Taking care is quite an old English idiom. In the *Authorized
Version* the Good Samaritan brought the man who had fallen
among thieves to an inn, and 'took care of him'. Ideologues of
the New Right argue that he could do this not because he had

compassion and a bleeding heart, but because he had a fat
wallet to pay the landlord. In one of his letters, Lord Chester-
field, that worldly wit, whose advice was described unkindly
by Johnson as teaching the morals of a whore, and the manners
of a dancing-master, wrote: 'I recommend to you to take care
of minutes; for hours will take care of themselves.' Sound
advice that has become a cliché or proverb.

Taking care gradually acquired slang connotations by accre-
tion. In Victorian society 'take care of Dowb' came to be a slang
catch-phrase for number 1, or for one's chums in an old-boy
network. The story was that some VIP wanted to look after an
officer called Dowbiggin, and sent to Lord Raglan in the
Crimea the message, 'Take care of Dowbiggin.' Communications broke down in the middle of the transmission of the
message, as they tended to in that incompetent campaign, so
that all that arrived was, 'Take care of Dowb.' The generals
assumed that Dowb was some part of the Russian force or
position, and looked anxiously out for it. When the truth about
the full message came out, 'Take care of Dowb' became current
as a euphemism for nepotism, or jobbery of some kind or
another, or keeping an eye on the main chance for oneself seen
as Dowb.

In this crooked century to take care of somebody has become
euphemism, or sardonic meiosis, for killing somebody in
gangster or espionage circles: cf. to eliminate, to account for,
to neutralize, to put away, to take for a ride, to take for an
airing, to take out into the country, to turn off, to demote
maximally, and dozens of other cosmetic phrases. In espionage
jargon if those to be assassinated are from the opposition, the
murders are called sanctions; if the target is one of ours, the
murder is called a maximum demote. Take care.

'Take care' as farewell seems to have originated in Canada
late in 1973 or very early in 1974. It spread at once, and may
have connections with such American phrases as 'to take care
of Numero Uno', and 'The Lord helps them that take care of
Numero Uno.' In British use it is related to such valedictions
as, 'Mind how you go', and 'Have a nice/good day.' I suspect
that Alan Ross and Nancy Mitford might have classified 'Take
care' as Non-U. But the world has changed in the twenty-five
years since Mitford reprinted in *Noblesse Oblige* Ross's seminal
article in the *Bulletin de la Société Néo-Philologique de Helsinki*, of

all places. All classes tend to say 'Take care' as goodbye. We are less keen on class, and more keen on appearing one of the lads at all costs.

That is why wearing the old school tie is done only by the very old or the very insecure. As soon as we left school we rushed to the shirtmakers to buy the old school tie as a badge of freedom and adulthood. Now the young would not be seen dead in it, except perhaps at weddings, and then only sheepishly. And the older have followed the fashion, and discarded their neckties with slanting stripes of unsuitable mixtures of magenta and emerald and old gold, obsolete flags of an exclusive status. Even in the City of London, that surviving brass tower of snobbery, it is a solecism to wear an old school or regimental tie before Friday, when it is considered just okay, on the mysterious grounds that everybody is off in the lunch-time rush to the country cott.

The modern terror of being thought élitist also explains why we never address people by their surnames: it would sound unfriendly and snobbish. Old-fashioned gents of a certain class still address one by one's surname *tout court*, and we recognize that this is the most intimate appellation that they have. They would give the handle Mr only to tradesmen; and they may still address their wives as Mrs followed by her married name, like gentlemen in Jane Austen. So we start even our letters with 'Dear Philip Howard' in case 'Mr Howard' looks cold; and Terry Wogan, and other show-biz shepherds of 'celebrity' interviews, are on first-name terms with archbishops and presidents even as they meet them for the first time.

A striking example of this modern tendency towards seeming to be demotic and terror of appearing snooty (a welcome tendency in view of the past history of English class snobbery) is the remarkable progression of 'Cheers'. This developed early in the century as a friendly exclamation or exhortation to be cheerful, especially as a salutation before drinking. It was cognate with 'Cheerio' and 'Cheero' or 'Cheerho', which were used either as drinking toasts or informal goodbyes. Nice philologists trace the development of 'Cheerio' out of 'Cheero' to the officers in the First World War. Nowadays 'Cheerho' sounds the U version, and 'Cheerio' the demotic.

Here are some contemporary examples of the uses: 'Cheero! I wish they'd killed you in a decent show.' (Siegfried Sassoon in *Counter-Attack*, 1918.) An advertisement in the *Sphere*, 1919: 'Cheers – I'm longing to see you and Kenilworth together – the two nicest things on earth.' Since the Second World War 'Cheers' has become the dominant word, and since the Seventies it has started to be used as a less formal, less élitist word for 'thank you'. 'Cheers' is what people say when given change in the supermarket, or in acknowledgement of any small favour. It means, 'Thanks'. Quite recently 'Cheers' has started to be used to mean 'Sorry' for some small accident or inconvenience. 'Sorry' apparently sounds a bit haughty, and 'Excuse me' intolerably patronizing. If somebody bumps into you on the escalator, or pushes through the door before you, a common idiom is for him to say, 'Cheers'. The correct reply is not, 'Two-and-a-half cheers', or 'One hand clapping'.

Let us not fuss too much about the vogue valedictory phrase, 'Take care', or the vogue thank-you or sorry, 'Cheers.' Like most vogue phrases they will soon begin to sound old-fashioned. They are not really so very different from such old phrases for saying goodbye as 'goodbye', 'farewell', 'adieu', and the Latin *vale*. Remember the haunting, sobbing line of farewell, full of elisions, from Catullus ci: *Atque in perpetuum, frater, ave atque vale* (And so, my brother, hail, and farewell evermore). Come to think of it, it is no odder than the private idiom or idiolect favoured by some of us, 'Go well.' Cheers.

# WHITE KNIGHTS

## Sir Lunchalot

'So they shook hands, and then the Knight rode
slowly away into the forest. "It won't take long
to see him *off*, I expect," Alice said to herself, as
she stood watching him. "There he goes! Right
on his head as usual! However, he gets on again
pretty easily – that comes of having so many
things hung round the horse – "'
*Through the Looking-Glass and What Alice Found There*, chapter
8, 1871, by Lewis Carroll (Charles Lutwidge Dodgson)

Outsiders, and even some insiders, were confused in the 1980s
by squadrons of White Knights that started to gallop around
the City and financial pages of the newspapers, without ever
once falling off their horses. For example, from the *Guardian*,
dealing with some City drama that seemed immense at the
time and was forgotten a month later: 'Thomas Tilling emerged
yesterday as the White Knight appointed by Berec to save the
Ever Ready battery-maker from the clutches of Hanson Trust.'
Here is a cognate example from *Backlash*, a book published in
the United States in 1977: 'Woody would like nothing better
than to play the White Knight to my damsel in distress.' The
context here is not financial and industrial wheeler-dealing.
But the White Knight is still seen as some sort of Saint George,
or Perseus coming to the rescue of an Andromeda.

A White Knight has become Stock Exchange slang for a
champion or hero, in particular a company that comes to the
aid of another company facing an unwelcome takeover bid. In
1986 Guinness was described as a White Knight coming to the
help of the Distillers' Company faced with takeover; prema-
turely, as it happened, since the surcoats of the managing
director and his chums on the board were subsequently found
to be pretty grubby. But the use is being extended from the
financial world to mean good guys generally. For example,

from *The Times*: 'The Italian Communist Party will take its members into the regional election campaign next month as White Knights dealing with the joint evils of corruption and reaction.'

I think that this increasingly fashionable cliché is at best illiterate, and at worst misleading. What its users have in mind is the hackneyed phrase, 'a knight in shining armour'. But a White Knight brings irresistibly to the mind of anybody who has read Lewis Carroll (which means pretty well everybody, even in the City) a quite different sort of figure. Come on, you remember the White Knight. An enthusiastic but bumbling old fool. Always falling off his horse. Ineffectual, very. Forever inventing things like boxes for keeping clothes and sandwiches in, which he carries upside-down so that the rain can't get in. Sandwiches and clothes all fall out, of course. Devises way of getting over gate by putting head on top of gate, then standing on head which raises feet high enough to surmount obstacle. Sings that haunting song called 'Ways and Means', but with the name 'The Aged Aged Man':

> Whose look was mild, whose speech was slow,
> Whose hair was whiter than the snow,
> Whose face was very like a crow,
> With eyes, like cinders, all aglow,
> Who seemed distracted with his woe,
> Who rocked his body to and fro,
> And muttered mumblingly and low,
> As if his mouth were full of dough,
> Who snorted like a buffalo –
> That summer evening long ago
>    A-sitting on a gate.

It is fine nonsense verse. I think there is an echo of it in Tennyson's poem about Catullus:

> Row us out from Desenzano, to your Sirmione row!
> . . .
> Tenderest of Roman poets nineteen-hundred years ago.
> 'Frater Ave atque Vale' – as we wander'd to and fro
> Gazing at the Lydian laughter of the Garda lake below
> Sweet Catullus' all-but-island, olive-silvery Sirmio!

Catullus was a great deal more than tender and sweet. Be that as it may, if the White Knight we know and love from

Lewis Carroll were to offer to come to the help of a company, prudent directors and shareholders would get out at once; and emigrate if they had any sense.

Protesting about this recent ambivalence of White Knights is more than a pedantic itch to verify one's literary references. The new meaning is potentially confusing because White Knight is at the same time used in its endearingly dotty sense: '"I believe I have made a really significant discovery," cried Dr Otterley with the infatuated glee of a White Knight': Ngaio Marsh in *Off With His Head*. And this from the *New York Times*: 'The Rangers' problems stemmed from the habit that the team's general manager had of hiring ineffectual cronies to coach the club, and then replacing them with himself when they failed – a kind of White Knight compulsion.' Those New York scribes and jocks are better-read and more careful with their slang than London stockbrokers: surprise, surprise. With White Knight being used at the same time to mean a) an enthusiastic idiot and b) a conquering hero, there is scope for misunderstanding, which is the sin against the Holy Ghost in using a language.

Other popular phrases may have influenced the shift in meaning. 'The man on the white horse', the politician, usually with military connections, who is going to solve all the country's social, political, and economic problems at a stroke, was a popular image for political journalists from the late nineteenth century until fairly recently. He seems now to have disappeared. Maybe he has been conflated with the knight in shining armour to make the new-style White Knight. A White Hope was originally a white boxer who might beat Jack Johnson, the first Black to become world heavyweight champion (1908–15). He is now a person who, or thing which, it is hoped will achieve much, or on whom or which hopes are centred.

White Nigger has nothing to do with the phrase; nor does White Lady, which is used to mean two kinds of alcoholic drink, one geriatric Sloane, and the other meths, and a killer. A White Sergeant is a bossy 'breeches-wearing' wife: Francis Grose, the antiquary, draughtsman, and very early collector of slang, defines her in the first edition of *A Classical Dictionary of the Vulgar Tongue*: 'A man fetched from the tavern or ale house by his wife is said to be arrested by the White Serjeant.' Nor do I think we should waste time on White-Haired Boy, which is antipodean in origin, or White-Headed Boy, which is Irish.

Americans, who have no medieval knights in armour on white horses in their native history, have their own metaphor of approval for good guys: White Hat. This comes from the only native American art form of western movies, in which, symbolically, heroes wear white hats and villains wear black. The phrase was popularized during the Nixon administration, when there were a lot of cowboys in business. The TV commentator and cougar-hunting hostess, Barbara Howar, once invited William Safire to a party with the gloss: 'Wear your white hat.'

The original Americans, the Apache and Ute Indians, described anybody of Caucasian origin as White Eyes. I do not think they meant it as a compliment. But we should make up our minds about whether a White Knight is a hero or a bumbler. I vote, Bumblers Rule, OK?

# PART 2

# NEW USAGES

# AFFIRMATIVES

## The answer's in the infirmative

> 'And I thought well as well him as another and
> then I asked him with my eyes to ask again yes
> and then he asked me would I yes to say yes my
> mountain flower and first I put my arms around
> him yes and drew him down to me so he could
> feel my breasts all perfume yes and his heart was
> going like mad and yes I said yes I will Yes.'
> *Ulysses*, 'Penelope', closing words, 1922, by James Joyce

I worry about the future of the short inoffensive, useful little
word, peculiar to English, imported by our Anglo-Saxon forefathers, as they waded, dripping, ashore in Kent and Essex
and Suffolk. The word is 'yes'.

Yes expresses an affirmative reply. It is derived from the Old
English *gese, gise, gyse*, probably abbreviated from *gia sie*, 'yea,
may it be so', and was formerly used specifically in response
to a negative question. Modern grammarians classify it as a
reaction signal, one of a group of little words that are important
because of their high frequency in spoken English. Reaction
signals stand at the beginning of a reply, and include: yes, no,
yeah, yep, m, hm, mhm. Initiators stand at the beginning, and
kick off an exchange: yes, well, oh, ah, oh well, well then,
why.

The trouble is that the high frequency of yes is declining.
Nobody uses it any more. Politicians, journos, and others of
the public waffling classes, when performing their chatterbox
trade on radio or television, and wishing for once to agree with
something somebody else has said, and then go on to develop
their own point at length, no longer say 'yes' to assent. Instead
they say: 'That's right.' And they say it with a mid-Atlantic
pronunciation, and an unusual stress on the second word.

It is trendy. It sounds like sunrise slang, forward-looking
and high-tech and gung-ho. It is a pox of a vogue phrase. We

humans are creatures of fashion: pack animals. Even those of us who are ostentatiously unfashionable in our clothes follow the fashions of language unconsciously. I suspect that 'That's right' became the fashionable nod-phrase for politicians a few years ago in the States, from where most of our fashions in language come. It has caught on in the United Kingdom like February 'flu. If it follows the usual pattern, it will be so over-used that it will become boring.

'That's right' has a longer pedigree than you might have supposed from its modern fad. In *The Diary of a Nobody* by George and Weedon Grossmith, published in 1892, the fatuous Mr Padge says 'That's right', and that's about all he did say the entire evening. Not many challenge Belloc's yes to Pooter when he described him as an immortal achievement.

The other current catch-phrase of agreement and assent is, 'There you go.' It can mean, 'There you are', when giving something, e.g. change or a BLT down, no lettuce, hold the mayo (a bacon, lettuce, and tomato sandwich on toast, but without the traditional dressing of lettuce and mayonnaise). It can be a phrase of approbation, generally of some specific action. It can be said to someone who has been struggling with something for a while (to open a jar or bottle, for instance, or to fix a gadget), who has a sudden, late success. It can be said to someone who has been slow to grasp the meaning of what he is being told or is reading, but suddenly tumbles to it. It can mean yes. It can mean 'Cheers', which itself seems to have moved on in English-English to mean 'Sorry'. It is a piece of multi-purpose linguistic putty, useful for filling in the interstices of social intercourse. It has already become something of a bore.

It sounded a very British rather than American idiom to me. But I was wrong. Eric Partridge found a transatlantic example of 'There you go' from as long ago as 1844 in *Peter Ploddy and Other Oddities* by Joseph Clay Neal, the Philadelphia journalist and humorist, whose work Dickens reprinted in this country. It is a phrase associated with harassed but cheerful New York waitresses dealing frequent plates off their elbows. It was recorded early in Australia, particularly Queensland, meaning 'There you are.' It may have been spread around the world, like so much other slang, by the international, roving, laid-back surfing community. Why it should have caught on so strongly among the feckless young in the South of England over the past few years is an oddity in itself. It would be nice, but as difficult as discovering what song the Syrens sang, to pin down one of these vogue catch-phrases at the moment of birth.

For example: 'The greatest thing since sliced bread.' The man and the moment that produced the notion of sliced bread as one of the landmark inventions of our century are puzzling questions beyond all conjecture. Pre-sliced bread was introduced by British bakers in the Twenties. In 1981 Sainsbury's the English grocer and hypermarket chain, ran an advertising campaign around 'The greatest thing since sliced bread.' (The answer turned out to be, boringly, unsliced bread.) But Sainsbury's used it because it was already a popular catch-phrase.

The phrase does not go so well in translation. The Conservative Party recently proposed to broadcast an election slogan in Punjabi asserting that Conservative policies were the country's most important discovery since the introduction of sliced bread. It was withdrawn at the last minute when somebody pointed out that the Punjabi version went: 'Conservative policies are the country's most important discovery since the advent of circumcised nans' (slightly leavened Indian bread shaped like a large flat leaf).

Often these phrases are picked up from some charismatic or otherwise ghastly figure on television, from advertising slogans, or graffiti. We shall never know about sliced bread. Its originator is lost in the backward and abysm of time. Nor shall we ever know which brave Noah or Mrs Noah first launched out and started the fashion for 'There you go.'

We can do better for once with the most popular and characteristic of American reaction signals, OK, and its swarming progeny, okay, okey-doke, oke, and the rest. Because it is such a typical American phrase, much ingenuity and misplaced folk scholarship have been devoted to its origin. One school says that it represents the Choctaw Amerindian *oke*, 'it is'. Another school says the French *au quai*, 'to the quay or wharf', as in 'to the woods', I suppose. Another roots school derives OK from a word in the West African language Wolof by way of slaves in the southern states of America.

All of these etymologies, as the lexicographers say, lack any form of acceptable documentation: i.e. they are monstrous towers of bogus scholarship erected on foundations of painted smoke.

The true etymology of OK was set down definitively by A. W. Read in *American Speech XXXVIII* (1963), XXXIX (1964), and subsequent issues. This has in no way stopped the amateurs riding their hobby-horses round and about the OK corral. Mr Read published detailed evidence that OK first appeared as a jocular alteration of the initial letters of 'all correct' (i.e. orl korrect) in 1839. In 1840 the Democrats adopted OK as their slogan in a rowdy and funny presidential election campaign. Their candidate was Martin Van Buren (1782–1862), who was born at Kinderhook in New York State, and nicknamed Old Kinderhook.

Democrats formed the OK Club to campaign for Van Buren's re-election, and broke into a Whig meeting shouting: 'Down with the Whigs, boys, OK.' The slogan was at first a secret codeword, and attracted attention in all the papers. Some of the suggestions of its meaning were: Out of Kash, Out of Kredit, Out of Karacter, Out of Klothes, and Orful Kalamity.

The *New York Morning Herald* gave the fullest and most whimsical explanation:

'THE OK CLUB – OK LITERATURE

'This gang of loafers and littérateurs, who broke in upon the Whigs at Masonic Hall on Friday evening last, and kicked up the row there, are said to number 1,000 bravos . . . The origin of their name, OK, is curious and characteristic. A few years ago, some person accused Amos Kendall to General Jackson, of being no better than he should be. "Let me examine the papers," said the old hero. "I'll soon tell whether Mr Kendall is right or wrong." The General did so and found everything right. "Tie up them papers," said the General. They were tied up. "Mark on them, OK," continued the General. OK was marked upon them. "By the eternal," said the good old General, taking his pipe from his mouth, "Amos is *Ole Kurrek* (all correct) and no mistake," blowing the smoke up the chimney's cheek. After this the character of Amos was established on the rock of Gibraltar. Harvard College, on hearing of this event, was thrown into extacies (sic), and made the General an LL.D., which he is to this day.'

Orl Korrect Rules, OK? as we say in British graffiti.

The newest trendy nod-word and reaction signal among British teenagers is 'brill', an abbreviation of brilliant. Brilliant replaced magic and epic as the vogue word for excellent among the young around the end of the Seventies. It was soon shortened to 'brill' in Liverpool, whence it has spread; but not, I think, outside the United Kingdom. It was popularized by the British television tragedians Little and Large. There is no need to be irritated by it. Like most vogue affirmatives it will have a merry life, but a short one. It is already being replaced in parts of London by 'boss'. Australians in the Earl's Court Road district known as Kangaroo Valley also may have had an influence on 'brill'. They tend to shorten their reaction signals to brill, splend, wond, and marv. Americans in London seem to tack on a 'y', as in 'marvey'.

Assenting is a tricky and delicate business always. Sidney and Beatrice Webb were founding parents of British socialism. Sidney was founder of the Fabian Society and the London School of Economics. Asked to account for the harmonious front that the Webbs presented on the important issues of the time, Beatrice explained that they had agreed early in their married life always to vote alike on great issues. 'Sidney was to decide which way we voted. I was to decide which were the great issues.'

Well, there you go; cheers; at this moment in time; let's be honest; tell it like it is; I turned round and said: 'You must be joking'; that's a big help; thanks a lot, mate; not if I see you first; you didn't, did you?; you should have seen his face; well, look after yourself; take care; have a nice day; there you go; cheers.

# ALPHABETS

## Knot the alphabet

'And after thousands and thousands and thousands of years, and after Hieroglyphics, and Demotics, and Nilotics and Cryptics, and Cufics, and Runics, and Dorics, and Ionics, and all sorts of other ricks and tricks (because the Woons, and the Neguses, and the Akhoonds, and the Repositories of Tradition would never leave a good thing alone when they saw it), the fine old easy, understandable Alphabet – A, B, C, D, E, and the rest of 'em – got back into its proper shape again for all Best Beloveds to learn when they are old enough.'
'How The Alphabet Was Made', *Just So Stories*, 1902, by Rudyard Kipling

Kipling's short stories made the conventional assumption that writing evolved from prehistoric art and pictographs. Not all modern linguists accept this pattern, and the origin of alphabets is lost. Man is a writing as well as a talking animal; but when and how *Homo sapiens* became *Homo scribens* is still a matter of controversy and speculation. The peoples and countries that discovered writing prospered. There is still a correlation between poverty and illiteracy and analphabeticity.

Perhaps writing began with history, in Sumerian cuneiform. An alphabet started to replace pictograms in the Sinaitic world at the North end of the Red Sea between 2,000 and 1,700 BC. This North Semitic alphabet had only consonants, but was based on phonetic and syllabic principles. Its O has remained unchanged, and is accordingly the oldest of all letters. From then on alphabets and writing spread across the face of the earth. Of the commonly used languages still in use Sinhalese has the most letters with 54, and Rotokas in central Bougainville Island the fewest with eleven, sc. A, B, E, G, I, K, O, P, R, T and U. Amharic has 231 formations from 33 basic syllabic forms, each of which has seven modifications. So it cannot be described as a proper alphabet. The extant language with the most consonants is the Caucasian language, Agul, with 78. The one with the most vowels is the nearly extinct Brazilian language Caxinana, with 15. Tamahaq, the language of the Nomadic Saharan people, the Tuareg, has no vowels and no fixed order for putting down its consonants, which may explain why the Tuareg never stay in one place for long.

Our alphabet of the English language is the Roman alphabet. The Romans gave a suspiciously exact date for the legendary foundation of their city that became a world empire: 753 BC. They learnt their letters from the Etruscans, their cultivated neighbours whom they wiped off the face of the earth as completely as the colonists of America wiped out the original inhabitants, or the convicts and settlers destroyed the Aborigines of Australia. The Etruscan script, based on an early form of the Greek alphabet, was modified to suit the needs of Oscan, Umbrian, and, above all, Latin. Our modern version has 26 letters of the alphabet.

The alphabet is one of the first things that a child learns. It is one of the few cultural possessions that he shares with the rest of the English-scribbling world. Accordingly, there are many childish games played with it. For example, there is the punning alphabet, packed with ghastly paronomasia.

A for 'orses
B for mutton
C for -th Highlanders
D for mation
E for brick
F for vescence
G for a horse
H for stealing my girl
I for Jones
J for orange
K for teria
L for leather
M for sis
N for lope
O for the wings of a dove
P for comfort, or Pan

Q for fish, or a bus, or almost anything
R for mo
S for Rantzen
T for two
U for me
V for la France
W for quits
X for breakfast
Y for husband
Z for breeze

In a language as old, and hospitable to other languages, and complex as English, written words often give little indication of their pronunciation, and sometimes are as misleading as the signposts that were all turned around in 1941 in Southern England in order to baffle a German invasion. The complexity of English spelling and pronunciation is illustrated by the definitive Unhelpful Alphabet, which I am trying to compile.

A is for aisle, or aegis, or, for that matter, anything
B is for Bdellium (pronounced Dellium)
C is for Czechoslovakia, or ctenoid, or cygnet, or chair
D is for Djinn, or Djibouti, or Djebba, or Djati, and several
 other oriental and Middle Eastern immigrants, which are
 cheats because they are proper names
E is for Europe, or ewe, or eyrie, or either (pronounced either
 of the two most popular ways), or Ewell, or ewer, or
 euphony, or eulogy, or Eulalie
F is for ****, or Fhred (Gaelic vocative of Fred, pronounced
 Red), or Felin-foel (pronounced Vellinvóyl according to the
 BBC Pronouncing Dictionary of British Names) and many other
 place-names in Wales.
G is for gnat, or gnu, or gnome, or Gnocchi
H is for honour, or honest, or hour, or hotel when it is
 pronounced by the old-fashioned or pretentious
I is for Iupiter, or Iynx (an otiose variant and homophone of
 Jynx, a wryneck), or Iatmul (a New Guinea people pro-
 nounced Yatmul)
J is for Jojoba (Mexican bush) or Jipijapa (either an Ecuadoran
 palm tree or a Panama hat) pronounced Hohoba and
 Hipihapa

K is for knickers, or knot, or knee, or dozens of others

L is for Llanfairgollyiwishiwerethere on Blessed Mona, and dozens of other Welsh place-names; and please don't write; I can spell them correctly if I want to

M is for mnemonic, or Mneme, and several cognate words

N is for misprint, or Nkomo, or Ngaio, or Nkonze (Lichtenstein's hartebeest, and don't look at me like that; I didn't make it up)

O is for Oedipus, or oestrus, or oeuvre, or Oeufs en Cocotte, or Oerlikon, or oestrogen

P is for psalm, or pseudonym, or pneumatic, or psittacosis, or Pseud, or psephology (the last two are psynonyms)

Q is for quay, or queue, or quiche, or Quebec (pronounced the Frog way), or Qatar (pronounced Gutter)

R for mo, or Rzeszów (pronounced Zhéshoof, and several other places in Poland)

S is for Schmaltz, and 'Sdeath (pronounced Zdeth, according to the *OED*), or Siking, a city in north-western China formerly called Changan, and now called Sian, which must be unsettling for the natives

T is Tzigane, or Tsar, or Tzitzis (tassels on ceremonial Jewish garments)

U is for urn, or Uitlander, or Usquebaugh, or Ur, or Ukiyoe (Japanese artistic movement pronounced Ookeyoya)

V is for Volkswagen, or Volkslied and all that lot, or von Ribbentrop, or vlei (in South Africa an area of low marshy ground, especially one that feeds a stream)

W is for write, or wrap, or whole

X is for Christmas, or xylophone, or xyster (a surgeon's instrument for scraping bones), or xyst or xystos (a long portico used for athletics in ancient Greece), or Xerxes, or Xhosa (pronounced with a click, if you can manage it)

Y is for you, or Yule, or yclept, or Ytterbium

Z is for Zigeuner, or Zaragoza, or Zweibrücken (I hope the two cities are twinned), or zopilote (pronounced sopilote, the turkey-buzzard or urubu), or zambomba (a simple Spanish musical instrument, made by stretching a piece of parchment over a wide-mouthed jar and inserting a stick in it, sounded by rubbing the stick with the fingers, and pronounced thambomba), or zugzwang (a position in chess in which

whoever has the move is at a decisive disadvantage; pronounced Tsuktsvang, or sounds to that effect)

If we had world enough and time, I suppose we could devise
another kind of Misleading Alphabet in which the first syllables
of the definitions sound like the names of the letters they
define.

C for see-saw
F for effluent
G for jee
H for aitch
I for eye
L for elephant
M for empty
N for entity
O for aubergine
Q for Kew
R for Aardvark
S for espouse

But that is quite enough of that.

Over the centuries we have dropped a number of letters that
became otiose from our alphabet, for example the thorn (pronounced th) from the Anglo-Saxon runic alphabet, called a
*futhorc* after the names of its first six characters: *feoh* wealth, *ur*
aurochs, *th* thorn, *os* ?month, *rad* riding, and *cen* torch. As the
centuries roll on, we may drop some and introduce others as
the need arises. All the elements of language change constantly
to suit the new world as it arrives. VDUs and computers are
already affecting punctuation, and may change our alphabet.

I suppose that the most unnecessary letters in our alphabet,
as we spell and pronounce at present, are J, K, Q, W, X, Y,
and thou whoreson zed, thou unnecessary letter. Tidy-minded
organizers sometimes suggest reforming English spelling to
make it simpler and more logical. I think that this would be a
pity, since it would destroy the twenty centuries of history and
evolution that each letter carries like a knapsack on its back. It
is interesting and potentially useful to spell connexion and
similar words with an X, to indicate that they are derived from

actual Latin nouns in -xio, and not from the present stem of Latin verbs. The spelling is a signpost, even though it is not one that is used very often. It is interesting and potentially useful to end verbs in -ize if they are derived from a Greek verb ending in -izo, or from a Latin, or French, or English imitation of such a Greek verb. At *The Times* until quite recently we used to spell the Monna Lisa (sic) with a double NN, to swank that we knew the historic Italian spelling of a mistress. Nobody else spelled the lady that way, not even the Italians, who call her La Gioconda.

It would be agreeable if English spelling were closer to its pronunciation. But such an old and complex language is bound to have old and anomalous spellings, which hold clues to the history of the words. English spelling will never be reformed to make it phonetic. For one thing, language does not evolve by such political diktats. And for another, whose pronunciation will this brave new spelling represent: Oxford English, Boston, Black, Oz, Belfast, or Glesga.

# APPELLATIONS

## Pardon me for esqing

'I am Robert Shallow, sir, a poor esquire of
this county, and one of the king's justices
of the peace. What is your good pleasure
with me?'
*King Henry The Fourth*, Part Two, III, 2, 54, c. 1598, by
William Shakespeare

'If you read the superscriptions to all the
offices in the kingdom, you will not find
three letters directed to any but esquires.'
*The Tatler*, no. 19, p. 2, 1709, by Sir Richard Steele

Our handles and appellations are in a terrible state of chassis.
What we call people, how we label them, are delicate, complex,
and movable conventions. Ever since Adam named the animals, and decided to call Eve Woman 'because she was taken
out of Man', there has been trouble. Adam's derivation, at any
rate when he was speaking the English of the 47 revisers of the
*Authorized Version*, is the earliest example of bogus folk etymology. And the name he chose still infuriates fanatic feminists.
Our names and appellations are labels that validate us: we feel
threatened and alarmed when people get them wrong or
offend our conventions.

For example, take that frowsty and snobbish old suffix label,
Esq. Secretarial shortage in our brisk new world where we
have got rid of overmanning (sorry, overwomanning – sorry,
overpersonning) means that I spend too much of my day
addressing envelopes for very short and increasingly testy
letters. If I address a self-consciously proletarian Northern
novelist as Esq., he will be livid. On the other hand, if I
address Pinkmantle Pursuivant at the College of Arms as plain
Mr, he will flinch with fastidious distaste.

The conventions about Esq. are old and complex. In days of

old, when knights were bold, or at any rate had good PR agents in Geoffrey of Monmouth and Malory, an esquire was originally a title of function. An esquire was a knight's attendant, and carried his gear. In detail he was a young man of gentle birth, who, as an aspirant to knighthood, attended upon a knight, carried his shield, and rendered him other services. This function is long obsolete. In historical and romantic writing the functionary's title is usually shortened by aphesis to squire. This is also done as a sarcastic form of address in the pub. The esquire or squire was an Englishing of the Latin *armiger* or armour-carrier. Kings and noblemen employed various officers, as esquire for the body, esquire of the chamber, and esquire of the table.

As knights lost their function, esquire became a title of rank, scilicet a man belonging to the higher order of English gentry, ranking immediately below a knight. As you can see from the quotation from *The Tatler* at the head of this chapter, by the eighteenth century the English class system had broadcast Esqs widely throughout the nation. The Victorians systematized the use of Esq. into a grand hierarchy. One eminent Victorian authority (and any authority into the use of defunct titles is largely self-appointed) restricted the use of Esquire to five classes:

1 Younger sons of peers, and their eldest sons.
2 Eldest sons of knights, and their eldest sons, and so on, in perpetuity: a class that must by now be large.
3 Chiefs of ancient families, by prescription.
4 Esquires by creation or office, as heralds and sergeants of arms, judges, officers of state, naval and military officers, justices of the peace like Robert Shallow, barristers-at-law.
5 Esquires who attend the Knight of the Bath on his installation – usually two specially appointed.

This enumeration was greatly disputed, even in the nineteenth century, which cared more about such distinctions. For example, barristers are entitled to use the suffix Esq., certainly after they have taken silk; there is some doubt about the outer bar. Solicitors are never more than gentlemen and mere Mr. I have an acquaintance who claims to be thrice an Esq., once as a Lieutenant-Colonel, once as a CBE or Commander of the British Empire, and once as the son of a clergyman. Garter King of Arms declares his opinion that sons of clergy are not entitled *ex officio patris* to an Esq. It became so difficult to know who was an Esq., because of some eldest son of a knight lurking up there in the higher branches of the family tree, that we eventually promoted the entire adult male population, apart from tradesmen, when written to *qua* tradesmen, to this once select and coveted status.

They manage these things differently in the United States, where a bias against titles is written into the constitution (Article I, 1789: 'No state shall grant any title of nobility'), but where, nevertheless, anybody with a flag such as Senator or Judge wags it more vigorously than in the United Kingdom. My bible of etiquette, *Debrett's*, reports that Esquire, usually contracted to Esq., as in Britain, is customarily used in social correspondence especially in the eastern part of the United States, but not in business circles. In the Department of State, the term is reserved for Foreign Service Officers serving abroad, and is not abbreviated. I suspect that *Debrett's* is a bit out of date in this matter, and that Esq. is not used much in social correspondence anywhere in the United States, not even in Boston. It has also not noticed the remarkable consequence of the feminist revolution in New York, where qualified lawyers of both sexes are dignified with the label Esq.

There is even a distinction about where to put the Esq. In ceremonious use, e.g. in legal writings or in genealogy, where the name of the person's estate or of his place of residence is given, the title is, by English custom, placed last, as, 'A.B. of C., Esquire.' In Scotland, on the contrary, the title immediately follows the surname, 'A. McB., Esquire, of C.' Similarly, in England the Esq. follows the designations 'Junior' or 'The Younger', whereas in Scotland it precedes them.

I think that Esq. is dying. Let him die, poor old complicated and vulgarized fool. It will be a great relief to those of us who have to decide whether to Esq. or not to Esq.

Thomas Paine wrote, in the first chapter of *The Rights of Man*, with resolute egalitarianism and shocking male chauvinism: 'Titles are but nicknames, and every nickname is a title. The thing is perfectly harmless in itself, but it marks a sort of foppery in the human character which degrades it. It renders man diminutive in things which are great, and the counterfeit of woman in things which are little.'

Then, how do you start the letter? Old-fashioned gents and

pseudo-gents favour the plain surname ('Dear Howard') to equals, and Mr for tradesmen. In Jane Austen's time husbands and wives addressed each other as a stranger would: Mr Bennett, but Sir Thomas. Mr sounds unduly formal to some in our increasingly informal age. The growing convention is to start the letter with first name, surname, and no handle: 'Dear Philip Howard.' This suits our unbuttoned age, when one of the deadly sins is to be seen to be élitist or snobbish. However, this practice annoys some people greatly (epistolary conventions are among the subtlest shibboleths of the intricate English class system), and it has been described as an unspeakable usage and an odious practice.

Nor can you win with the new female handle, Ms. This is a very rare example of a word that has been artificially introduced into the language for social and political reasons, rather than growing naturally from usage. Half the women in the country want to be addressed as Ms, on the reasonable grounds that they do not see why they should have to declare their marital status in their title, while men do not. The other half are affronted whenever they see a Ms, and write to complain. Speaking very generally and provocatively, the younger, liberated generation of women support Ms; the blue-rinse brigade cling obdurately to the distinctions they were brought up to adhere to. Other European countries solve the problem by according the married woman's handle, e.g. Madame, Signora, Frau, to all women of a certain age, above about thirtyish, irrespective of their marital status. The pronunciation Mizz seems to be winning over the trickier Merz.

> How to pronounce Ms? It is
> A funny word, which rhymes with Liz.
> Vowel-less Ms – this is no fable –
> Sounds like the 'mis' in mis-erable.
> If Ms is widely used, I fear
> It will require a subtle ear
> To tell the Mss from the Misses,
> And to distinguish both from Mrs.
> Some may confuse the Ms with Mr,
> So I shall call myself Magister.

There is a similar conflict between generations about how to sign off letters. Some will find 'Yours sincerely' stuffy. Others will find the 'Luv' of the Sixties excessively familiar and flip. I was taught that you signed 'Yours faithfully' on business letters; 'Yours truly' when it is not a matter of business and you do not know the recipient, and 'Yours sincerely' (optional initial capital 'S') for social letters. For signing off to the Queen and other dignitaries, there are complex rubrics beginning 'I remain'. For example, for signing off official letters to and from ambassadors, the stately formula runs: 'I have the honour to be, with great truth and respect' (or 'with the highest consideration'), 'Sir' (or 'Your Excellency' or 'My Lord')', 'your' (or 'Your Excellency's' or 'Your Lordship's') 'obedient servant.' An ambassador writing to the Foreign Minister of the country to which he is accredited must not sign off without giving this assurance: 'I avail myself of this opportunity to renew to Your Excellency the assurance of my highest consideration.' Diplomacy has been streamlined into practical business rather than old fool network, and few ambassadors adhere to the traditional formulae any more.

It is not just the British who are silly about conventional appellations and titles. Although citizens of a republic, the French are just as bad. They are, of course, crashing snobs. Sophie-Charlotte, Duchess d'Alençon, preferred death to losing her handle and status. On 4 May 1897 she was presiding over a charity bazaar in Paris, when the hall accidentally caught fire. There was hideous panic, stampede, and holocaust. Some rescuers reached the duchess, who was still sitting calmly behind her booth. They wanted to help her get out. She refused: 'Because of my title, I was the first to enter here. I shall be the last to leave.' So she was burned to death, along with 120 others, mainly women and children.

French handles are just as pompous. A junior officer, on posting, will write to his new Commanding Officer: 'Mon Colonel, It is with the most profound gratification that I learn that I am to have the honour of serving under your distinguished command – but please can I have six weeks' leave?' Or words to that effect. Note that 'Mon Colonel' does not mean 'My Colonel'; it is short for 'Monsieur le Colonel.' You use 'Monsieur le' as a handle unabbreviated only in the unlikely event of having to address a Marshal of France, when you would, of course, address him as 'Monsieur le Maréchal.'

These are tricky conventions, which involve politics and

class quite as much as language. The tide, pushed by the media, is towards informality. One of the good things about our Age of the Common Man is that we find it unpleasant and ridiculous to emphasize publicly that some men are more equal than others. We waste less time on trivial distinctions. On television pap-shows you call everyone by his or her first name, and kiss, on first meeting, whether or not you know her or him from Eve or Adam: anything more formal is felt to be hostile. On radio there is a growing convention to address people by first name and surname, Miranda Moneypenny; and to do so more often than one would in normal conversation. This is to help the unseeing audience identify the speaker.

By the next cybernetic century the problem will be solved: we shall address each other by our personal identity codes, which will have as many otiose digits as an electricity bill. And we shall look back with nostalgia to our silly old conventional appellations. Even then, it will still be possible to be either polite or familiar. Noël Coward showed the way. When T. E. Lawrence (of Arabia) had become an airman (to escape from his legend, or his lies), Coward wrote to 'John Hume Ross' a letter which began: 'Dear 338171, or may I call you 338?' Noël Coward did not know the tricky RAF convention by which the first shall be last. He should have written: '. . . may I call you 171?'

# CLICHÉS

## Seasick of clichés

'What does it behove us to proclaim?
Our faith.
In what does it behove us to proclaim our faith?
Democracy.
From what vertiginous eyrie does it behove us to
proclaim our faith in democracy?
From the house-tops.
At what time should we proclaim our faith in
democracy from the house-tops?
Now, more than ever.'
The Myles na Gopaleen Catechism of Cliché, 1968, by Myles na
Gopaleen

We all quote, partly because quotation is the parole of educated men and women, and partly, I dare say, to show off our literary credentials. The latter is a foolish reason. But some things have been so well said that they cannot be said better; and we wish to share our pleasure in them with others. The danger is that we become so fond of a hackneyed quotation that we trot it out without thinking, at every opportunity.

I have two favourites at the moment, which I have to guard against. The first is the one about the life of man being solitary, poor, nasty, brutish, and short, just to let everybody know that I am an intellectual sort of chap who reads Hobbes in the bath. The second is David Hume's fork: 'Does it contain any abstract reasoning concerning quantity or number? No. Does it contain any experimental reasoning, concerning matter of fact and existence? No. Commit it then to the flames: for it can contain nothing but sophistry and illusion.' When we notice one of our friends getting stuck in the groove of a favourite quotation, we are doing him or her a kindness by pointing it out, so that she or he can move on to fresh fields and pastures new: which is a hackneyed MISquotation.

148

There has recently been a pox of sea-changes in the public prints, echoing the thunder of the surf of *The Tempest* I, ii, 400:

> Nothing of him that doth fade
> But doth suffer a sea-change
> Into something rich and strange.
> Sea-nymphs hourly ring his knell:
> Ding-dong.

Sea-change means a change wrought by the sea, coined for Ariel's magical song. It has become the most intrusive and importunate of hackneyed quotations and irrelevant allusions. I doubt whether sea-change can ever be used, even when, unusually, the context has some remote connection with water, without vexing one's readers with the glutinous jocularity. Ariel must turn somersaults of glee at the incongruous uses to which his phrase is put.

Sea-change has been a hackneyed quotation for more than a century. Another sea-quote is having a belated and surprising vogue. It is the one about sea-green incorruptibility, and it crops up all over the place. It was applied in a leader in *The Times* recently to a bunch of trade-union leaders. And I am sorry to say that a book reviewer in *The Times* slipped a sea-green incorruptible past me recently; but, as he was using the irrelevant allusion to describe an admiral, I suppose he would have tried to justify it.

Since the curse has come upon us, it is worth looking at what 'sea-green incorruptible' originally meant, before it became a mindless cliché, and reminding ourselves that in its first use there was no connection between the greenness and the incorruptibility other than chance and a bad pun. Carlyle is writing, asking which of the Six Hundred at the States General looks the meanest: 'Shall we say that anxious, slight, ineffectual-looking man, under thirty, in spectacles; his eyes (were the glasses off?) troubled, careful; with upturned face, snuffing dimly the uncertain future times; complexion of a multiplex atrabiliar colour, the final shade of which may be the pale sea-green. That greenish-coloured (*verdâtre*) individual is an Advocate of Arras; his name is Maximilien Robespierre.'

Later, when Robespierre is about to get his comeuppance, and Louvet strides towards the tribune, taking papers from his pocket, 'The Seagreen became tallowgreen.'

They don't write like that any more. Correction: nobody but Bernard Levin can get away with such marvellously complex and ornamental periods these days.

However, when Carlyle exclaims of Robespierre, 'O seagreen Incorruptible', he is making a botanical pun that will be recognized by keen gardeners. He is playing on another meaning of seagreen, which is one of the names for the common or garden saxifrage, the houseleek or 'sengreen'. The *Oxford English Dictionary* conjectures that seagreen in its gardening sense entered the language as a misprint for sengreen.

The sengreen (which Johnson defines in his dictionary, with characteristic prolixity, as 'a plant') also has other names: 'aygreen' and 'everlasting'. Those plants are described as everlasting which retain their shape and colour when dried. They are incorruptible in the primary sense offered by the *OED*: incapable of undergoing physical corruption; that cannot decay or perish; everlasting.

Please note that Robespierre was seagreen because his digestion was rotten, and he had a bilious complexion. He was incorruptible because he was a zealot and a fanatic. There was no necessary connection between his seagreenness and his incorruptibility, and they had nothing to do with the sea. Carlyle's esoteric gardening pun about the common saxifrage, if he meant it, must be taken to mean that an inflexible commitment to tough policies, and a belief in TINA (There Is No Alternative) are signs of mental desiccation as dead as an everlasting flower. A foolish figure – But farewell it, for I will use no art. Of course, Seagreen Incorruptible is a vivid phrase, with or without reminding us of the garden saxifrage. That is why it has become a hackneyed quotation. I think we should give it a rest.

# COINAGE

## Phrasing a coin

'Life is short, and so is money.'
*The Threepenny Opera*, 1928, by Bertolt Brecht

'Old pennies have a picture on the back of
a lady riding a bicycle. Her name is Ruby
Tanner.'
Anonymous schoolgirl, 1986

There is a general tendency in the modern world to reduce the
size of our coins, in order to make them handier to carry
around now that we do not like being lumbered with money-
belts, scrips, and great bags. I vote that this is a good idea, if
only to abate the agony when my trouser pocket springs a
leak, and the money cascades down the inside of my trouser
leg and into the crevices of the escalator. Britain decimalized
its currency and introduced new coinage in 1971. I suspect that
we are not really fond of the new coins yet. We have invented
few nicknames for them. The former duodecimal currency
acquired lots of affectionate and euphonious pseudonyms.
Their etymologies are often obscure, as is usually the case with
vernacular slang.

Bob as nickname for shilling is old enough to have appeared
in Grose's *Dictionary of the Vulgar Tongue*. Sessions' Papers of
1789 suggest a criminal origin: '*Bulls* and *half bulls* are half
crowns and half crowns in coiners' language, and a *bob* is a
shilling.' Bob may be connected with bobstick, a shilling's
worth in eighteenth-century low-life slang. But nobody knows
the origins of the words. *Bobe* was the name of a small coin in
Old French of the fourteenth century. Its survival in English
slang seems very unlikely. Bob was also slang for a shoplifter's
assistant, perhaps because he bobbed in and out of the shop
without paying. The best guess is that it is an abbreviation of
the Christian name Robert, as seems to be the case with wet-

bobs and other bobs, bob in this case being slang for a chap or
fellow, cf. Jack, and Tom, Dick and Harry. The old shilling has
long gone. But bob lingers on in the Scouts' bob-a-job week,
bob-a-nob when collecting small contributions e.g. for a leaving
prsent, two bob as a rough estimate of a smallish sum of
money, and as queer as a three (or nine)-bob watch. It survives
in Australian as the term for a subscription to a common fund;
and in New Zealand English in such phrases as, 'He left her a
bob or two.'

Tanner, the slang name for the old 6d piece, has shown less
staying power than the bob, and is now obsolete except among
the incorrigible old and Cockney street traders. Its origins are
equally obscure. John Camden Hotten's *Slang Dictionary* of
1859 suggested the gypsy *tawno*, young and hence little. The
next edition of a year later had shifted to the Latin *tener*, young
and hence little. It came into written English at the beginning
of the nineteenth century, making its first appearance in *The
Lexicon Balatronicum*, or fourth edition of Grose, of 1811, and
Vaux's *Flash Dictionary* of 1812. Dickens used it in *Martin
Chuzzlewit* in 1844: "How much a-piece?" The man in the
monument replied, "A tanner." It seemed a low expression,
compared with the monument. A nice scriptural etymology
connects it with an old joke about St Peter's banking transaction at Joppa, when he lodged with one Simon a tanner. Simon
was eighteenth-century slang for a sixpence, but it cannot be
derived from tanner, since simon got into the first edition of
Grose in 1785. But tanner could well be derived as a joke from
simon. Joey, slang for the old 4d piece, came from Joseph
Hume, the politician and financial expert (1777-1855). Quid, a
guinea, and when guineas went out a pound, is probably a
Latin joke from *quid?*, what?; cf. the wherewithal. Half-a-quid
was ten bob. Half a dollar for half a crown must be borrowed
from the Americans.

Of course, it takes time for a nickname to gain currency, and
arsy-versy for a currency to gain a nickname. Twenty years is
not long in the development of a language. Cash is less central
to our lives than it used to be, because more people have
cheque-books, plastic, and other substitutes. But it is also
possible that we still do not much like the new coins, atavisti-
cally resenting them as one of the improvements imposed on
us from on high without consultation, like the wanton changes

in British county boundaries and names in 1974. I still cannot think of darkest Ayrshire as Strathclyde, or Bath as being in Avon.

One new and quite irritating monetary saying is: 'When a pound was worth a pound', which came in during the great inflation of the Seventies. Users of this phrase are imprecise about the date of this golden age, when you could have a dozen oysters at Scott's, and a ticket to a West End theatre, and still have change from a pound. But, as with those who look back to a supposed vintage year for English grammar, it usually turns out to have been in their salad days, when they saw the world and the pound in their pocket with the optimism of youth. What they are suffering from is not really inflation, or the death of English, but middle-aged grumpiness. It was Harold Wilson who introduced the pound in your pocket into the lexicon, in a Ministerial Broadcast explaining his devaluation in 1967: 'That doesn't mean, of course, that the pound here in Britain – in your pocket or purse or in your bank – has been devalued.'

Other recent coinages which may be about money include: 'You don't get many of those to the pound.' This is a sexist remark between males when a particularly protuberant pair of pneumatic female breasts passes by. This probably comes from weights and measures rather than money. A very recent variant is: 'You don't get many of those to the kilo.' Is this a sign of inflation? I dare say that the male chauvinist saying is not all that recent. The rough boys at Pompeii were probably cracking the same bad joke with *sestertii*, in the same way that *Marcus hic fuit* was probably the origin of 'Kilroy was here.'

The most spectacular change in the language introduced by decimal currency has been the death of the penny, and its replacement by either 'pee' or 'pence'. During the transition the Decimal Currency Board encouraged us to 'speak of one p', in order to avoid confusion with the old duodecimal penny which is now dead. The new p is inscribed 'one penny'. But, if you call it that at the Post Office, you run the risk of being reproved: 'The penny went out with decimalization.' People speak of 'one pence change'. I have even heard, 'One pounds, one pence.' What other words have evolved three ambivalent plurals: pence, pennies, and pees?

The tendency for plurals to be treated as singulars and so

become singulars is not an unknown phenomenon in the language. But it does seem a pity that we are losing the subtle distinction between five pence (collective) and five pennies (individual one-penny coins). Presumably we shall all eventually be saying five one-p pieces, five one-ps, or even five one-pences, instead of five pennies. However, before wringing our hands in linguistic *Angst*, it is worth remembering that the Russians have been cheerfully treating our collective plural pence as a singular for years. *Odin pens* to them means the same as *odno penni*, i.e. one penny; and they do not hesitate to use it in the Russian plural, *pensy*.

Pre-decimal, we never spoke of 'Five l, two s, and six d.' The French managed when *Mille francs* became *dix francs*, without resorting to *dix f*. For a few years the adjective *nouveau* was prefixed, and still is when necessary. Over in the United Kingdom we coined the p. There are those who object because they think the p is ugly. Whether it is or not, aesthetics have nothing to do with the way we coin our language in the hurly-burly of usage by Everyman. I suspect that the objectors to p are fussed by the leguminous, or more probably micturitional, homophone of p. Others object to one pence having become an illiterate singular. Like it or lump it, ugly or illiterate, the biggest effect on the language of the large social change of the decimalization of British currency has been the arrival of the p, and the singularization of pence.

# COLLISION

## Collision course

'Tickler was a wax-ended piece of cane, worn smooth by collision with my tickled frame.'
*Great Expectations*, chapter 2, 1860–1, by Charles Dickens

I have a correspondent who is fighting a war to the death with the Oxford lexicographers over what he takes to be sloppy journalistic misuse of the words 'collide' and 'collision', and its being made respectable in their dictionaries. One of the glorious disadvantages of being an Oxford lexicographer is that one is generally mistaken as an umpire rather than a recorder of the language, which belongs to all of us. My friend objects to the use of collide and collision with a stationary object. He thinks that the prefix col- (*cum*, with) implies joint or mutual bashing together of two moving objects, not simply one. So that a moving car can collide with an elephant, if the elephant is also moving. But a car cannot collide with a lamp post, he asserts.

The argument is that idle and misguided journos suppose that, if they write that a car crashes into a lamp post, they are implying that the car driver was responsible for the accident. So they prefer to write 'collide', which implies no blame, and will pacify the lawyer. And so the well of English is being defiled yet again by hacks. It seems to me that my pedantic correspondent takes too Ptolemaic a view. It doesn't matter whether 'collide' can be used only of two moving objects or not. Even a lamp post is travelling at 18.5 miles a second in an elliptical orbit around the sun. *Eppur si muove.*

The Oxford lexicographers write ironically back, saying that they have some evidence from their unpublished files that reputable writers have referred to collision with a stationary object. Cecil Day-Lewis in his autobiography, *The Buried Day*

(1960), wrote: 'My father collided with an ass which was lying asleep in the middle of the road.' And John Wain wrote in *The Smaller Sky*: 'His head came into painful collision with a wooden crate.' We need not attach too much value to this evidence. You could condemn the Day-Lewis sentence as badly constructed. The quotation from Wain could refer to a crate that was moving. Oxford says that if a usage is widely accepted by careless writers, but generally avoided by careful ones, its policy is to include it in dictionaries, but to label it as disputed. They are having a careful look at collision, to see whether they should give it a warning label in the next edition.

I do not think that they need to bother too much. There is no implication in the prefix col- that both objects have to be moving when they clash together. There are examples from an early date of good writers using collide and collision about one moving and one stationary object. 'The Blood collides against the Sides of the Aorta', 1746. 'The collision of the waters against the lips of the orifice', 1677. My friend is barking up the wrong tree. But I am pleased to see that Sir James Murray, who edited this volume of his dictionary himself, notes that when the word was first used of railway trains or ships in collision in the first half of the nineteenth century it was objected to as an Americanism.

It is a wild goose chase. But if you catch sight of a wild goose, however pedantic, it is worth giving chase for the sake of tidiness and getting things right. We should look at the early literature of collisions. In 1849 Thomas De Quincey published his famous essay, 'The English Mail Coach'. In it he describes at some length a collision between a mail coach and a gig containing a pair of lovers, which had previously been creeping on at one mile per hour but, on perceiving the onrushing mail coach, endeavoured to turn, and then stopped. 'Already in resignation he had rested from his struggle.' De Quincey describes the crash: 'Oh, raving of hurricanes . . . Even in that moment the thunder of collision spoke aloud. Either with the swingle-bar, or with the haunch of our near leader, we had struck the off-wheel of the little gig; which *stood* rather obliquely . . .' (My emphasis.) Looking back upon the scene, De Quincey records that 'the horse was planted immovably, with his forefeet upon the paved crest of the central road'. There appears, therefore, to be no doubt that the gig was stationary at the moment of impact or collision.

De Quincey also uses the word 'collision' earlier in the same passage, though not when the opposing vehicle was known to be stationary: 'Our frantic horses swept round an angle of the road which opened upon us that final stage where the collision must be accomplished and the catastrophe sealed.' His essay was published at a date when it is possible that his use of 'collision' is derived from railway parlance, and does not establish that the railway usage was descended from that of the highway. The trouble is, of course, that collisions were a relatively minor hazard of coaching, and so do not find much mention in the literature. Greater perils were misbehaving horses, overturning, falling off, being shaken to bits or to death, getting stuck in the mud, and highway robbers. You could try claiming that De Quincey was a sloppy journalist. Certainly he was sloppy, and arguably he was a journalist. But whether the conclusion follows from these premises I doubt.

If we turn to the early railway literature we find pristine uses of collision. In 1833 an anonymous work was published entitled *The Railway Companion, describing an excursion along the Liverpool line, by a Tourist. London: Published for the Author by Effingham Wilson, Royal Exchange, and James Fraser, 215 Regent Street.* It includes the passage: 'The last carriage of every train carries a revolving lamp, one side of which is red, the other blue. As long as the train is in motion the red light presents itself to whatever follows, but at the instant of stopping, the blue light is turned outward; the engineer of the next train instantly sees this change, and is enabled, by checking the velocity of his engine, to avoid a collision that would be tremendous.' 'A Tourist' may, I suppose, have been an American. But his use of the word 'engineer' for driver is not evidence of this. At this date many words (such as 'railroad') that later became characteristically American were commonly used in this country. That he was a journalist is hardly credible, since he seems to have paid for the publication of his own work.

1835. March 2, minutes of the Liverpool and Manchester Railway's Board: 'The Horsley Engine, the Star, which was proceeding with the Train to Manchester, was jerked off the rails and ran across the opposite side of the road when she came into collision with the Caledonian Engine and Tender.' That the Caledonian (this was the name of the engine, not of the later and geographically remote Caledonian Railway) was in motion at the time seems unlikely. This would surely have been stated as a very relevant circumstance.

1849. The word 'collision' occurs at least three times in the Rules of the London and North Western Railway, in Rules 21, 33, and 41. There are probably more occurrences; but Rules make tedious reading. I quote Rule 41: 'If any part of a train is detached when in motion, care must be taken not to stop the train in front before the detached part has stopped, and it is the duty of the guard of such detached part to apply his Break in time to prevent a collision with the carriages in front, in the event of their stopping.' Obviously a collision with stationary carriages is here envisaged. The spelling of 'Break' for brake was very common at this period in railway literature. It does not warrant a sic.

In short, or rather at length, the reply to the assertion that a collision can take place, if you are using the language exactly, only between things that are both in motion is pshaw and tilly-vally.

# DIFFERENT

Preposidioms: O! You must wear your
difference with rue

'By different methods different men excel:
But where is he who can do all things well?'
*An Epistle to William Hogarth*, 1, 573, 1763,
by Charles Churchill

No two people speak or write exactly the same English. Each
of us differs from all other English-users in vocabulary, grammar, pronunciation, slang, idiosyncrasy, misunderstandings,
solecisms, family jokes, and dozens of other parts of the
language. A man's version of English is called his idiolect; and
it is far more strikingly peculiar to him than his fingerprints.
Some make a living out of their peculiarities: for example,
Jimmy 'Schnozzle' Durante, 1893–1980, the US comedian,
known for his big nose and his inextricable entanglement with
the English language. Durante was once one of the two guest
experts on the radio programme *Information Please*. They were
asked: 'Can you touch your scapular with your patella?'
Durante replied in his voice like calico being torn: 'I hope your
program ain't getting off-color.'

We tend to think of our particular idiolect as standard, and
everybody else's as aberrant. Everybody's out of step except
our Johnny. We try to pass on our idiolects to our children. I
remember my father working himself into a passion about the
Suffolk Ow his children were acquiring instead of the smarter
metropolitan long O. I recently met an undergraduate of St
Hilda's who was being given a hard time by her mother, a
graduate of that noble college beside the Cherwell, for saying
and writing 'different to' rather than 'different from'. Then I
met a distinguished English teacher who also had a hobby-
horse about 'different from' in his idiolect. We had better look
into the matter.

The brisk answer to this particular foible in people's idiolects is that it is a superstition, if not a fetish. The *Oxford English Dictionary* reports that the usual construction is now different 'from', but that different 'to' is found in writers of all ages. Its first example, from *Pilgrim Perfect*, published by Wynkyn de Worde in 1531, favours 'to': 'His lyght is moche different and unlyke to the lyght of the holy goost.' On the other hand, in *The Comedy of Errors* V, 1, 46, Adriana, the wife of Antipholus of Ephesus, describes her Protean husband and pseudo-husband: 'This week he hath been heavy, sour, sad, And much different from the man he was.' Coming forward to a great writer nearer our own time, George Eliot, in *Silas Marner* chapter 9: 'It is a different sort of life to what she's accustomed to.'

The *OED* records examples of different 'against' and different 'with'; but obelisks them as obsolete. For those who turn purple and hiss at the supposed American barbarism different 'than', I regret to tell you that 'different than' is found in such professional masters of English grammar as Fuller, Addison, Steele, Defoe, Fanny Burney (being generous with the definition of professional masters), Coleridge, Southey, De Quincey, Carlyle, and Thackeray.

Let us try to get to first principles, which is always a perilous trial in such an unprincipled matter as English grammar. The grammatical argument for different 'from' is that the preposition stays the same after morphologically related verbs, adjectives, and nouns: I differ from; different from; difference from. But this correspondence is so erratic as to be useless as a rule: full of, but filled with; proud of, but pride in; this accords with, but according to; I neglect, but negligent of; this derogates from, but derogatory to; inconceivable to, not to be conceived by; she pleases, suffices, neglects me, but pleasant to, sufficient for, negligent of. The prepositions that go with certain words are matters of idiom, taste, idiolect, and aberration; and they are all in a state of constant flux.

My teacher friend, who is a good classicist as well as an English purist, adheres to his idiolect: 'I remain obdurate (or fairly so) that the likes of Ovid and Shakespeare are allowed to break rules and make them, but lesser mortals should be more diffident. The prefix dis- has essentially the implication of "apart", separation from, and this must take from and not to. The latter, except from the pen of a master of literature, sounds cacophonous. You would not surely accept "to" after distinguish, disconnect, disagree, and other such dis- verbs? You may retort with disadvantageous or disallow; but I would distinguish these as having the prefix ad- dominating.'

Pushing this line of argument as far as it will go, let us assert that 'different to' is an oxymoron, and therefore, like all oxymorons, meaningless: its two parts cancel, leaving emptiness. If somebody writes of a 'small giant', the small conjures up tininess; then along comes this giant, who neutralizes the first image, and leaves you with no image at all, or at the most a poetic paradox for special occasions. Similarly, precisians can say that 'different' falls on the ear as a moving apart, a separateness, a disparity; while 'to' means a coming together, an approach, a meeting. Put together they are like acid and alkali: they neutralize into nothing. 'A is different to B' has as much meaning as 'A is similar from B': i.e. none.

I found myself writing 'different . . . than' the other day, because there was a thumping big parenthesis between the adjective and its preposition, which was followed by an elliptical clause. I looked at it again, and decided that it sounded right, or suited my idiolect, and let it stand. I regretted it, because I then had to write several letters justifying the usage to irate readers.

Different than is a particularly Amerrican idiom; and it is the only way to say it, when different is followed by a comparative than-clause, particularly an elliptical clause. She's quite a different girl than she was five years ago. If you want to use 'from' you will have to write: 'She's quite a different girl from what she was five years ago.' 'The unions are taking a very different attitude than the bosses (sc. are taking).' If you want to avoid 'than' you will have to write: 'The unions are taking a very different attitude from that of the bosses.' You could write: 'The unions are taking a very different attitude than the bosses'' (with an apostrophe, sc. than the bosses' attitude).

Women are different than they used to be. They are playing in a very different way than (sc. they played) before. There are however very widespread and indignant objections to using different 'than' when only a noun phrase follows: 'Tabloids are very different than serious newspapers.' The argument is that 'than' is inappropriate and wrong in contexts where it can be viewed as a preposition. It is not a preposition.

I suspect that our difficulties with what to do after 'different' come from false analogy, which is a sore corrupter of English grammar. It causes the careless writer to write: 'Questions in which an intimate acquaintance of bureaucratic reforms of the Emperor Claudius was essential'; when the poor sap should have written 'acquaintance with' or 'knowledge of'. Analogy makes the hack in a hurry scribble: 'He smashed his boundaries to all parts of the compass'; when the cliché he is searching for is either 'all parts of the park' or 'all points of the compass'. 'They showed no inclination to throw in the sponge.' No, you either throw up the sponge, or you throw in the towel, if you have any sense, when you are getting thumped, and the world starts to move beneath you.

I suspect that the attraction of than after different is because, by false analogy, we confuse different with a comparative adjective such as 'other', which means much the same as different, and in some of its senses is used as a comparative, with a than-clause after it. 'He will never be other than he is now' is idiomatic and 'correct' grammar. So is: 'We are other than we should be', a sentence true, alas, as well as grammatically correct. By analogy with the correct construction after 'other', we start to say things like: 'Your reading of the election is different than mine.' Vice versa, by false analogy, different often improperly influences other, so that many use 'from' after 'other'. George Saintsbury, a fine idiomatic writer as well as a funny man, in his introduction to Thackeray's *Virginians*: 'Yet dress, habits, politics, other things, were still, as it were, of another world from ours.' You could say that that is incorrect. He should have written: '. . . than ours'. I prefer to say that that was George's idiolect of the day, or perhaps he did not read his piece through with due care and attention.

Different is not a comparative adjective; it is a positive adjective. It does, like all adjectives, have a comparative, 'more different' (which has nothing to do with 'very different'). 'She's quite a different girl than she was five years ago!' 'You may not think she's different, but I can tell you that she's more different than anyone else you know.' 'Quite' doesn't make a comparative; 'quite' means somewhat or rather, and doesn't figure in the comparison of English adjectives. 'She's more different than the girl she was five years ago.' If that makes sense to you, then go for it.

What one does after different is not a matter of morality, but of idiom and idiolect. 'Different than' makes British hackles rise, because it is a signal that the speaker belongs to a different educational tribe, and that we must therefore be cautious about his attitudes in general. Such little idiolects are shibboleths, and have considerable social and historical importance. My idiolect these days is to say and write 'different from'. But that is mainly from the cowardly motive that it saves the trouble of writing explanatory letters of justification to indignant shibboleth hunters. If a context arises in which 'different to' or, perhaps, 'different than' seems to express the meaning better, *Fiat idiolect, ruat coelum*. On second thoughts, I shall rephrase the sentence so as to avoid 'different than'.

# DOWN TO 1

## When down is up and in

'For promotion cometh neither from the east,
nor from the west: nor yet from the south.
And why? God is the Judge: he putteth down one,
And setteth up another.'
*The Book of Common Prayer*, Psalm 75, 7–8, 1662

We seem to be in the process of changing our ups for our downs. The sense I have in mind is that listed as 17.d in the majestic entry, measureless to man, for 'up' considered adverbially for the second time in the *Oxford English Dictionary*. The idiom in question is 'up to' meaning that something is obligatory or incumbent upon somebody, or the responsibility of someone. As in: 'It's up to you, squire.'

Until recently people would say things like: 'It is up to the Prime Minister to do something about unemployment, or the weather, or sex on television, or whatever.' I note that the young today say: 'It is down to the Prime Minister' to do something about these matters. I do not think that this is a sign that English is falling apart at the seams and prepositions. But I think it is interesting; and it may be instructive to try to see what is going on.

The entry in the appropriate fascicle of the *OED*, which was one of the last published, in 1926, describes this idiom, which seems standard today, as colloquial. It derives it from poker: 'So with the poker terms "ante up" and "it is up to you".' It asserts that the phrase has been in common use from c. 1913 (I like that learned, or bluffing, c.). And it states that the use is an Americanism, with an example from as early as 1908: 'It was "up to him", then, as an American would put it, to say that he had done this thing.' If it was necessary for the *Westminster Gazette* to quarantine the phrase in brackets, and apologize that this was an American speaking, it indicates that 'up to' in this sense is not built into the roots of Anglo-Saxon, but a recent arrival. The 1933 *OED Supplement* found an earlier example of 1896 from George Ade, the Indiana author whose books are noted for their racy use of the vernacular, and their sympathetic portrayal of country characters: 'Up to me – see!' Eric Partridge agrees that the 'up to' idiom comes from poker, and has nothing to add, apart from describing Ade as inimitable. Volume IV, *Se-Z*, of R. W. Burchfield's *Supplement*, published in 1986, could take the matter no farther back than Ade.

I have two other citations to add illustrating the recent arrival of 'up to' in British English. On 10 July 1908 Gilbert L. Jessop, the mighty smiter of the cricket ball, wrote to the Editor of *The Times*: 'It seems to me that as the MCC were invited to send a team to Australia it was "up to them", if I may for once borrow a Yankee colloquialism, to return the invitation.' In May 1914 H. H. Asquith, the Prime Minister, sent to Miss Venetia Stanley a list of expressions headed *Locutiones B.V.S. valde deflendae necnon vehementer cavendae*, sc. 'Expressions used by B.V.S. which are much to be deplored and emphatically to be guarded against.' There are twelve items on the list (ten slang words such as 'biffo', or phrases, and two endearments addressed to people other than the Prime Minister); and the first expression on the list is: 'It's up to you.' Venetia (full initials B.V.S.) was much younger than Asquith, twenty-six at the time of the list, and a member of the 'Coterie'. She liked to win money at cards, so presumably this is poker jargon.

The only other 'up to' idiom in English is Etonian slang, meaning to be taught by a beak, or master. For example, a letter from Aldous Huxley, aged fourteen: 'This half we are all up to that ignorant creature Heygate. I have successfully proved his ignorance.' This is esoteric, peculiar slang, and has nothing to do with the case.

So what in the world are we up to, giving up our once racy slang from poker that once excited the disapproval of the Prime Minister, and substituting 'down to'? Here is an example from a free sheet in 1987: 'A spokesman told the *Trader* that many faults may actually be down to vandalism, but didn't get reported as such.' In their 1966 album *Aftermath*, in a song called 'Under my Thumb', the Rolling Stones sang: 'It's down to me . . . the difference in the clothes she wears.'

I first came across 'down to' used not so much to mean

'responsible for', but rather 'on account of' or 'because of' in a novel called *The Crust on Its Uppers*, published in 1962 by New Authors Ltd (now Century Hutchinson). It is by Robin Cook (b. 1931), an Old Etonian; and it is an extremely funny, as well as sad, account of upper-middle-class crime and low life, and authoritative on the contemporary slang of that caste. Eric Partridge drew extensively on the glossary that is provided in the book, but failed to note the use of 'down to', with which Cook makes great play as a characteristic idiom of the moment in those circles. This was either because Partridge missed it (unlikely), or because he thought that it was synonymous with 'down to' as low slang for 'wide-awake, suspicious, aware', as in 'Down to every move' (1850); which it is not.

The phrase 'down to' is clearly not from poker or any other card game. The idiomatic use of 'down to' until recently has been as an adverb and preposition indicating, 'Even including the final item of a comprehensive list of things', for example, down to the last woman, the youngest man, the last detail, the final stages, the present day.

The modern use of 'down to', meaning that when you get down to the bottom line, it is down to you, i.e. it is your responsibility, may have come from sevice jargon for putting somebody down on some roster: 'You are down to whitewash coal today, Howard'; 'Latrine fatigue is down to you.' Auctioneers knock down a lot to the highest bidder; if they detect that a bidder, in a fit of enthusiasm, is bidding against himself, they say: 'It's down to you, sir.' Generous boozers say to the barman, when a friend comes in and orders a drink: 'Put that down to me.' Collectors for charity ask: 'May I put you down for a donation?' The idiom is in bookmakers' jargon: 'A hundred pounds to thirty on Blue Tarquin, down to Howard', i.e. written down in the book. Policeman use it. Detective Constable to suspect: 'This burglary is definitely down to you. You could make it easy for yourself if you tell me all about it.' The idiom clearly comes from low life, and lumpen London, I think, not the provinces. In drinking slang 'Down to Larkin' means 'free'. 'Who's paying for this round?' 'Shush! It's down to Larkin.' Larkin's identity is lost in the mists of time or a forgotten music-hall song. But he may be connected with 'larking', which is a rich word in thieves' cant. Captain Francis Grose defined 'larking' as 'cunnilingus' in the first edition of his *Classical Dictionary of the Vulgar Tongue*. Since 1920 criminals and the Metropolitan Police have used 'larking' to mean theft. 'Down to larking' means wrongly convicted, and may be the origin of the free drink Larkin.

In its original meaning 'down to' denoted responsibility; 'up to' denoted choice. Builder to client: 'It's up to you, squire'; i.e. you choose whatever colour/units/finish you like. But: 'It's down to you, squire'; i.e. you must pay for the extra work. It is up to the Prime Minister whether to cut taxes or increase public spending. But mass unemployment or raging inflation is down to the Prime Minister. Here is a nice little idiomatic distinction, which is widely ignored.

Why have the young suddenly started to say 'down to' where we all said 'up to' before? Misunderstanding of low Cockney slang? Ignorance, madam, pure ignorance? Is it that there is something more condemnatory and obligatory in down than up? 'It's all down to the Government, now' sounds rhetorically more minatory than 'It's up to the Government.' In part, I think, it is merely an example of the constant, copy-cat chase for trendiness in language, even in tiny prepositions and adverbs. The racy old poker term has begun to sound staid and boring, even though it vexed Asquith. At any rate, those of us who prefer 'up to' can carry on using it, without sounding hopelessly square – for the present, at least.

# ETYMOLOGY

## Rooting around

'Etymology has been briefly defined in this book
as "the origin, formation, and development (of a
word)". Some of the words going back to Old
English are as old as time, and are represented in
many of the Indo-European languages.'
*The Oxford Dictionary of English Etymology*, introduction, 1966,
edited by C. T. Onions

Etymology is a notorious adventure playground of eccentricity.
English, of all languages, because of its mongrel mixture of
Germanic and Romance and all the languages of the world,
has words with very rum roots indeed. 'Bosh' comes from the
Turkish word meaning empty or worthless; and gained currency from its frequent use in James Justinian Morier's Middle-
Eastern romance, *Ayesha*, 1834. 'Grotesque' comes from the
Greek verb *kryptein*, to hide, and hence *krypte*, a vault or place
where something might be hidden. The noun was taken into
Latin as *crypta*, and in Late Latin became *crupta* or *grupta*. From
the latter English derived grotto, a cave or cavern. Grotesque,
formerly also spelled crotesque, is a combination of grotto and
crotto and the Romance suffix -iscus, resembling or having the
characteristics of. Originally grotesque was narrowly applied
to a form of fantastic wall paintings found in ruins excavated
by the Romans, and imitated by Italian painters in the sixteenth
century. This sixteenth-century *pittura grottesca*, or grotty paintings, typically combined monstrous human and animal forms
with elaborate floral patterns. Hence in the seventeenth century grotesque acquired the generalized meaning of bizarre,
incongruous, absurd, and later gained the added connotations
of unpleasant, ugly.

Lunch comes from a Scottish word for hunk or thick chunk,
perhaps derived from the Spanish *lonja*, a slice. It was length-
ened to luncheon, by analogy with punch and puncheon,

trunch and truncheon, because the longer form sounded more genteel. A chapel is derived from the cloak or *cappella* that the soldier, St Martin of Tours, divided with his sword in order to give half to a beggar. Originally it was the sanctuary devoted to the preservation of the *cappella*. By about 800 AD it began to be extended to oratories attached to palaces or the like, and to parochial places of worship other than churches.

Admiral comes from the Arabic *Amir al Bahr*, or transliterate it as you will. *Amir* equals prince (as in Abdul the Bul Bul . . .). *Al* equals (of) the. *Bahr* equals sea. However, John Julius Norwich in *The Normans in the South* maintains that in origin *ammiratus* had nothing to do with the sea, but was just the word for the office of an emir, e.g. the Emir of Palermo, who under the Norman rulers was a Greek Christian. The -d- added in English and German is said to come from confusion with the Latin *admirabilis*. Or is this just a Navy joke?

False etymologies are almost as much fun: a belfry does not come from bells; a salt-cellar has nothing to do with cellar; and a gillyflower is ultimately derived from the Greek *karuophyllon* or clove-tree – the flower is a corruption.

But at least there is no problem about philately. Or is there? You will know the authorized version of the bizarre etymology? The first postage stamps to pay in advance to have a letter delivered were introduced in 1840. Shortly afterwards loonies started to collect them: I suppose it was more intellectually demanding, and less of a public nuisance, than jogging. George V was an enthusiastic stamp-collector. A private secretary once remarked to him: 'I see in *The Times* today that some damn fool has given fourteen hundred pounds for a single stamp at a private sale.' 'I am that damn fool,' said the king.

To start with the hobby of stamp-collecting was called *timbromania*. In 1865 the Frenchman M. Herpin coined the word *philatélie* in his *Le Collectionneur de Timbres-Poste*. He derived it from two Greek roots: *phil*, meaning a lover or fan of some activity, and *ateles*, free from tax or charge, or *ateleia*, a exemption from payment.

*Ateles* was taken as a passable Greek equivalent of 'free' or 'franco', which was formerly stamped on prepaid letters to show that the addressee need not pay, before the introduction of the impressed receipt stamp, or its successor, the adhesive label with perforated edges that will not tear and silly pictures.

A philatelist was a person who was dotty about stamps that showed that a letter was untaxed and could be received free of charge. That is the orthodox account of the etymology of the word: no more ridiculous than those of many words that have come into English. Philately was adopted into all the European languages except one: its mother language, Greek. They order these matters differently in Greece.

The Greek words are PhilOtely and PhilOtelist, sc. the love or lover of charges or taxes. Look them up in the big Greek dictionaries if you don't believe me. They define *philoteleia* as the love of collecting stamps, and explain: 'The word *Philoteleia* is more correct in Greek, although it is derived from the French *Philatélie*, which although wrong etymologically, has been adopted by nearly all European countries. *Philoteleia* magazine was established in 1924, and is published by the Greek Philotelic Society, which was founded in 1926.' And so on.

There does seem to be a radical difference between the love of the untaxed and the love of the taxed. Perhaps the Greeks don't understand their own language as well as the rest of us; in the same way that we are evidently better at looking after their marbles than they are. It goes to show that etymology is a science into which the prudent man gangs cannyways, and tries to make not too many unqualified assertions.

The trick is to notice the changes that are going on beneath our very eyes and into our very ears. Most language goes in one ear and out the other without causing a ripple on the wetware in between. We need to keep our eyes and ears open all the time, if we are not to snooze the day away beneath a duvet of clichés.

The other day I spotted my first 'completist', unrecorded by the latest dictionaries. It was in the *Book Collector* magazine: 'Clarke also contributed drawings to a wide variety of ephemeral publications in Ireland, which are all very scarce today, and mainly of interest only to completists.' A completist is a collector, originally of books, now of stamps, or anything, who sets completeness or completion as his goal. A veteran collector of science fiction described himself as a forty-three-year-old completist: 'That means I buy everything that comes out in the field, and never throw anything away.'

The word has started to be used attributively about magpies of things other than books: 'The completist attitude, which has governed several projects, finds the company (Columbia Records) in the position of either having finished or nearing the end of the complete recorded work of Stravinsky, Varèse, Webern, Schönberg, and Copland.' The word was clearly born in the United States. The earliest English reference I have found is in *Time Out* of 7 November 1985, where a review of Stephen King's book *Cat's Eye* included the fighting sentence: 'The result is liable to induce catalepsy in all but the most hardcore of King completists.'

Collectors are prolific inventors of new jargon, perhaps to keep profane outsiders away from their dotty hobby. Look at the semantic rubbish created by philatelists, or philotelists, such as 'setenant'.

I came across a Chelseafy the other day in property jargon. It sounds like a new sort of salad leaf to be found in trendy *nouvelle cuisine* restaurants. It means, I take it, to do up a house or a district in the twee fashion of Chelsea, a specific variation on the more general 'gentrify'. It can be only weeks before we spot our first Fulhamize.

And, Good Grief, what have we here? We have Imperial Chemical Industries advertising black polythene sheeting for mulching. I have always taken the view that mulching, like stamp-collecting, was an activity best left to those who like that sort of thing. But I thought I knew what it meant. It is well defined in *Chambers*: collecting loose material, straw dung, cowpats, earth, and mixing it up with water, to lay around the roots of plants as protection. Old English and German roots, no doubt, meaning half-rotten straw, and related to the dialect word *melsch*, or mellow. There sounds something onomatopoeic about sploshing the nasty stuff around with a trowel or fork. Granted that its function seems broadly similar, in keeping roots damp and stopping weeds: but how can black plastic sheeting ever be mulch? It provides no sustenance, and it sounds wrong.

The place where language changes fastest is among the young. They are learning words at a prodigious rate. They get bored quickly. They play trends and codes and insiders like adults. I report from a primary school in Swindon the latest vogue words for 'excellent'.

Skill

Ace

Radical, with optional abbreviation to rad
Raredos

By the time you read this, that school will have moved on to new slang. Primary schools around the English-speaking world have their own lingos, and change them continually. I can see the origins of the first three hurray-words in a Swindon primary school in 1986. But what is the fourth, this thing that sounds like a choir-screen? I think we should be told. But it is already too late. The slang of Wiltshire kids has changed. And I dare say that raredos is already passé.

# GRAMMAR

## Grammar: rules, OK, but not rule

'Word has somehow got around that the
split infinitive is always wrong. That is a
piece with the outworn notion that it is
always wrong to strike a lady.'
James Thurber

I dare say that our education system is hopelessly old-fashioned, and that the children we are turning out from school
are feckless, illiterate, and ill-prepared for the modern world.
At any rate, it is comforting for our vanity to think that we
were so much better educated than they are. The extreme
argument that standards are falling would be more impressive
if the ideologues who put it used English better. It is an
agreeable irony that devotees of the three Rs, flogging, cold
baths, Christianity, cricket, and grammatical studies are not
distinguished for any remarkable felicities of expression.

When was this supposedly golden age of English grammar?
It usually turns out to have been when the angry old men and
women were at school themselves. In fact they are mostly
male, and almost entirely white and middle-class. Their problem is not falling standards, but the male menopause. They
find themselves surrounded by bewildering new knowledge
and younger competitors; and the only change they can
confidently attack in this threatening new world is the change
in the supposedly adamantine rules of grammar.

In fact we were taught very little grammar. At primary
school we parsed, and learnt by rote long spelling lists of
difficult words like 'diarrhoea' and 'eschscholtzia' (better with
the 't' in the middle, I think), so that to this day I can write
them down confidently without snatching for the dictionary.
An impressive trick, no doubt; and about as useful as Heather,
the Jack Russell, being able to bounce a football on her nose six

times without it touching the ground. Opportunities to write 'diarrhoea' and 'eschscholtzia' do not come every day.

At secondary school we were taught no 'English', apart from being required to write Sunday Questions (essays on a pious or scriptural theme), and essays for a General Paper. An anxious mother once asked the Head of Greek whether it was right for a boy to pass through the Old Coll. from the age of 12 to 18 without ever having to read Shakespeare or Dickens, except for the purpose of translating them into Greek or Latin verses or prose. Richard Martineau replied imperially (and unrealistically): 'They can read them in the holidays.'

Alas, mortification and dammit, there is little evidence that the children coming out of our schools are worse than we were. They may be worse at some things. But they are knowledgeable over a far wider range of subjects. Far fewer of them learn Latin and Greek, and there is alarming evidence that they are not sound on the dates of the kings and queens of England, and maybe know less history generally. They are probably worse spellers. But a learned Greats examiner at Oxford declares emphatically that standards are as high as they were 30 years ago. The sixth-form children I meet seem frighteningly bright, and more articulate than we were. What has happened is that there has been a reaction from the *ancien régime* of the three Rs and learning 'diarrhoea' by rote to self-expression and a let-it-all-hang-out radicalism.

We could have done with a bit more self-expression and thinking for ourselves instead of plagiarizing our textbooks to pass exams. But, like all reactions, the reaction from the old grammatical purism has been taken too far by some enthusiasts. What is needed is a sensible advance towards the noble goal of universal literacy and articulacy for our children. It is worth remembering that this is a very recent goal indeed.

Grammar was made for man, not man for grammar. It changes continually. In its history so far English has changed from a fully inflected to an almost completely non-inflected language. Grammar is not a moral virtue or a Golden Rule. All it means is the consensus of a particular period about the way to put words and sentences together. There is often no consensus, but variants and disagreements and fetishes.

And grammar can be taken too far. On his death-bed the great French grammarian, Dominique Bouhours, announced portentously: 'I am about to . . . or I am going to . . . die; either expression is perfectly good grammar.'

When John Horne Tooke, the British radical politician and philologist, was at school in the middle of the eighteenth century, a master in a grammar lesson asked him why a certain verb governed a particular case. Tooke answered: 'I don't know.' 'That's impossible,' said the master; 'I know you're not ignorant, but obstinate.' Tooke, however, persisted in saying that he didn't know. So the master beat him. After the beating was over, the master quoted the rule that covered the verb in question. 'Oh, I know that,' said Tooke at once: 'but you asked me the *reason*, not the *rule*.'

And the grammar of the Golden Age was not all that hot. The schoolboys who became the literary stars of the Elizabethan Age learnt from Horman's *Vulgaria*, translating English into Latin badly: We will play with a ball of wynde: *Lusum erit nobis follis pugilaris spiritu tumens*. This game was handball, not football, which was considered barbarous, and forbidden by Act of Parliament at the time. The contemporary *Book of the Governor* speaks of: 'Football, wherein is nothing but beastly fury and extreme violence; whereof proceedeth hurt, and consequently rancour and malice do remain with them that be wounded.' Our common standards of grammar and football have improved greatly since those days, *pace* the grumpy old shell-backs of the New Right, which differs from the Old Right only in its meanness of spirit.

Nevertheless, one palpable disadvantage of the decline in classics teaching is that we are increasingly unsure about the names of different parts of speech, and the way to use them and grammatical forms. Take such a simple thing as the superlative. In the days when we all worked our way through the comparison of adjectives in *Kennedy's Shorter Eating Primer*, I think we got into less of a muddle.

Here is a recent example from the Anniversaries Column on the Court Page of the thinking man's (and woman's) paper: 'Canada, the world's second largest country after the Soviet Union . . .' Because we are uneasy about those damned superlatives, we put a spanner in the works with the word 'second', which implies that there is some country in the world larger than Canada but smaller than the USSR. Delete 'second', and the illogicality is removed.

175

Ambiguity over comparatives and superlatives is not new. There was the schoolboy puzzle about the circus proprietor who spoke of 'the greatest elephant in the world except himself'. Even Milton, the most classical of English writers, got into a muddle with his superlatives:

> Adam, the goodliest man of men since born
> His sons; the fairest of her daughters Eve.

(Something not quite right here, Ed.)

Superlative confusion is not new; but there seems to be more of it around these days. I think this may be partly due to the fact that every child in the kingdom is no longer taken through the comparison of adjectives by Mr Quelch in Shell, or Miss Beale in the Lower Fourth.

Here is an example of another common type of superlative illogicality: 'Lord Peregrine Philanthrope's gift of £1 million to the Sunset Homes for Overworked Hacks is only the latest of many acts of splendid munificence by which he has benefited his fellows before now.' Pestilential purists, such as Fowler, reply to such a sentence: 'If it is the latest of Perry's munificences, it is one of them; if one of them, it must have been given before now; but it is in fact given now, not before now, which is absurd. QED.'

The other superlative rule that was whacked into us by Old Chalky, but has now faded from common usage, is that the superlative is only for three or more persons or things; for two persons or things, use the comparative. Thus: 'Zola Bulb is the faster runner of the two.' 'He is the cleverest boy in the whole class.' As for 'former' and 'latter', they are quite out of fashion, and are beginning to sound quaint.

Not all these superlative distinctions are of the first importance, which is why they are fading from English grammar. But anything that reduces the flexibility and options of the language impoverishes us all. And superlative mistakes that produce illogicalities must be a bad thing, and annoy your readers.

Each generation evolves its language's grammar to suit itself and meet new needs. It is possible that as a result of the decline of classics in schools we need to teach a bit more of the nuts and bolts of English grammar. It would be more sensible and more fun to revive a bit of Latin and Greek grammar for everyone. They are doing so in the United States, where they find it is a very useful subject for deprived and polyglot children of the decaying city centres. Not only is it a good way to learn the nuts and bolts of grammar, with a language that is not marked with racial and class distinctions. But it opens the door to the roots of our Western languages and cultures.

# HISTORY

## Too serious to be left to historians

'Henry VIII was a strong king with a very strong sense of humour and VIII wives, memorable amongst whom are Katherine the Arrogant, Anne of Cloves, Lady Jane Austin, and Anne Hathaway. His beard was, however, red.

In his youth Henry was fond of playing tennis and after his accession is believed never to have lost a set. He also invented a game called "Bluff King Hal", which he invited ministers to play with him. The players were blindfolded and knelt down with the heads on a block of wood, they then guessed who the King would marry next.'
1066 and All That, 1930, by W. C. Sellar and R. J. Yeatman

How does one write history these days? It was so much easier when the world was simpler: And Bela died, and Jobab the son of Zeräh of Bozrah reigned in his stead. Herodotus, Father of History, Father of Lies, simply packed his reporter's tablets, and went off on a jaunt, to gossip about crocodiles with Egyptian priests, or sketch the topography of Babylon.

In the days when history was supposed to run on royal railway lines, as in Sellar and Yeatman, it was simplified into Good Things and Bad Things: Alfred had a very interesting wife called Lady Windermere (The Lady of the Lake), who was always clothed in the same white frock, and used to go bathing with Sir Launcelot and was thus a Bad Queen. Intellectuals sometimes reversed the simple moralities of history at school. In *Portraits from Memory*, his delightful memoir, Bertrand Russell remembered school: 'Broadly speaking, anything done against kings was to be applauded – unless, indeed, it were done by priests, like Becket, in which case one sided with the king.'

Gibbon, Macaulay, and our other giant historians dealt with vast and complex matters, but gave them a compulsive course that makes their histories hard to put down even for the general reader, though Gibbon does eventually run out of steam with all those *fainéant* Byzantine emperors. 'Gibbon's style is detestable; but it is not the worst thing about him . . . When I read a chapter in Gibbon, I seem to be looking through a luminous haze or fog; figures come and go, I know not how or why, all larger than life, or distorted and discoloured; nothing is real, vivid, true; all is scenical, and, as it were, exhibited by candlelight.' Well, I disagree, Silas Tomken Cumberbatch, and I suspect a little jealousy.

It is not that history is not being written these days. More of it pours off the academic presses in a year than used to be published in a century. One trouble with history today is that it has become increasingly specialized and esoteric for the general reader: for example, *Early Victorian Water Engineers* by George Morse Binnie, published in 1981. Or how about *Millennium Charisma Among the Pathans*, 1976, or *Faith, Reason and The Plague in Seventeenth Century Tuscany*, 1979? Or care for a bite at *Cannibalism and the Common Law* by A. W. Brian Simpson, 1986? All good stuff, no doubt, for fans of the subjects. But the general reader would need to be omnivorous or very bored to tackle them. There are few books for the intelligent general reader in the desert that stretches between romances for visitors to Madame Tussaud's and academic works for the specialists, or at least for the purpose of getting the author a doctorate. Are there any?

Another trouble is that prosopography and the other modern historiographic techniques, intended to make history more scientific, tend to make dry reading, except from the pen of a genius like Ronnie Syme or Fernand Braudel. I suspect that to write big history you need a bee in your bonnet rather than academic objectivity: Macaulay, Gibbon, and Tacitus certainly had queen bees in their bonnets. If this theory is true, why are Marxist historians, and other modern historians, who certainly have swarms of bees in their bonnets, and a procrustean attitude to their material, unreadable?

But the principal difficulty with trying to write history today is that there is too much of it. The world is no longer run by a handful of rulers in Western Europe. And there is more to history these days than who beat whom in which battle, and who succeeded whom on what throne – there always was, but it was deemed irrelevant. Most history has been a record of the triumphs, disasters, and follies of top people. The black hole in it is the way of life of mute, inglorious men and women who made no nuisance of themselves in the world.

International politics and economics from all around the world are vital, no doubt. But they are hard to turn into compulsive reading. And that is why people who used to read history have turned to the comparatively new literary genres of biography and historical fiction. The life of one person, and the fictional re-creation of past time, are more alive than international treaties, and more fun to read. They may also be more truthful, in that they get nearer to the heart of the past.

This confusion about what is important in the long eye of history also affects the hod-carriers of history, the journalists. *The Times* is supposed to be the paper of record; but which of our records will be considered significant by a historian in a century's time? Most of the things we work ourselves into a sweat of excitement about, whether Fudge succeeds Mudge as leader of the Neanderthal Party, what the Budget will contain, whither the Salt talks, will seem as remote as and less interesting than the laws of Lykourgos in Ancient Sparta thirty centuries ago. Let us hope that the poor Noah who survives the cataclysm of events to write our history has a sympathetic imagination, to see us as we are, and make allowances.

There is no such thing as exact history or a paper of record. Take one of the simplest things that journalists try to report: a speech. In the High Victorian times, when there was more leisure, and public speeches were the only means of communication for politicians, *The Times* used to report their speeches at great length, sometimes almost verbatim. But these were still not exact records. They were translations of the spoken into the written word. They left out emphasis and intonation, nudge and wink, the meaningful pause, the tricks of the trade, the vocal and non-verbal signifiers. They left out the reactions of the audience. You can write in 'Applause' or 'Uproar' or 'Dissent', but that is inadequate. Written reports leave out the connotations and implications carried on its back by every word used, the echoes and allusions, some of them going back twenty centuries. To give a full report of a speech would take every page of today's *Times*, and it would still be nowhere near an exact report. And most historical events are vastly more complicated to record than a speech.

It is a serious matter in the United Kingdom that politicians no longer know and refer to their history, and school-children are no longer taught so much history, even of the old-fashioned and slighty ludicrous royal genealogies of Willie, Willie, Harry, Ste . . ., and great British victories and their dates. The cement that holds an old, complex society like Britain together is made partly from its history. Things are different in the United States, where the citizens have very little common history, and are bound together instead by noble philosophical ideals and a belief in the future.

In the same way it is a serious matter that the classics, Latin and Greek, have declined so disastrously as subjects for study in British schools, particularly in the state sector, where 94 per cent of our children are educated. The classics suffer by reaction because they were once pre-eminent, the king and queen of the curriculum in Victorian and early twentieth-century public schools. They were the education of the ruling élite, and of the idle rich, who could get through life with a private income and a few tags from Horace. In reaction to this snobbery and extravagant emphasis on the classics, they have been demoted too far. It is possible also that some of the education administrators and politicians have sour memories of all those pages of irregular verbs set in bold type in their school Latin and Greek grammars. Since Oxford and Cambridge ceased to make Latin a compulsory subject for entrance into our two most famous universities, the classics have dwindled away.

It is worth rehearsing a few of the arguments for the classics for short-sighted people who think of them as out-of-date accomplishments of old-fashioned ladies and gents:

1 Latin and Greek are the roots of Western European languages. They are the mother tongues. It is impossible to understand English, or any other Western European language, fully without some knowledge of the classics. They help in every department of subsequent languages, from spelling to idiom to metaphor to deep grammatical structures.

2 Latin and Greek are the roots of Western culture. From iconography to politics, and from the theatre to philosophy

and history, a Westerner with no knowledge of the classics is a rootless person, and blindfolded in a garden of delights.

3 State education systems elsewhere, from Japan to the United States, are increasingly offering *more* classics. Surveys in urban areas of the United States have demonstrated beyond argument that acquaintance with a fully inflected language such as Latin helps the backward and educationally disadvantaged to understand their own language. It teaches them the roots of grammar. They are languages without class or racial shibboleths. The demand for Latin teachers in the United States has increased by 10 per cent for each of the past five years.

4 Classics are fun. Children with an aptitude for language get more pleasure out of them than from any other subject, and in so doing open the door to the garden of two of the greatest literatures in the history of the world.

5 Greek and Latin are the very much alive, and international, languages of the sciences (viz. particularly Greek in physics and chemistry, particularly Latin in anatomy and botany). Anyone professing these disciplines can hardly understand what he is talking about without some acquaintance with the etymology and history of his terms. Moreover, this process continues: new words are continually being coined and added to the pool from the classical sources. For example, recent newcomers, a small band of fuglemen to represent a mighty army, include cybernetics, topos, hermeneutics, and axonometric.

6 Classics help you to solve British cryptic crosswords (joke). There should be a typeface, called Ironics, possibly italics leaning backwards rather than forwards, to indicate to the reader that a joke is being attempted.

One could extend the list. But the point is that history and classics are important and delightful disciplines; and that education systems and national cultures neglect them at the peril of reverting to barbarism.

# INDIAN ENGLISH

## In Indian country

'India is no more a political personality than Europe.
India is a geographical term. It is no more a united
nation than the equator.'
Speech by Winston Churchill, 1931

Churchill was accosted at a wartime reception by an overbearing American lady. 'What are you going to do about those wretched Indians?' she demanded. 'Madam,' replied Churchill, 'to which Indians do you refer. Do you refer to the second greatest nation on earth, which under benign and munificent British rule has multiplied and prospered exceedingly? Or to the unfortunate North American Indians, which under your present administration are almost extinct?' The Indian subcontinent has enriched British life from Sezincote and the Royal Pavilion, Brighton, to the latest pagodas and beautiful launderettes; from poppadums and butter chicken to great novels and films; from famous cricketers to the corner newsagent and grocer who opens earlier and shuts later than any other shop.

I was reminded how it enriches the English language by a letter from the Wilco Shipping Agency of Madras, soliciting my custom under a misapprehension of my needs, but with the full flower of Indian politeness: 'Reputed owners have either gone bankrupt or landed in receivership. Our brochure is enclosed to regale you about the prevalent modus operandi. Owners can always confide in us for any matter. They may whisper anything and we will not even allow the walls to eavesdrop . . .'

This is a typical, ornate Indian *babu* business letter, using some words in a slightly exotic sense, eg 'reputed' for 'reputable'. The last sentence is perfect, with its vivid image of even the walls listening in some treacherous Mogul corridor. You can imagine the pronunciation of 'eavesdrop', with the 'drop' stressed, and rhyming with carp. 'Indian shipping scenario is fraught with episodes, where owners face some exigencies and need immediate assistance.' The unique strength of English is that it has so many lively national and regional dialects enriching the central core.

We forget how much of the British vocabulary comes from India. Indian words have been insinuating themselves into English ever since the reign of Elizabeth I, when such terms as *calico, chintz,* and *gingham* had already found their way into the London docks and English shops, and were lying in wait to enter English literature.

Bungalow, khaki, jungle, and cummerbund are reasonably well known. But remember shampoo, which is the anglicization of *chāmpō,* the imperative of the Hindi verb *chāmpnā,* meaning to massage, as the Romans used their *tractator* to knead and soothe their aching muscles. The process is described in *A Voyage to East India,* by Edward Terry, 1616: 'Taking thus their ease, they often call their Barbers, who tenderly gripe and smite their Armes and other parts of their bodies instead of exercise, to stirre the bloud. It is a pleasing wantonnesse and much valued in these hot climes.' Strabo referred to the practice; but the historians say that the connection between lubricity and massage parlours that existed in Rome, and has been revived in Soho, was not made in India. The first use of the word in English that I have found is in *A Voyage to the East Indies* in 1747 and 1748: '*Shampooing* is an operation not known in Europe, and is peculiar to the Chinese, which I had once the curiosity to go through, and for which I paid but a trifle. However, had I not seen several China merchants *shampooed* before me, I should have been apprehensive of danger, even at the sight of all the different instruments.' Lieutenant-Colonel A. Beatson in *View of the Origin and Conduct of the War with Tippoo Sultan* described the custom: 'The Sultan generally rose at break of day: after being *champoed,* and rubbed, he washed himself, and read the Koran for an hour.' I wish I had a *tractator* or Indian Barber to gripe and smite my aching parts tenderly at the end of a hard day at the word laboratory. As it is, I have a hot bath, shampoo my hair, and bless our Indian roots.

We owe cash to the Indians in the linguistic as well as the pecuniary sense. The letters of the young, light-hearted masters of the East India Company are full of references to 'cash', the sundry coins of low value and amazing shapes in various parts of India. Cash, of course, is what they were there for. 'In this country (Calicut) a great number of apes are produced, one of which is worth four *casse*, and one *casse* is worth a *quattrino*', *The Travels of Lodovico di Varthema*, 1510. The Indian word for coin was affected by the existence of the distinct English word 'cash' meaning money-box, from the French *caisse*, and the Italian *cassa*.

The great vocabulary of English is enriched by Indian. *Hobson-Jobson*, the Glossary of Colloquial Anglo-Indian Words and Phrases, by Colonel Henry Yule and A. C. Burnell, was first published in 1866, and has frequently been reissued. The imperial connection, by which most British families had a relation who had served in India, has long been broken. But the historical and family connection, with our own native British Indians, remains as strong and enriching as ever. English usage in India, and also in Pakistan, Bangladesh, and Sri Lanka, affects our common stock of English in vocabulary, accent, idiom, syntax, semantics, grammar, and all the other departments of language. I sometimes wonder, in my more extravagant moments, whether the trick of leaving out the definite article in TUCSpeak, as in Conference and Congress *tout court* without an introductory 'the', may not be an echo of Indian English.

In India there are fifteen official languages, and a thousand or so others. English is the only common linguistic ground from Bombay to Calcutta, and from Delhi to Madras. Only about two or three per cent of the population speak it. But it is this educated élite that provides the men and women to run the country. You could write a whole book about the Indianization of English, the particular and delightful dialects of English spoken in India. Learned professors have. They noted the grammatical and syntactical idiosyncrasies of Indian English, such as leaving out the pronoun with reflexive verbs (enjoy, exert); the peculiar syntax of verbs by which 'I am doing it since six months' is used for 'I have been doing it for six months'; and the powerful tendency in Indian English to dispense with pronouns in noun compounds such as 'glass-pane' and 'beer bottle'.

In style and tone they catalogue such Indian idiosyncrasies as:

1 Latinity, by which an Indian might prefer demise to death, or pain in one's bosom to pain in one's chest.

2 A propensity to polite forms. The main reason for this is that originally the registers of English introduced into India were administration and the law, both polite and formal registers.

3 Grammatical differences: for example, aircraft is sometimes pluralized into aircrafts in Indian, never in British English.

4 Lexical variation. A thing to warm the bed on cold nights is called a hot-water bag by many Indian-English speakers; to the British English it is always a hot-water bottle.

5 A tendency to phrase-mongering, such as Himalayan blunder; nation-building; change of heart; and dumb millions.

6 Variations of idiom: British English say, 'He's always had a soft spot for her'; the Indian English idiom is, 'He's always had a soft corner for her.'

7 Initialism, the passion for offical initials and acronyms that exceeds even the officialese of American English. 'HE's PA has written DO to the ASP about the question of TAs. The DC himself will visit the SDOPWD today at 10 AMST.' Expanded for the benefit of slow British-English speakers, this means: 'His Excellency's Personal Assistant has written a demi-official letter to the Assistant Superintendent of Police about the question of Travelling Allowances. The Deputy Commissioner himself will visit the Sub-Divisional Officer of the Public Works Department today at 10 am Standard Time.'

8 Variations of style, for example in different levels of formality in the two varieties. For example, Indian English says, 'She was felicitated on bagging the first prize.' In British English 'felicitate' is extremely formal; while 'bag' is extremely informal and old-fashioned; so that the two words would be unlikely to occur in the same sentence.

9 A moralistic tone: Indians cannot keep God out of it.

10 Clichés: Indian English has a tendency to elaborate clichés, such as 'better imagined than described' (easily imagined); 'do the needful'; 'each and every' (pleonastic for 'each'); 'leave severely alone' (for 'leave alone').

11 Deletion of pronouns and other contractions, by which,

for example, 'an address of welcome' in British English becomes 'welcome address' in Indian English; 'a bunch of keys' becomes 'key bunch'; and 'love of God' becomes 'God-love'. Some pundits think that this tendency follows Sanskrit compounds.

12 Yes-no confusion in answering questions: 'You have no objection?' 'Yes, I have no objection.'

13 Reduplication and repetition, as in, 'Who and who came to the party?' This feature is common to all South Asian languages, and has been adopted into Indian English.

14 Bookishness: most Indians are taught their English formally from books, using authors such as Shakespeare and Milton. It is not surprising that their dialect is somewhat bookish, and often more accurate and beautiful than British English. Indian English does not sound conversational, because English has seldom been taught as a spoken language in India.

15 Social and cultural variations: Indian English refers to events and phenomena that do not happen in other English-speaking countries. For example, 'He's so angry with them he's threatening to have them shoe-beaten.' To beat someone, or threaten to do so, with a shoe or slipper is considered grossly insulting in India. The idea, and the language used to express it, would not be understood by British-English speakers.

16 Differences of collocation: collocation in linguistics refers to the way that certain words tend to be found in the company of other words: 'milk' collocates frequently with 'cow', but not very often with 'tiger'. Here is an example from an Indian newspaper: 'It was alleged that the police had been awarded bribes by the gamblers.' The collocation of the verb 'award' and the noun 'bribes' would be most unlikely in British English.

17 Differences of meaning: some words mean different things in Indian and British English. For example, in Indian English a 'busybody' means somebody who is extremely busy. In British English a 'busybody' means somebody who meddles in the business of others, perhaps even a mischief-maker.

18 Registers: some words that have specialist meanings in British-English registers are used in general everyday language in Indian English. For example, 'cover', which has a specialized

meaning in postal and philatelic jargon in British English is widely used to mean an ordinary 'envelope' in Indian English. In British English a 'bogie' is the technical term of railway jargon; in Indian English it is used generally for a carriage or coach.

19 Loan-words. Indian English adopts thousands of loan-words from Hindi, Urdu, and the other languages of the subcontinent, most of them unknown to speakers of the other Englishes. For example: *bandh*, *lathi*, *lakh*, *crore*. They often form compounds with British English words: *lathi*-charge, double-*roti*.

20 Neologisms: Indian users of English have been particularly productive in creating new English words that are not generally known to other speakers of English. For example: freeship (a free studentship, i.e. a scholarship with full remission of fees); delink (to remove or abolish the link between something and something else); batch-mate (a fellow in the same group or batch, i.e. a class-mate or fellow student).

You could make a case for arguing that people with two languages and two cultures are more creative linguistically than dull monoglots. It is clearly the case that many Indians, because they have been taught from old-fashioned textbooks by old-fashioned teachers who still believe in the Great Queen's English, write formal English of a certain kind better than your average Englishman, whose education has largely given up the writing of formal prose. Yā Hasan, Yā Hosain, or as we say Hobson-Jobson, for our old and rich Indian connection.

# JANUS WORDS

## Quiddities in

> ' "I don't know what you mean by 'glory'," Alice said.
>
> Humpty Dumpty smiled contemptuously. "Of course you don't – till I tell you. I meant 'there's a nice knock-down argument for you'."
>
> "But 'glory' doesn't mean 'a nice knock-down argument'," Alice objected.
>
> "When *I* use a word," Humpty Dumpty said in rather a scornful tone, "it means just what I choose it to mean – neither more nor less."'
>
> *Through the Looking-Glass and What Alice Found There*, chapter 6, 1871, by Lewis Carroll (Charles Lutwidge Dodgson)

I take it that we are interested in the quirks and quiddities of language; otherwise, what in the name of Hermes are we doing in a book like this? Because of the vast size of its vocabulary, and looseness of its grammar, English is richer in the qs and qs of language than any other tongue. Here is a quiddity-hunt to exercise you. I am looking for what we might call auto-antonyms; that is words or phrases with two meanings that are the opposite of each other. I give you eclectic examples of all sorts, before we consider how and why auto-antonyms happen.

**Affection**: love – malady.
**To anticipate**: to foresee and act in advance of – to expect.
**To back up**: to support – to reverse: 'Back your car up.'
**A bomb**: particularly in theatrical slang can mean both a complete flop, particularly, in the United States, and a raging success in the United Kingdom. This Janus effect of looking in opposite directions at the same time can cause confusion and offence in transatlantic congratulatory cables after first nights.

**To buckle**: to fasten – to bend.

**To chop**: chop the tree down – then chop it up.

**Chuffed**: is used to mean both gruntled and disgruntled, though the former meaning seems to me to be prevailing.

**To cleave**: to cling together or adhere to – to split apart.

**Contemporary**: at that time – now.

**Disinterested**: impartial – uninterested.

**Down**: upland, as in Sussex Downs – low-lying place. Q: 'Have you ever seen a man with a feebly-growing down on his chin?' A: 'I don't think so; what is a feebly?'

**Dyke/dike**: wall – ditch.

**To draw**: to close the curtains – to open the curtains. If the curtains are half drawn at 6 p.m. on a summer's day, what are you expected to do, when asked to draw them?

**To dust**: to take off the dust, like a char – to put on dust, as when pollinating a rose.

**Fairly**: Chairman of Industrial Tribunal: 'But your employer says you were fairly dismissed' – aggrieved appellant (probably an Aberdonian farm worker): 'I was fairly dismissed.'

**Fascination**: I have a fascination for actresses (or misericords, if you prefer) – actresses (or misericords) have a fascination for me.

**Fast**: speedy – stationary.

**Good deal**: 'It cost £10, which I thought was a good deal.' A bargain, or overpriced?

**Handicap**: an advantage – a disadvantage.

**To hew**: to sever – to conform to (chiefly American and Canadian).

**If not**: and also 'This play is certainly the liveliest, if not the most subtle, in town.' – but not also: 'At times she was highly irritating, if not downright exasperating.'

**Impartable**: something that cannot be parted – something that can be imparted or shared.

**To infer**: to conclude or deduce – to imply.

**In charge of**: who is in charge of whom? From *The Lost Girl*, by D. H. Lawrence: 'Alvina went to bed at about 9 o'clock in the morning, leaving James in charge of Miss Pinnegar.'

**Inflammable**: a notorious Janus word. It is widely used to mean both something that can be set on fire, and also something that cannot be set on fire. This is dangerous as well as silly. Sooner or later somebody's fingers will be burnt because of the confusion.

**Ingenerate**: born – not born.

**Insurer**: in the jargon of the insurance business, means either the company, or the insured person, though, mercifully, the latter meaning is obsolescent.

**To lay**: to give birth (an egg) – to destroy (lay waste).

**To let**: to allow (ME *leten* AS *letan*, *laetan*) – not to allow, to prevent, as in 'without let or hindrance' (ME *letten* AS *lettan*).

**Lost, as in 'lost time'**: reduced, as when an allocated period is cut – increased, as when a competitor in a timed event makes a mistake.

**Mild**: warmish – coolish.

**Modern**: now – then, before the Post-Modern Movement.

**Moor**: low-lying plain, as in Somerset – upland, as in darkest Ayrshire.

**Mortar**: material for sticking things together – a device for blowing things apart.

**Naughty**: nice, as in Soho advertisements – nasty, as in the *The General Epistle of James*, I, 21: 'Wherefore lay apart all filthiness and superfluity of naughtiness.'

**Now**: now, now – now, then.

**Outgoing**: friendly – retiring, as in the outgoing president.

**To overlook**: to fail to notice – to look after.

**Oversight**: an omission or mistake – supervision.

**Patron**: a benefactor – a client or customer.

**Pediment**: a low-pitched gable, usually triangular, as on the Parthenon and other classical architecture – a gently sloping rock surface, formed through denudation under arid conditions.

**Pravda**: truth – lies.

**To pressurize**: to make resistant to high pressure – to break down resistance by applying pressure.

**To prevent**: to keep from happening, hinder, impede – to precede, anticipate.

**Priceless**: of inestimable value – valueless.

**To protest**: in Britain a convicted felon protests his innocence – in the United States he protests his sentence.

**Quite**: moderately: this chapter is quite amusing – extremely: this chapter is quite fascinating. Is a jigsaw that is quite complete all there, or not? She's quite pretty, I s'pose, but I shall never understand why Jeremy prefers her to Jacynth, who is quite lovely. The evening started quite well, but Henry later got horribly drunk, and made a quite hideous scene.

**Quiddity**: itself: the essential nature of something – a petty or trifling distinction.

**To ravel**: to tangle – to disentangle.

**Ring**: a circle – a square, as in boxing.

**Riverine**: of, like, relating to, or produced by a river – of, like, relating to, or produced by a bank.

**Room**: enclosed space – open space.

**Sanction**: final permission – coercive measures.

**To save jobs**: to prevent unemployment – to create unemployment.

**To scan**: to read systematically – to read hastily.

**To shelve**: to put off – to put in, as librarians shelve books.

**To skin**: to take the skin off – to put the skin on, as in a sausage factory.

**Slated**: badly reviewed – scheduled, chiefly AmerEnglish, as in, 'New show slated for Broadway.'

**Slice**: cut – piece cut off.

**To stand by**: You said you would stand by me. But when I needed you, you just stood by.

**To slow**: to slow up – to slow down.

**To stone**: to take the stones out of (plums) – to throw stones at (adulterers).

**Through**: transatlantic telephone operator: 'Are you through?' Howard: 'Yes, thank you.' So she cuts you off.

**To throw out**: I throw out 'throw out' as an auto-antonym; but if you don't agree, you can throw it out.

**Topless**: topless towers of Ilium – topless model has prominent and supposedly interesting tops.

**Trying**: working hard – irritating.

**Ullage**: the volume by which a liquid container falls short of being full – the quantity of liquid lost from a container due to leakage or evaporation.

**Unarguable**: incapable of being argued – incontestable.

**Unbending**: he is so unbending: I wish he would unbend.

**Undone**: ruined – unfastened.

**Up**: speed up – slow up.
**To yield**: to give in – to give out.

There is a fine, knock-down farrago of Janus words or auto-antonyms for you. You could add many more. Any word with a long, complex history has a great many different meanings for a great many different groups of people; and some of those meanings are going to be opposites, or startlingly incongruous. The notorious Janus or Chameleon word 'nice' has meant everything from silly to fastidious, and from agreeable to disagreeable. In the seventeenth century a nice man was a bad-tempered one; but a nice woman, I regret to say, was fast.

We could divide our list of Janus words into two main groups: words which are used in different ways by people: and quite distinct words that are spelled in the same ways. A third group in our list consists of jokes and whimsies. Words and phrases in the first group tend to be complicated and long, and are therefore instinctively avoided for those reasons as well as for their ambiguity. Words in the second group tend to be shorter and clearer; and the double meanings seldom cause a problem.

For example, 'cleave' comes from two quite separate Anglo-Saxon words: *cleofan*, to split; and *cleofian*, to stick fast. There was no confusion ten centuries ago, especially as the former verb is strong (p.p. *clofen*) and the latter weak (p.p. *clifen*). The words were quite separate, and all attempts to connect them are fanciful. The two meanings of 'down' are, of course, connected, though they come from different parts of the OE word, *daun*, a hill. The adverb and occasional preposition are aphetic corruptions of *adune* and *ofdune*: *adown*. 'Fast' originally meant being fixed, firm, strong; the speedy Gonzales sense was derived from the adverb, and the idea of running with great effort, a use that arose by analogy with holding fast.

Words are kittle cattle, and any word with a long history will have acquired some ambiquities. Another way to corral double-edged Janus words or auto-antonyms is to notice that there are two varieties. The first kind are words that have opposite meanings such as sanction, handicap, dyke, cleave, fast, and oversight. We could also call these antithonyms (sc. naming opposites). The second sort are pairs of apparent opposites that have identical meanings, such as passive and impassive, inflammable and flammable, shameful and shameless, and bend and unbend. These are really pseudo-antonyms, and actually synonyms.

Dr F. Waismann noted an extreme case of ambiguity in what he called the antithetical sense of primal words. There is evidence that in the oldest languages opposites such as strong/weak, light/dark, large/small were expressed by the same root word. For example, in ancient Egyptian *keu* stood for both strong and weak. In Latin *altus* means both high and deep, *sacer* means both sacred and accursed. Compare further *clamare* to shout, but *clam*, secretly, quietly; *siccus* dry, but *succus* juice. Ambiguity is built into the roots of language.

# METAPHORS

## Mad maxims

Proverbs are the folklore of simple, rural societies, providing incantations instead of thought. Perhaps that is why we are so bad at them these days. I keep on hearing, 'We must cut our cloth', which – if you stop to think about it instead of nodding and yawning – conjures up an obscure image of some batty Tailor of Gloucester. The original proverb, which goes back in written records more than four centuries, is: 'I shall cut my coat after (or according to) my cloth': a prudent, though not a very dashing maxim.

Everybody now says: 'It is too late to shut the stable-door after the horse has bolted.' Sensible horses, if that is not a contradiction in terms, bolt home towards rather than away from their stables. The original proverb referred to horse-stealing and the futility of shutting or bolting the stable-door after Blue Tarquin the Third had been stolen. It is a very old proverb, its origin lost in the midden of the Dark Ages: *Maxima pars pecore amisso prasepia claudit*. Today, less used to horses and horse-thieves, we get it wrong. We need a new proverb about traffic wardens and wheel clamps.

Similarly, people refer to somebody being hoisted by his own petar(d), giving me the unworthy suspicion that they imagine a petar to be some kind of crane or spring trap that hoists you feet first into the air. A petar is a thoroughly modern weapon, still used by terrorists:

> For 'tis the sport to have the enginer
> Hoist with his own petar: and it shall go hard
> But I will delve one yard below their mines,
> And blow them at the moon.

The proverbial catchphrase that we are at present getting wrong, or at any rate altering the meaning of, is the one about shooting one's self in one's foot. Over the past few years this metaphor has become widely used by the political classes to describe a self-inflicted wound caused inadvertently and by stupidity, and clumsiness, and lack of foresight. Shooting one's self in one's foot is the act of a silly-billy.

In fact the phrase was originally used to describe cowardice rather than stupidity. In the trenches in the First World War the cheapest ticket home to Blighty was to shoot oneself in some inessential part of the body like the foot. In fact it is quite hard to shoot oneself in the foot by accident these days.

It is possible that the modern alteration of the phrase comes, like so many macho political metaphors adopted by Ronald Reagan from B-movies, from the Wild West (cf. trigger-happy, High Noon, walking tall, shooting from the hip or the lip, and so on). The people who used to shoot themselves in the foot by accident rather than design were the gun-slingers of the Old West. Silent, in the white sunlight of their empty high-noon streets, they were so anxious to beat each other to the draw that they quite often pulled the trigger too soon and shot their own feet. Clay Allison was only one of many gun-fighters who limped because he had fewer toes than the regulation issue through pulling the trigger too fast.

Those old six-shooters, and any hand-gun even today, were remarkably inaccurate. Doc Holliday, the answer to an undertaker's prayer, once emptied his Colt at a bartender six feet away, and missed with all six shots. Wyatt Earp was said to have survived because he always fired second, having taken time to aim. He kept all his toes until he turned them up for the last time in bed. From my memory of the pistol range in the Black Watch, you were more likely to hit something by throwing your dirk.

We are not a military nation, thank Venus, and we get our shooting and military metaphors and prognostications hopelessly wrong. Senior officers in the First World War, after watching a tank demonstration, reported: 'The idea that cavalry will be replaced by these iron coaches is absurd: it is little short of treasonous.' We potently and powerfully believe that it was the introduction of gunpowder into Europe in the thirteenth century that finished off knights in armour and the Age of Chivalry. Wrong again. It was the longbow. Froissart confused us by referring to artillery; but by that he meant crossbows and other such projectile weapons that did not use gunpowder. There were a few guns at Crécy, doing more bang than damage. When he had to refer to them, Froissart called them 'kanons'.

Now we have got hold of the wrong end of the rifle in our firing lines. Recently *The Times* has put, among others, Militant Tendency, judges, and the Royal Ulster Constabulary in the firing line, when it is clear from the context that they are being shot *at* rather than doing the shooting. This is the exact opposite of what a firing line originally meant. In the days when British troops marched through bush or veld in scarlet and tartan, they deployed into firing line for line-firing at the enemy. The Boers finally persuaded our generals that this stately parade-ground manoeuvre was not practical. This use of firing line for those who were doing the firing, rather than those who were being fired at, persisted for as long as civilians were liable to be called up to do their bit of biffing. For example, Robert Wilkie, joiner of Campbeltown, Argyll, formerly private, the Parachute Regiment, will tell anybody who cares to listen, again and again, about the night he came under heavy small-arms fire in Tunisia in 1943, although, in his own words, he was '*not* in the firing line'.

Here are some earlier examples of the old military firing line in its original sense. The *Daily Telegraph*, 1881: 'General Stewart was obliged to put every reserve man into the firing line.' G. W. Steevens of the *Daily Mail* on General Sir Hector Macdonald at Omdurman: 'He saw everything; knew what to do; how to do it; did it. At the "fire" he was ever brooding watchfully behind his firing line; at the "cease fire" he was instantly in front of it: all saw him, and knew that they were being nursed to triumph.'

In a similar misunderstanding of warfare, sub-editors on newspapers still find it convenient to write that a ship struck a mine. Modern mines are detonated by magnetism, acoustic influence, or pressure. To say that a ship struck a mine is as improbable as an insurance claim by a motorist that his vehicle had been struck by a lamp-post. But we think that SHIP STRIKES MINE has more journalistic impact. And anyway 'strike' is shorter for headlines than saying that the ship was sunk by a mine. Headline English from the tabloid newspapers is one of the many powerful influences that change the way we speak and think.

You can play an artificial game to illustrate the infinity of meanings and misunderstandings we construct with language. Take a simple sentence, for example: 'Watch the dark brown dog run down the street.' Now examine its meaning from a purely lexical point of view, one word at a time, without any deductive short cuts, as an alien from another world might. Even in common sense the specimen sentence has a number of different possible meanings. Is this dark brown dog a beagle, or a racialist reference to a human? Is it actually running, or running down in the sense of disparaging? Is the street that one over there, or the Street as in Fleet Street? Is this dark brown chap being rude about journos? And so on. Now look up the main meanings of each of the nine words in the sentence in an average-sized dictionary: 18 for watch, 118 for run, and so on. Now multiply them out to determine the total number of possible combinations of meaning and non-meaning: 223,665,152,256. With these possibilities of confusion, no wonder we sometimes shoot ourselves in the foot.

# MICROWORDS

## Meanwhile with just desert

'. . . be just, and fear not.
Let all the ends thou aim'st at be thy country's,
Thy God's, and truth's: then if thou fall'st, O Cromwell!
Thou fall'st a blessed martyr.'
*Henry VIII*, III, 2, 447, before 1613,
by William Shakespeare with John Fletcher

The little words are often the most complex. Few dictionaries venture to treat two of the most common little words in the English language, 'um' and 'er', which mean, among other things: 'Hang on; I've not finished yet; I'm just tidying my thoughts and hunting for the *mot juste*.' The definition and exegesis of the word 'a' by the *Oxford English Dictionary* is a masterpiece of concise scholarship in ten thousand words, and rank upon rank of distinct definitions, categories, and clauses. The pity of it is that nobody except masochists and professional grammarians ever reads the entry, because we all know what 'a' means, and how to use it, don't we, children?

I detect that we are drifting into muddle, or at least sloppy vogue use, with the simple little four-letter adverb and intensifier 'just'. We all know what it means, for heaven's sake. We drop it into our prose without thinking, or needing to look it up in a dictionary. And it shows. Here is a recent example from *The Times*: 'Just two-thirds (67 per cent) of American high school seniors.' On the same day a theatre review in the *Guardian* spoke of 'an audience of just one'.

And here are just six other examples of the pox of the little word in just one advertisement in just a single issue of a magazine: '*Business Opportunities Digest* can tell you just what others are making . . .*BOD* tells you just what these businesses are . . . working for just two days a week . . . How Steve, just 19, performs . . . At just one a day . . . for just a few minutes work a week.' (That's just about enough, Ed.)

You must have noticed the standard opening question by the radio or television interviewer: 'Just how seriously . . . ?' I have even heard: 'Yes, but just exactly what do you mean by that?'

Just what are we to make of all this?

1 It is not a linguistic or a moral crime. We do not need to whistle for the Vocabulary Police, poor old fellows (we never do).

2 Nice grammarians classify this slippery little 'just' in the following ways:

   a. As a diminisher subjunct in the class of downtoners. Downtoners have a lowering effect on the force of a verb or predication, and many of them apply a scale to gradable verbs. Diminishers, such as 'quite', 'only', and 'just', scale downwards and roughly mean 'to a small extent'. 'She'll just be powdering her nose for a few minutes.'

   b. As an emphasizer. That's just disgusting. I just can't believe it.

   c. As a restrictive subjunct. For that essay, you could get a Beta, just.

   d. As a time adjunct. The paper has just arrived.

   e. As a time subjunct. She just spoke to me about it. She's just stopped talking, thank God. She's just coming.

3 We do not need to be as nice as grammarians in distinguishing between adjuncts and subjuncts. In its popular modern use 'just' has lost so much of its cutting edge that it is hard to tell whether in a particular instance it is being used as a diminisher or an emphasizer.

4 It is a fashion. The chattering and scribbling classes are magpies, covetous of shiny words. They pick up and steal from one another tricks of language that look smart, and repeat them. After a while the bright new words begin to sound stale and boring. Nobody with any sensitivity to language can use them seriously any more. Example of phrases that have suffered this fate: 'Sick as a parrot', 'Over the moon', 'Leave no stone unturned', 'Explore every avenue'. (The fact that nobody with any sensitivity to language uses them any more does not imply that politicians and journos do not use them.)

5 'Just' is becoming not so much diminisher or emphasizer as a cottonwool word, like 'um' and 'er', intended to pad out a bit of space while the mind races ahead to the next point. The broadcaster who uses 'just' is saying at the same time, 'I am a professional media person who uses all the right jargon', and also, 'Hang about, I'm still working out my question.'

6 'Just' is becoming a bit of a bore. It is a tedious, mindless habit. 'An audience of one' is more striking, because it is simpler, than 'an audience of just one'.

7 I resolve never to use 'just' again. I shall almost certainly fail, as soon as I am faced with speaking extemporaneously, when there is no time to make the prose shipshape. We all use little cottonwool fillers, to pad out the time for thinking.

8 That eminent editor of the *Guardian*, A. P. Wadsworth, insisted that his staff could use 'just' only as the opposite of 'unjust'.

'With' is another silly little word that I worry about, together with the ablative absolute. Not in Latin, you understand, where it has a satisfying if dotty tidiness. The camp having been pitched, Labienus sent out his cavalry to look for the enemy. Right on, Labienus. But in English we are in the process of establishing an illogical and sloppy new idiom with the inoffensive preposition 'with'.

I had better give you an example before we plod much farther. 'Tomorrow will be cloudy, with further rain coming at the week-end.' Weathermen on the radio and television, those desperately egomaniac and modern prophets, are particularly fond of the new construction. I give you three more examples of the growing nastiness:

1 The President stepped from the helicopter, with the First Lady on his arm.
2 The President stepped from the helicopter, with the First Lady following immediately behind.
3 The President stepped from his helicopter, with the First Lady expected in a second helicopter later.

Of these specimens, number 1 is clearly OK. Number 3 is clearly very odd. The First Lady is not with the old President, but without him, and expected later. Number 2 is the transition. Here is an example of the phenomenon from *The Times*:

'Phil Mahre (a skier) won the gold in the slalom, with brother Steve taking silver.' Well, he cannot have been quite 'with' him, or it would have been a dead heat. I suppose that we cannot expect grammatical exactitude when a chap is composing a picture caption in a hurry. But newspapers are foolish not to pay more attention to the grammar and sanity of their picture captions. David Ogilvy, the advertiser, wrote, and I believe him, that nobody notices headlines, but everybody reads picture captions.

Let us analyse what is happening in a grammarian's way. Like many syntactic changes, the shift probably took place because certain kinds of clause introduced by 'with' were syntactically ambiguous. They admitted both the old and the new grammatical analysis of 'with'. In the picture caption, 'Phil Mahre won the gold in the slalom, with brother Steve taking silver', that 'with' introduces a clause indicating an attendant circumstance that has no direct link with the main clause. It is not the normal, comfortable, old-fashioned use of 'with' to indicate a circumstance directly accompanying the subject, as in the acceptable sentences, 'Phil Mahre won the gold in the slalom with his arm in a sling'; or '. . . with his legs tied together'; or '. . . with his scarf billowing behind him'.

The transition stage between the normal 'accompaniment' use of a with-clause and the new 'attendant circumstance' use is provided by clauses that contain a participle, and are semantically, and therefore syntactically, ambiguous. For example, 'The President stepped from the helicopter with the First Lady following immediately behind' can be taken as expressing accompaniment. The President, with the First Lady who was following behind, stepped . . . But it can also be taken as a much looser construction indicating attendant circumstances: the President stepped . . . incidentally, the First Lady was following behind. This kind of ambiguous clause remains tolerable so long as the 'with' can denote or connote accompaniment. The First Lady may have been lagging behind, making eyes at the National Guard, but she was still with the President.

There are varying degrees of acceptability. 'It would be foolish to go climbing with blizzards due (or expected) this afternoon' is at the tolerable end. But, 'Tomorrow will be cloudy, with further rain due (expected) at the weekend' is at the intolerable end. The main reason for not using the bare absolute participial construction is that it is difficult to hear in informal speech. 'Phil Mahre won the gold, brother Steve taking silver' would be difficult to parse mentally, apart from the ludicrous conjunction of the formal absolute construction with the highly informal 'brother Steve'.

It is natural for words to change their meanings like this continually in the ebb and flow of life and language. We know, Philip, we know. But the changes are not all for the better. And sometimes they are mistakes, errors, wrong, deleterious, and pig-ignorant weasel words. 'Meanwhile', a plain little adverb short for 'In the meanwhile', is going through the same sort of change as 'just' and 'with', and for the same sort of media cottonwool reasons.

Meanwhile is normally used to indicate that something is (or is not) happening pending the beginning, continuation, or ending of something else. Its alias is 'meantime'. What it ought naturally to mean is either during the intervening time, or at the same time, especially in another place. Recently it has started to be used on radio and television to mean 'while we are on the subject', or 'to change the subject slightly', or even 'to change the subject altogether'.

Here are three examples of that old chameleon 'meanwhile' from a recent issue of The Times. A Conservative MP has tabled a motion, 'meanwhile' Tony Benn has written to the Prime Minister on the same topic. This is the normal use. The President is in hospital, 'meanwhile' the condition of the Vice-President is said to be comfortable. Here the adverb appears to mean 'changing the subject slightly'. The badgers an animal rescuer cares for are always returned to the wild if possible; 'meanwhile' they stay at her field centre. This example has no temporal sense, and appears to mean 'on the other hand', or 'taking a contrary view', or 'if that is not possible'. It is a good example of the new badger word 'meanwhile'.

'Meanwhile' is used in this vacuous new way partly as verbal cottonwool to pad out time. It is used as a bogus link in radio and television chat shows. The presenter has to pretend that a succession of celebrities being introduced are linked by some common factor other than being prepared to take the money for appearing on the ghastly Babel. 'Meanwhile' suggests that they are there by a deliberate plan rather than at the whim of chance and the director. I suspect that this 'meanwhile' may also be influenced by the popularity of 'Meanwhile, back at the ranch . . .' as a catch-phrase. In the old and very popular silent movies, after a shot of a bloodcurdling fight with the Apaches or Sioux, cut to the anxious little woman back home, possibly being molested by a baddy, introduced by the famous and irrelevant caption: 'Meanwhile, back at the ranch . . .' Agitated violins. The cinema is one of the most potent influences upon our languages this century.

# MYSELF

## Myself, I'd rather be me

'If I am not for myself who is for me; and being for my own self what am I? If not now when?'

*Pirque Aboth*, i, 15, (?70BC–AD10?) saying of Hillel 'The Elder'

What song the Syrens sang is not a puzzling question at all, old Thos Browne, when you think about it. It must have been that well-known hymn, 'Rock of Aegeus'. That was a joke. Making jokes in print is a tricky business, liable to be misunderstood, unless you are very sure of your audience.

More puzzling than the singing Syrens is the daily shift of language in semantics, grammar, idiom, and all its other departments. Everyday existing words take on new meanings: casual, necklace, and hacker, for example. New compounds are joined together: e.g. lap-top and off-the-wall. And completely new words evolve: greenmail, megamerger, octopush.

Sometimes a word is invented to fill a new need. 'Schemant' is such a word, worth keeping your eyes and ears open for. A schemant means somebody who is being instructed in a Youth Training Scheme of the kind introduced by the British Government in the 1980s. You will meet it *passim* in articles and broadcasts dealing with employment and related topics. There is no need to turn purple and protest, sir. It is a natural piece of official jargon, which is shorter and simpler than saying or writing in full every time, 'a young person, male or female, who qualifies under the Act and is being instructed on a Youth Training Scheme'. You are allowed to complain that the word sounds ugly, and that it is incorrectly derived from its original Greek root. But make sure that you are not complaining merely because schemant is new; and remember that judgements about what sounds ugly are subjective. That which we call a rose by any other name would smell as sweet. But would it?

Would a rose smell as sweet if we called it an onion? There is an obvious linguistic need for some such noun as schemant now that Youth Training Schemes have been introduced. If you can invent a better and more euphonious word than schemant, introduce it. Myself, I'd settle for trainee.

In the constant flux of language, here is a grammatical as opposed to a lexical novelty. There is a remarkable new vogue for reflexive personal pronouns: the ones ending in -self. We say and write 'myself' and 'yourself' all the time, where a few years ago the simple subject and object pronouns, 'I, me, you' etc., were correct and all that was required. What are we up to? Is this a concession to Irish practice? Do we think that 'me' *tout court* sounds a bit common? Are we trying to be genteel?

One reason for the sudden vogue for reflexives is that people are uncertain of the grammar of the personal pronouns; and hedge their bets with 'myself'. They are not sure that it is, 'My wife and I like reading detective stories', but 'Detective stories are the best read for my wife and me.' So they take refuge in 'My wife and myself', which is horrible.

Another reason is found in the rat-race of status and getting on in Yuppiedom. Some people seem to think that 'me' implies a subordinate role, and cannot stoop to describe themselves as me. At the same time they know that 'I' is wrong in the accusative. Accordingly, they fall back on 'myself'. The test of whether gentility, or assertiveness, or arrogance predominates in the choice of 'myself' is given by the order in which a person lists himself or herself when referring to other people also. 'I and McGonagall will prepare the report.' 'The boss wants myself and McGonagall to prepare the report.' One minor reason for the excessive popularity of 'myself' is the linguistic politics of managers jockeying for position.

The solecism is not as new as I supposed. In a Reuter's report of 27 April 1897 about the precipitate Greek retreat before the German-trained Turks, I found the otiose reflexive twice in the same short paragraph: 'Then suddenly their weight overbalanced the vehicle, which overturned, and was smashed to pieces, all the occupants, including *The Times* Correspondent and myself being thrown out . . . Keeping together, *The Times* Correspondent and myself got into the roadside ditch, but we had only walked forward a short distance when we were thrown down by a rush from behind.' I think that the Reuter's man chose 'myself' because it sounded more impressive for his dramatic report. It was choice of the unnecessary (and erroneous) grandiloquent.

Your reflexive pronouns are rare and sensitive beasts in the linguistic jungle. Some of them, such as the rare 'royal we' singular reflexive 'ourself', should be used only if oneself is sure that one is entitled to it, and allowed to make statements such as, 'We are not interested in the possibilities of defeat', and, 'We are not amused ourself.'

In the classic grammar of English, reflexive pronouns have two distinct uses: the basic, and the emphatic. In the basic use, the reflexive pronoun stands in for the object of a sentence or clause, and refers back reflexively to the subject. He saw himself in the mirror. In 'He saw him in the mirror', the 'him' necessarily refers to some chap other than the one doing the seeing. She saw herself in the mirror. But she could not, by any stretch of grammar or unsexist language, see himself in the mirror. Help yourselves! is grammatical. Help ourselves! or Help themselves! is disconcerting and ungrammatical.

A noun clause as well as a verb can take a reflexive. 'Philip's extravagant hero-worship of himself.' 'Alexander's confidence in himself moved mountains.' 'Your gratification with yourself is disgusting.' Sometimes the reflexive 'oneself' (informal 'yourself') refers to an implied human subject of the most indefinite kind. 'Voting for oneself (yourself) is unethical and bad form.' 'Pride in oneself (yourself) was counted as a deadly sin.' Americans use a personal instead of the reflexive pronoun as an indirect object that is coreferential with the subject in informal contexts. 'She got her (herself) a new outfit.' 'He got him (himself) a good seat.' 'We're going to elect us a new President next year!'

Some verbs, called reflexive verbs, take an obligatory reflexive object. 'She always prides herself on her academic background.' 'She prides her on her academic background' sounds like some Mummerset county dialect in *The Archers*. With semi-reflexive verbs, the reflexive pronoun can be left out with little, or no, change in the meaning. Behave now: behave yourself now. He has to shave twice a day: he has to shave himself twice a day. Dress: dress yourself.

The second conventional use of reflexive pronouns is to

emphasize, in apposition to a noun or pronoun, and with heavy stress. Unlike the basic reflexive pronouns, they can float around their clauses. I myself wouldn't eat that. I wouldn't eat that myself. Myself, I wouldn't eat that. The last example sounds New Yorker jinglish to me. Do you mean to say that you had tea with the Queen herself?

When the reflexive comes first, referring forward to something that is to come, it is usually in a literary or intellectual context. You could call it mannered or pretentious. 'Himself a fervent believer, Newman was nonetheless able to sympathize with those who . . .' 'Myself is thus and so, and will continue thus and so' (Saul Bellow). 'Oneself did not die; that, like the very quiddity of otherness, was for others' (Anthony Burgess).

Some teachers describe this second, emphatic sort of reflexive pronoun as an Emphasizing Adjective. I myself think there is a lot to be said for this approach, which distinguishes the two distinct uses.

Today there is a vogue for using reflexive pronouns instead of the plain subject or object pronouns. I think that this is an exaggeration of the emphatic use, intended to give artistic verisimilitude to an otherwise bald and unconvincing interview on the telly or column in the blats. Sometimes the prevalence of reflexives is not merely irritating, but also ungrammatical, and erodes the language.

# NAME GAMES

## Crossed lines in the name game

'A yeomanry colonel introducing his officers to an inspecting general stopped before one of them shaking his head and snapped his fingers. "This is Captain . . . Captain . . . memory like a sieve. I'll be forgetting the names of me hounds next."'
*The Oxford Book of Military Anecdotes*, 1985

'Good morning – my name is Neddy Seagoon.'

'What a memory you have.'

I wish I had a memory for names. I have a copious rubbish-tip of a memory full of such useless information as the punishment of Erisicthon, the kings and queens of England, and the diagram for electrolysis. But I suffer from onomastic aphasia: I have difficulty remembering people's names. It is a grave disadvantage in my trade: a journalist has to get on intimate or at any rate gossipy terms with a vast range of people very fast, write the story, and then move on to new people. It is a bad start to wheedling a story out of somebody if you can't remember his name. I envy friends who have not only a prodigious memory for quotations, oddments, and tags of information, as I have in part, but also an eagle's eye and an owl's retentiveness for names and faces.

I am not consoled by the fact that forgetting names is quite a common condition. In his later years Ralph Waldo Emerson, transcendentalist philosopher and exponent of individualism, known as the Sage of Concord, grew increasingly absent-minded. He used to refer to his 'naughty memory' when it let him down. He would forget the names of things, and have to refer to them in a circumlocutory way, saying, for instance, 'the implement that cultivates the soil' for plough or, as he would have spelt it, plow. Worse still, he could not remember people's names. At Longfellow's funeral he remarked to a friend: 'That gentleman has a sweet, beautiful soul, but I have entirely forgotten his name.' Most poignant was his name for his umbrella: 'The thing that strangers take away.'

John Gilbert, the great screen lover of silent films, could learn his lines for stage parts, but could never remember the proper names. He was called upon at short notice to play the part of the heroine's father in a Chicago production. He learned the lines in record time, but was still struggling to remember the name of the character he was playing, Numitorius, when the play opened. A colleague suggested the *Book of Numbers* as mnemonic. Gilbert strode on stage with renewed confidence on the first night, and delivered his opening line: 'Hold, 'tis I, her father – Deuteronomy.'

The most daunting introduction for those of us who are nominally forgetful is for a complete stranger to come up and say: 'Hullo, you're Philip Howard, aren't you? Do you remember me?' There is no satisfactory answer to that which does not sound rude. You can try: 'I haven't got your telephone number', open your diary, and wait for dictation. If this is just digits, you have waded deeper into trouble. You can try: 'How *do* you spell your name?' This risks the answer, 'Without the H', or worse, a cold stare and, 'S-M-I-T-H.' You can say: 'I'm most awfully sorry, but I've forgotten your name.' When he says, 'Howard', you say: 'Don't be silly; of course I know it's Howard, it's your first name I can't remember.' These onomastic problems are the reason why some of us use the vocatives 'dear boy' and 'dear girl' and 'old thing' more than seems necessary to those who have a good memory for names. The last appellation should be used only to those under 30.

Disraeli, when greeted by an apparent stranger claiming prior acquaintanceship, used to say: 'Well, and how's the old trouble?' Everybody has some old trouble or other that looms large in their interests. Dixon Wright, the famous surgeon at St Mary's Hospital who was much in demand as a raconteur, used to say in after-dinner speeches: 'As you get older there are three things one finds difficult. Firstly, you recognize someone but cannot remember his name. Secondly, a name is mentioned of someone you know well, but you cannot recall who he is. And thirdly, ah – um – er – I am afraid that I cannot recall what the third thing is.'

For persistent and intrusive 'Don't you remember me?' nuisances, the only effective counter is the 'phrop' (phrase that means the opposite of what it appears to mean): 'Of course. Hullo. We must have lunch some time, old thing' (but I haven't got my diary for the year 2000 yet).

I have tried to think of reasons why I am so bad at names. I was brought up in a large and matey and extended family, in which all sorts of strange grown-ups who were not kin were known upon first introduction as Uncle Frank or Aunt Phoebe. This may have confused me about names at an early age. Apart from that, I read, or at least do the crossword, as I walk, because I do not get enough time for it in the rest of my life. This means that I bump into trees a bit, and joggers give me a wide berth (for which relief, much thanks), and that I am not very observant about what is going on in the world outside my head. Also, I am often weeping, because of a mote in my contact lens, or for general *lacrimae rerum* reasons.

Special pleading apart (and I rather like special pleading), I suspect that a bad memory for names indicates deplorable self-absorption. Absent-mindedness equals selfishness. Instead of doing the crossword or reading Plato, I should be enjoying the sun rising like a great blood orange over the Post Office Tower, watching the swans nesting opposite Peter Pan, and saying a cheerful 'What ho' to the joggers, all of whose ugly, contorted faces I would remember. (Why is it that joggers and those who enter for the London Marathon are so ugly that you would have to blindfold the baby before it would suck?)

There are advertisements, with pictures of a worried-looking man, offering to improve your memory and turn you into a whizz-kid high-flier. I do not think that we should bother with these, since it is merely a matter of strength of mind, deciding to look out rather than in. I resolve to do better: 'Of course, I remember you. At the Old Coll, wasn't it? Or perhaps in Berlin with the Black Watch? Don't tell me. Deuteronomy, wasn't it? We must have lunch some time.'

Professor William James of Harvard, the philosopher and psychologist (brother of Henry), was walking along a Cambridge, Massachusetts, street with a couple of students. A large, imposing figure, white-bearded, swinging his cane, talking to himself, paying no attention to the rest of Cambridge, approached them. A girl student said: 'Whoever he is, he's the epitome of the absent-minded professor.' 'What you really mean,' replied James, 'is that he is present-minded somewhere else.'

Of course, some names and faces are better forgotten. A copious, retentive memory may be a good thing. But the ability to forget is the true token of greatness.

Name games are played most strenuously on the telephone. Telephone technique is the modern equivalent of the duel and the tiltyard. 'Her telephone is engaged: will you wait?' The question expects and hopes for the answer: 'No.' 'OK, I'll wait for a bit, but not too long.' You wait for three minutes. It feels like an hour. At the other end of the line there is a silence as deep as the eternal silence of infinite space. Should you give up and put the telephone down? It seems a little rude to the overworked operator, who will come back to you eventually, and find you fled and never called him 'Mother'. In any case, sheer stubbornness makes you hang on, to see whether you can break the world record for waiting for a telephone conversation by a publisher's publicity director to come to an end.

Then there is the problem of answering machines on the telephone. Few people manage to record a cool, sensible message that is not coy, and does not panic nervous callers. To play them music is naff and wastes their time. There is an answering machine message in California, where they are frightened of burglars, recorded from 1984: 'You have reached the Blankety family. What you hear is the barking of our killer Dobermann Pinscher, Wolf. Please leave a message after the tone.'

It is cheating, and rude, to get your secretary to do the waiting for you to drag somebody to the other end of the telephone. It is a game of chicken between secretaries to see who can get the other's big boss on to the other end of the line first. The correct answer, when a secretary asks you over the telephone, 'Is that Mr Howard? I have Tom Maschler for you . . .' and leaves you dangling in infinite space, is, 'Congratulations; you can keep him', and then to put the telephone down. A man telephoned a friend at two o'clock in the morning. 'I do hope I haven't disturbed you,' he said, cheerfully. 'Oh, no,' the friend replied, 'that's quite all right. I had to get up to answer the telephone anyway.' In this marvellous new world of telecommunications it is a miracle that we ever get anything done at all.

An ugly new phrase of telephone technique is: 'Your name is . . . ?' It is used *passim* and *semper* by secretaries and operators over the telephone in answer to the question: 'Hullo, may I speak to Samuel Johnson (or, as it might be, Edward Gibbon) please?' It is used *semper* and *passim* by operators and secretaries who are telephoning you, in reply to the courteous (or harassed, or grumpy, or suicidal) opening shot: 'Hullo, *Times* Books Page; can I help you?'

The first few times that it was said to me, I thought that the caller was going to make a statement, and tell me my name. I waited politely, not understanding this new technique of telephone duel, until she repeated, impatiently: 'Your name is . . . ?'

The irritating and confusing vogue phrase clearly comes from television – specifically from television quiz shows, in which the question master puts one arm effusively around the shoulders of the next contestant, thrusts the microphone into his or her face with the other, and prepares to astonish her with the news that she stands to win a week's holiday in Alicante; second prize two weeks' holiday in Alicante. I dare say that 'Your name is . . . ?' is the conventional locution in television quiz shows. But television quiz shows are the lowest form of entertainment, lower far than the circus, the Space Invaders arcade, and the brothel; and television question-masters are the lowest form of animal life, lower far than the chimpanzees or footballing poodles at the circus. On the whole, one should robustly resist the view that the world is going to the dogs; and that every day, in every way, things get worse and worse. But the proliferation and popularity of moronic quiz shows on the box is powerful evidence for the pessimistic view. 'What name, please?' asks the question implied by the dreadful telly-question 'Your name is . . . ?' It is more polite, if slightly less economical.

In fact, the most businesslike and helpful telephone technique is to state the number first clearly, for the benefit of those waiting to put coins into a public telephone, in case they have got the wrong number, and can save their money, and then to state your surname, without handle, loud and clear, like old-fashioned gents or Cheltenham ladies educated before the war: '837 1234 . . . Howard.' 'I answer the 'phone "Dickerson here" because I'm Dickerson and I'm here. Now what the

hell do you want, Martha?' This method of telephone technique sounds so brusque to wet modern manners that it has
the additional benefit that often the caller puts the telephone
straight down, without speaking, in terror.

# NEW BIBLE

## The pretty good book

Newsreader: 'Good even. Here beginneth the
first verse of the news. It has come to pass that
the seven elders of the seven tribes have now
been abiding in Sodom for seven days and seven
nights. There seems little hope of an early settle-
ment. An official spokesman said this afternoon,
"Only a miracle can save us now."
    At the weigh-in for the big fight tomorrow,
Goliath tipped the scales this even at 15 stone 3
lbs and David at 14 stone 3 lbs. David's manager
said this even, "The odd stone could make all the
difference."
    The news in brief: Lamentations 4: 18–22 and
II Kings 14: 2–8.'
*I'm Sorry I'll Read That Again*, BBC Radio, by Bill Oddie and
John Cleese

The two most influential books in the English language are:
*The Book of Common Prayer*, evolved piecemeal in the sixteenth
century until its settled form of 1552, with revisions under
Elizabeth in 1559, minor changes under James I, and the final
text of 1662; and *The Authorized Version* of the Bible, initiated at
the Hampton Court conference convened by James I in 1604,
and published in 1611. The language and images and stories of
the two books are the bedrock of English-speaking culture. *The
New English Bible* published in 1970 (*New Testament* originally in
1961) and the various new prayer-books and forms of service
introduced over the past twenty years will not have such a
profound effect upon the English language. There are vastly
more competing influences today than in 1611, when the Bible
and the Prayer Book were likely to be the only books in a
house. And the quality of the language in the new books has
been widely attacked for its banality, and for not being as
memorable as the old sacred cows.

*The New English Bible* is the first new translation of the impregnable rock of holy scripture ever officially commissioned by all the main churches in the United Kingdom. King James's 47 scholars were instructed to follow the text of the Bishops' Bible (prompted by Archbishop Parker to counteract the popularity of the Calvinistic Genevan Bible, and published in 1568) wherever possible, and also used Tyndale's, Coverdale's, and other earlier versions as a basis for their text. So their English was archaic when it was written, which may account for its numinous dignity.

The new Bible was begun in 1946, when the General Assembly of the Church of Scotland accepted a proposal that a translation of the Bible should be made in the language of the present day. In the following year a joint committee of the major Christian bodies in the United Kingdom – other than the Roman Catholic – across the theological spectrum from the Church of England to the National Bible Society of Scotland was set up to direct the operation. The Roman Catholics joined the committee as observers in 1966. The University Presses of Oxford and Cambridge, as experienced Bible publishers, and also as learned bodies that do not distribute profits, were invited to join the committee, and bore the cost of the enterprise, about £1,500,000.

The purpose of our generation's new Bible is not to rival, replace, oust, compete with, or destroy *The Authorized Version*, that indestructible book of which Macaulay said that, if everything else in our language should perish, it would alone suffice to show the whole extent of its beauty and power. It is intended to be complementary to King James's Bible, a more accurate version in contemporary language that ordinary people understand, avoiding archaisms, unreality, short-lived modern jargon, and pedantry; not aiming at preserving hallowed associations; not intended primarily to be read at public worship, though in fact it has produced some memorable and readable passages. The two fundamental reasons for producing a new translation of the Bible in the second half of the twentieth century were: 1) new knowledge that demands the production of a more trustworthy rendering; and 2) changes in the English language, which demand the production of a more intelligible text and a more effective instrument of propaganda. Three sections of the public are the main targets at which the new Bible is aimed: the large numbers who have no contact with any church; the young, with their passion for trendy language; and the many intelligent church-goers, for whom the traditional language is so familiar that it slides over their minds without causing a ripple (as the translators said: 'Words we have used, kept in the pocket, rubbed shiny with use, and forgotten').

The *modus operandi* was to set up three translation panels of the best qualified scholars available, regardless of denomination, for the Old Testament, the Apocrypha, and the New Testament. In addition the committee appointed a literary panel of people judged to have a good sense of English style, to help the translators express their meaning in contemporary English. As the preface to the new Bible puts it, delicately: 'Apprehending, however, that sound scholarship does not necessarily carry with it a delicate sense of English style . . .' A camel is an animal designed by a committee. *The New English Bible* is a version made by committees: but then so was King James's.

The procedure was that a single draft translator was appointed for each book. The appropriate translation panel went through his draft, revising verse by verse, word by word, until they reached a common mind that this was the best translation possible. The literary panel then scrutinized their draft, sentence by sentence, word by word, making sure that the language was the best possible, and was appropriate to the subject matter, whether it was narrative, poetry, law, or the many other different registers and types of writing found in the Bible. (A delicious example of colloquial language in a *conte*: the dirty old elders, with secret designs on Susanna, say to each other: 'Let us go home; it is time for lunch.') The literary panel's amendments were passed back to the translation panel to make sure that style had not distorted meaning. Particularly thorny passages went backwards and forwards between panels as endlessly as a ping-pong ball. The final agreed version was submitted to the Joint Committee of the Churches.

This Joint Committee met regularly twice a year, and had occasional extraordinary meetings. As well as supervising generally, it laid down certain fundamental principles for the translation. A good example is the decision whether to address

God as 'thou' or 'you'. There was a knotty debate, in which the pro-thou school pointed out that the archaic second person singular is still just alive in Northern England ('Dost tha know, lad?'), and perhaps among Quakers. It was felt that the public was not ready for the use of 'you' in prayers to God, with its overtones of familiarity, and connotations of casual speech. Eventually it was decided to play safe, and to retain thou, thee, and their concomitant verb endings. In all religious language there is an atavistic feeling that it is good to use the language of one's fathers and forefathers, and that stability of belief is somehow related to stability of language. When God is addressed in conversation rather than in prayer, 'you' is used. For example, Adam, passing the buck in the Garden of Eden, says: 'The woman you gave me for a companion, she gave me fruit from the tree and I ate it.' The committee had second thoughts, and reopened the 'thou' question. But by then it was too late: getting rid of 'thou' would have entailed too much rewriting of work already done. One of the reasons the new Bible outrages people who have not read the Bible for years, and never go to church, is that it smashes hallowed archaisms.

Other fundamental issues discussed by the Joint Committee included the decision to print in single, instead of the traditional double, columns; the retention of the traditional verse numbers (which are some 400 years old) for reference purposes, but to put them in the margin, in order to avoid breaking the continuity of the text; a few minor changes in the titles of books – for example, there is a partial return to the ancient practice of considering the prophets from Hosea to Malachi as one book, though they are renamed 'The Twelve Prophets', instead of what sounds a disparaging and supercilious name, 'The Minor Prophets'; chapter numbers, which are medieval anyway, are put in the margin like the verse numbers for reference; but, regardless of chapter and verse, the Bible is broken up into paragraphs, and main sections, each of which is given a short descriptive headline of not more than a line.

The committee also decided to print poetry in verse form, with an attempt to preserve the structure of the Hebrew rhythms: a decision that raised the whole purpose of the translation, whether, for instance, the psalms are to be used liturgically. Another difficult decision was the status of the

Apocrypha, which is not accepted by some churches as scrip-ture, but which was included as an integral part of the King James version. For this reason those editions of *The New English Bible* that contain the Apocrypha have a note opposite their pages, pointing out that its inclusion does not commit the sponsoring churches to any particular view of its canonical status.

The New Testament of *The New English Bible* was published in 1961. In 1970, as part of the complete Bible, a second edition of the New Testament was published, making a few minor changes that had been suggested since 1961. An example of a stylistic improvement: in the Sermon on the Mount the slightly ugly and awkward, 'You must therefore be all goodness, just as your heavenly Father is good', is displaced by, 'There must be no limit to your goodness, as your heavenly Father's goodness knows no bounds.' Neither version is the language of the supermarket or television chat show, and I much prefer the *Authorized Version*'s: 'Be ye therefore perfect, even as your Father which is in heaven is perfect.' But what sort of 'prefer' is that? Translating the holy in a world that has lost the language of holiness is an unholy mess. An example of increased precision of meaning in the second edition: when, in Luke, the angel announces the coming birth of Christ to Mary, she now replies: 'How can this be? I am still a virgin', which is what the Greek means, and just about what a contemporary girl might say; instead of, in the first edition, 'How can this be, when I have no husband?' which is not the same thing. This emendation was pointed out in a letter to the general director by T. S. Eliot.

Our new Bible destroys many favourite old pieces of mental furniture in the interests of either accuracy or intelligibility. The rose of Sharon is, in fact, an asphodel. Pharaoh's lean and ill-favoured kine have been transmogrified into lean, gaunt cows. The Heathen no longer furiously rage together; instead, the nations are in turmoil. The virtuous woman, whose price is far above rubies, turns out, disappointingly, to be a capable wife whose worth is far beyond coral. Strong red wine no longer bites like a serpent and stingeth like an adder; it bites like a snake and stings like a cobra. I did not realize that they had cobras in Palestine, but let it go. Haman is hanged from the gallows 75 feet instead of 50 cubits high. That something rich and strange, the pelican in the wilderness, has suffered a sand-change into a desert-owl. For cockatrice's den read viper's nest. The valley of the shadow of death is a valley dark as death. The nasty little boys jeer at Elisha: 'Get along with you, bald head, get along.' 'Emptiness, emptiness,' says the Speaker, 'emptiness, all is empty', which may convey his meaning more directly to the new generation, but has lost the magic and poetry. Delightful and dearly loved were Saul and Jonathan; in life, in death, they were not parted. Jael's butter in a lordly dish as described by Deborah has undergone metamorphosis to curds in a bowl fit for a chieftain. Behemoth was probably a crocodile, though a footnote raises a judicious eyebrow at the corrupt text. The Scripture has moved the translators of *The New English Bible* in sundry places to introduce many other hundreds of new interpretations based on new knowledge. Here is a brief, representative selection.

Daniel's lament over Saul and Jonathan traditionally starts: 'The beauty of Israel is slain upon thy high places.' The Hebrew word translated as 'beauty' can mean something like beauty or glory; or it can mean a gazelle. Previous translators and commentators thought it absurd, or impertinent, to call Jonathan a gazelle; so they plumped for 'beauty', though it does seem a rather emotional and soppy epithet for a young male warrior. Within the last thirty years the Ugaritic texts, written in a Canaanite dialect very like Hebrew, have been deciphered. One of them speaks of a king inviting his bulls and gazelles to a feast. This must be a metaphor for the king's grand magnates and princes, rather like the metaphor of a Regency buck. The new translators therefore rejected 'beauty'; decided reluctantly that it is impossible to say in English 'O gazelle of Israel'; and translated the verse as 'O prince of Israel, laid low in death.'

Take that enigmatic adage, *Proverbs* 26, 23: 'Burning lips and a wicked heart are like a potsherd covered with silver of dross.' Silver of dross is very odd. One would expect it, if anything, to be dross of silver. And, curiouser and curiouser, there is no evidence that any such substance, or anything like it, was ever used to coat earthen vessels in the Middle East, or anywhere else, for that matter. The Ugaritic texts now available make it clear that what has gone wrong is that a single Hebrew word has been split in two to make silver of dross. Taken together as one word, it is the equivalent of a Ugaritic word meaning 'like glaze'. So the verse can now be translated:

> Glib speech that covered a spiteful heart
> is like glaze spread on earthenware.

Which is not only better sense and better scholarship, but also a far more satisfactory, indeed a devastating text for preachers.

One of the crucial problems for the translators of the Old Testament was how to translate the divine name, represented in Hebrew as YHWH, probably originally pronounced Yahweh, which soon became ineffable anyway, and is incorrectly rendered in English as Jehovah. They decided to use LORD, printed in capitals, for God's personal name. But on two occasions with the name, and in four other place-names, because the name has to be explained, they have kept the traditional, but wrong, Jehovah. For example, in *Exodus* 3.15: 'You must tell the Israelites this, that it is JEHOVAH . . . This is my name for ever.'

Why did they not choose the more probably authentic YAHWEH? For three reasons:

1 It was felt that English readers might find the words uncouth, and perhaps think that it referred to some local Palestinian deity.

2 Although YAHWEH was probably the correct pronunciation of God's personal name in the early books of the Old Testament, by the later books the word had become unspeakable, and was no longer pronounced; so it would be incorrect to insert YAHWEH into these later books.

3 It was felt that YAHWEH might not be acceptable to Jewish readers, for whom the word is still unpronounceable. The Old Testament of *The New English Bible* is the first to be acceptable to the most orthodox and scrupulous of Jews, in that it contains no forward references to the New Testament. So Jehovah has triumphed once again.

Another crisis arose over the translation of the Hebrew word usually rendered 'cherub'. In English the word suggests a chubby, inadequately dressed, innocent, and nauseatingly pretty small boy, with midget and inadequate golden wings, who can be traced back through the *putti* and *amoretti* of

baroque and Renaissance painters to his fluttering and sentimental beginning with the Graeco-Roman Erotes or Cupids.
Unfortunately the archaeologists have recently discovered that
the Hebrew *cherub* was in fact a formidable winged lion with a
human head, as found in Syro-Palestinian art. In Psalm 99, for
example, 'he sitteth between the cherubims' means he is sitting
on a throne made out of two winged sphinxes as arm-rests. It
is a sobering thought to realize what one is actually doing if
one describes somebody's darling child as a cherub.

The vexing problem in the circumstances was how on earth,
or in heaven, to translate the Hebrew *cherub*. Would it be right
always to use the plural cherubim, with, where necessary, a
double plural, cherubims? Or should one spell it with a 'k', as
*kherub*, just to show that no allusion to Cupid is intended?
Another suggestion was to render the word as 'griffin' in one
of its many spellings (it is probably connected to it etymologically anyway). But griffin was felt to have ingrained avian
asociations; and anyway to most people the griffin brings
inexpungibly to mind the gryphon in *Alice in Wonderland*.
Eventually it was decided to translate the word as cherub, and
to hope that the public can be educated to appreciate the
religious symbolism alongside, if not in place of, the nursery
nuance.

The translation panels normally met for residential sessions
of two days or more, during which they sat around a table
piled as high as the little hill of Hermon (or, to be strictly up to
date, 'the Hermons') with Hebrew Bibles and lexicons. Sometimes they spent as much as half a day wrestling with as few
as three particularly tricky and elusive verses.

The Dead Sea Scrolls have thrown new light on a number of
passages, particularly in *Isaiah*, and have made it possible to
restore the original Hebrew. An example is at *Isaiah* 1.20,
where the Lord says:

> If you refuse and rebel,
> locust beans shall be your only food.

A footnote points out that the Scrolls support a variant reading,
'you shall be eaten by the sword'.

The new translation finally disposes of the doctrine that the
Virgin Birth was originally predicted in the Old Testament.
The traditional text, *Isaiah* 7.14, runs: 'Behold a virgin shall

conceive, and bear a son, and shall call his name Immanuel.' In fact the translators have now decided that the Hebrew word does not mean 'virgin'; it is 'a young woman of marriageable age'. This is the sort of passage that might be expected to provoke the Roman Catholics to disagreement. In fact the Roman Catholic *Jerusalem Bible* translates the disputed word as 'maiden' anyway, which does not have quite the same force as 'virgin'.

A great many changes in the new Bible are not changes of interpretation, but alterations into more direct and modern English. One of the main purposes of the Bible is propaganda, to convert people. And good propaganda needs to be clear, easily understood, and to call a spade a spade. A trenchant example: at *Numbers* 6.3 previous translators have proclaimed the rules for apprentice Nazirites: they must 'separate themselves from wine and strong drink'. *The New English Bible*, no longer beating about the burning bush, renders the phrase in the language of a modern, though not a trendy, G.P.: 'He shall abstain from wine and strong drink.'

Another delicious example is the whole of the serpent's treacherous dialogue with Eve. Eve tells the serpent that God has said that if she and Adam eat the fruit of the tree in the middle of the garden, they will die. In the classic version, the serpent replies, grandiloquently and pompously: 'Ye shall not surely die.' In the new Bible the serpent, who has become crafty rather than subtle, hisses with a contemporary and seductive sibilance: 'Of course you will not die.'

One of the problems of translating a huge work over twenty-five years is that even in such a comparatively short period the meaning of English words fluctuates and shifts. When the Old Testament translators started work, they wanted to translate as 'shelter' a Hebrew word that had previously been rendered as 'booth' or 'cottage'. For example, in *Isaiah* 1.8:

'And the daughter of Zion is left as a cottage in a vineyard, as a lodge in a garden of cucumbers.'

However, back in those days just after the war, a shelter meant one thing only to everybody, and that was an air-raid shelter. The translators decided they would have to use 'hut' rather than risk raising a laugh. Over twenty years 'shelter' entirely lost its connotation of air-raids, and now suggests either a bus shelter, or a charity that helps the homeless. So the translators were able to play 'shelter' after all, as a late substitute.

There were comparatively few amendments in the second edition of the New Testament, published as part of the whole new Bible in 1970. One of the delightful minor corrections concerned a colt. In the first edition at *Mark* 11.4 the two disciples find a colt 'tethered to a door' in the village. Somebody wrote in to the translators to ask what happened when the door was opened. So in the new edition the unhappy colt is tethered *at* a door.

The uproar that greeted the publication of the new Bible has not much abated since. The *literati* deem the translation to be not a patch on the English of *The Authorized Version* and iconoclastic of some of the most familiar phrases in our language, which are part of the cultural inheritance of any Englishman. The theologians, scriptural scholars, and clergymen and ministers like the new Bible for being closer to the original, and accessible to their congregations. You can at least read the Epistles and the more convoluted Prophets for the meaning as well as the thunder of the prose. We need both versions.

Similar outrage and uproar greet successive attempts by the churches to modernize their liturgies from the stately fifteenth-century formulae that are bred in the bone of an Englishman into something more modern, relevant, and meaningful. People, not necessarily frequent attenders at church, feel that the language of *The Prayer Book* is their heritage, and is being wantonly destroyed. For example, there is the problem of how to address God, which also occupied the translators of *The New English Bible*. It is one that has vexed God-bothering humans from the Hebrew Tetragrammaton, YHWH, vowelled Yahweh or, less successfully, Jehovah, the oldest four-letter word, to King David in Joseph Heller's novel *God Knows*, who addresses his maker in much the same terms as a New York taxi-driver addresses a fare. The question arises whether the Deity cares about traditional English grammar.

The revised *Book of Common Prayer* for use by the Church in Wales (Anglican) came into use in 1984. Its modernized usage removed obvious archaisms, and, in the opinion of purists, contained not only some very shaky syntax, but fundamental errors of grammar. In particular it was unsound on the person and number of its relative pronouns. The rule is that a relative pronoun always agrees with its antecedent in person and number. So we have: 'It is I who am wrong.' The archaic English of the *Book of Common Prayer* (final draft 1662) followed this rule invariably: 'O God who knowest . . .' (second-person singular); 'Through Jesus Christ who liveth and reigneth . . .' Fowler used the *Prayer Book*, with 'which art', 'who shewest', and scores of other examples, as overwhelming evidence that 'who' is not a third-person word, but a word of whichever person is appropriate.

The revisers modernized the second-person singular '-est' into the modern third-person inflexion '-s' throughout, so that 'O God who seest' becomes 'O God who sees'. You could say that this is ungrammatical, much like, 'You comes here often, doesn't you?' When you do say it, the modernizers reply: 'In seeking to remove the more obvious archaisms, our first instinct was to do what some previous revisers have done, and to transform a "Lord, who" clause into a "Lord, you" – petition into statement. But on reflection we concluded that this was banal, and presumptuous. In any case, we were told not to use "you" of the Deity. So we had a choice between "Lord, who make" (but "who" is indistinguishable in number in English, unlike *qui, quae, quod*) or "Lord, who makes" (with an implicit ellipsis – "Lord, (you are the one) who makes"). Classical construction would find this unacceptable, but it is acceptable in terms of evolving English usage.'

To this the purists reply indignantly that to address somebody, particularly somebody as important as God, in the vocative, and then to use the verb in the third-person singular is quite unacceptable, even in terms of evolving English usage. The Almighty himself has not yet pronounced on the matter. Though I think that if I were at a service at Lampeter or Llandaff, using the new *Prayer Book*, I might steal an apprehensive look at the vaulting when we came to the collect. We do not say: 'You pedant, who thinks you knows all about English grammar'; or: 'Miss, you has written the wrong word on the blackboard', even in terms of evolving English usage.

You could say that this is further evidence that the nice old distinctions of the relative pronoun are decaying fast, and that the younger generation do not know their 'who' from their 'whom' and do not care. You could say that devotion, relevance, and scholarship are more important than grammar. You could say (C. S. Lewis did say it in his first *Letter to Malcolm*, deprecating frequent alterations to the liturgy): 'The perfect church service would be one we were almost unaware of; our attention would have been on God.' You could say that, although no doubt God is no pedant, and understands our imperfect mumblings, we might as well get the grammar right when addressing him. And you could certainly say that the language of worship and the scriptures is a special register that takes into account matters beyond ordinary grammar and syntax, and speaks to something old and complex in Englishmen. You tamper with a jot or tittle of the ancient phrases and rubrics at your peril.

# NEWS

## No news is good news,
## and no journalists is even better

'In the old days men had the rack;
now they have the Press.'
*The Soul of Man under Socialism*, 1891,
by Oscar Wilde

'What is news?' said journo Pilate, and would not stay for an answer, because he had to get tomorrow's edition out. 'What news?' says Hamlet to his two-faced friends. 'Master, master, news! And such old news as you never heard of!' shouts Biondello, the boy servant in *The Taming of the Shrew*. The old answer to the question 'What's new?', dating from *circa* 1720, is, 'Queen Anne (or Queen Elizabeth) is dead', signifying that all news is stale. There are various American equivalents, for example, 'Bryan has carried Texas.' Delane, the great nineteenth-century Editor of *The Times*, is said to have cabled William Howard Russell, his correspondent in the Crimea, 'What are the news?' Back across the wires the electric message came, according to *Times* folklore: 'Not a damned new.' The same anecdote is told about American editors.

The anecdote is intended to illustrate the irritating way that words in English change their number, no matter how much pedants complain. News was originally a count noun and a plural when it came into English in the thirteenth century, so that Dryden wrote: 'The amazing news of Charles at once were spread.' As late as 1821 Shelley was writing: 'There are bad news from Palermo.'

Modern grammarians define nouns that are seen as individual countable entities as count nouns, and those that are seen as denoting an undifferentiated mass or continuum as noncount nouns. Book is a count noun; sugar a noncount. Some nouns have dual membership of the categories. 'Would you like a cake?' 'No, I don't like cake.' 'She was a beauty in her youth.' 'She had great beauty in her youth.' Concrete nouns tend to be count, and abstract nouns to be noncount. But there is no necessary connection between the classes of nouns and the entities to which they refer. In some related languages the nouns corresponding to information, money, work, and news, for example, are count nouns. But in English they are noncount.

What has happened is that over the last century news has shifted from count to noncount. There is nothing to be alarmed about. It has happened before to better words than news, for instance agenda and stamina; and it is in the process of happening to media.

As interesting as its grammatical class and number is the meaning, or are the meanings, of news. The Delane and Billy Russell anecdote also illustrates the irritating way in which journalists claim to be the only oracles of what is news. It is, after all, their *métier*. News sense is their professional skill. And jolly bad they are at it in general. Newspapers are predominantly run by middle-aged executives, almost all men, who have hardly mixed in the real world for thirty years. They work ridiculously long hours. Their favourite recreation is gossiping about journalism in the pub with other journos. The only art they have time for is television, which is a pseudo- and perhaps a non-art. They lead pitifully narrow lives. And their idea of what makes news was formed a generation ago when they were cub reporters being trained by crusty old news editors, whose ideas had been formed a generation before that. So Fleet Street, or whatever new topographical eponym we get for the Press now that Fleet Street is dead, runs on ideas that are as old-fashioned as Aesop's aunt. The British Press today most powerfully and potently believes that soap-opera stories about royals sell papers, but never carries a whisper of consti-tutional criticism of monarchy as an institution. A century ago it was the other way round. Crime has always been news. 'That was a good murder you had last week,' wrote John Thadeus Delane, the Editor who brought down governments and reformed the constitution, to his deputy. Most news is depressingly old-fashioned.

Take the inky axiom, devoutly believed by hard journos, that news sells papers. It is true that crisis and catastrophe are good for the sales of serious newspapers, because people are anxious to read as much as they can of the latest. But most people today get their news from television and radio. You have only to look in the newsagent's to see that it is not news that sells the pops, but bingo, royal rubbish, sexual scandal, and the intimate lives of actors and actresses playing characters in soaps. News hasn't sold papers of the pop variety for a generation, but the old journos still mumble the old lie piously. It was snobbish to say that the *Daily Mail* was written by shop assistants for shop assistants; but the pops reflect the values and views of the world of middle-aged, middle-class, suburban man. That is what popular means.

In fact news is not an absolute or objective value. One man's news is another man's tedium. For keen folk dancers the splash in *Petronella and Pas de Basque Proclamation* is more newsy than anything that comes out of Westminster or Wembley, even though it leaves the rest of us unmoved. There are readers around, hard though news editors find it to comprehend, who are not in the least exercised by Lady Di's latest frock or Joan Collins's latest husband.

News is a notoriously slippery concept. People try to define it, without ever arriving at an exhaustive, or even a satisfactory, definition. 'News is something that somebody somewhere does not want to see published.' Well, up to a point, in the case of investigative and exposé reporting of scandal and secrets in high places. But does the reluctance of peccant vicars and television celebrities to read scabrous revelations of their private lives in the grotty gossip columns *ipso facto* make such nasty tittle-tattle news?

The classic definition of news is: if a man bites a dog, that is news. The alternative and fuller version, ascribed to Charles A. Dana, Editor of the *New York Sun*, goes: 'If a dog bites a man it's a story; if a man bites a dog it's a good story.' I am not entirely persuaded by this definition either. In certain circumstances for man to bite beagle seems the natural and unremarkable thing to do.

There have been numerous other shots at news. George Orwell wrote: 'Early in life I had noticed that no event is ever correctly reported in a newspaper.' Rose Macaulay made the same point with characteristic indirection: 'You should always believe all you read in the newspapers, as this makes them more interesting.' People everywhere confuse what they read in the newspapers with the news. News is anything that makes a woman say: 'For heaven's sake!' Why only a woman, for heaven's sake? An editor is somebody who separates the wheat from the chaff and prints the chaff. No News is Preferable.

With characteristic good sense, Sam Johnson got close to the point that crisis concentrates the news sense of a diverse country, in *The Idler* of 11 November 1758: 'In a time of war, the nation is always of one mind, eager to hear something good of themselves, and ill of the enemy. At this time the task of news-writers is easy; they have nothing to do but to tell that the battle is expected, and afterwards that a battle has been fought, in which we and our friends, whether conquering or conquered, did all, and our enemies did nothing.' Everybody has his own idea of news; it takes national catastrophe or triumph to unite the mass of ideas.

News is such an elusive and subjective value judgement, and Fleet Street is such a competitive and insecure place, that you get fashions in news. Night newsdesks devour the early editions of the opposition to see whether they have been scooped, and to try to catch up if necessary. Next morning at conference there are post-mortems. When one dog barks, the whole pack starts howling. And so, for a brief fashion, until the pack moves on, the Bishop of Durham can preach no sermon, the President cannot talk about anything except Irangate, and the Prince of Wales can say nothing about anything, without finding themselves all over the front pages.

The Chief Press Secretary to Number 10 Downing Street recently accused the British Press of suffering from the Le Carré syndrome and conspiracy theory – that the government is always and inevitably up to no good. Watergate, he said, has a lot to answer for. In this case the Chief Press Secretary misunderstood the meaning of news and the role of the press. It is not to act as a megaphone for the government, but to ask itself, when told anything by officialdom or anybody with an axe to grind: 'Why are these lying bastards lying to me?'

News is what somebody will pay 30p to read. Since there's nowt so queer as folk, there is almost nothing under the sun or over the moon that will not be news to somebody. But newspapers that do not catch the news sense of enough people go bust. News is the aberrant, the unexpected, the novel. That is why public complaints that all the news is bad are misguided. Glasgow shuttle arrives on time, no crash, no hijack, is no news. The prophet Isaiah can say: 'How beautiful upon the mountains are the feet of him that bringeth good tidings', incidentally giving feet their only honourable place in literature. But he would have made a lousy news editor.

The other popular misconception about the Press is that it is written and run by trendy-lefty intellectuals, who are unrepresentative of the general public. There was a fascinating conference in the United States in 1984, entitled 'A Liberal Media Élite?' In it Rupert Murdoch, Ben Bradlee, and other captains of the inky trade debated with vim the proposition that American journalists, in their background, attitudes, and voting records, are divorced from the traditions of middle America.

It is probably true that the sort of people who go into journalism are different from the average: more literate and cleverer, for one thing, and on the questioning rather than the establishment side of life. But in my observation the best journalists are not party political but unbelievers in politics. A good journalist would come near to knocking over his grandmother and kicking out her teeth to get at the truth, or at any rate to get his story on the front page. He would certainly not be diverted from it by ideology. The fact that right-wing commentators complain about the 'liberal consensus' in the Press, and Vanessa Spart commentators on the Left complain about a right-wing 'meeja' conspiracy in the BBC and Fleet Street, suggests that the Press is performing its traditional, cynical, watchdog role. *The Times* was nicknamed the Turncoat, because it followed its own rather than any party line, long before it was called the Thunderer.

We had newspapers controlled by politicians in the eighteenth century, and wholly corrupt and dishonest they were, which is why Fleet Street was called Grub Street. At least junk journalism is better than giving somebody the power to dictate where responsible journalism begins. We all agree about the free Press: it's just the newspapers that are so dreadful. It is a sobering question why the British popular tabloid Press is about the most disgusting and dishonest in the world. People from almost any other country would be embarrassed to be seen reading it. It may come from the honourable old English tradition of John Bull knowing his own mind, not believing a word of the stuff, and enjoying looking down his nose at his newspapers.

The death of Napoleon was announced in a Paris salon attended by Wellington and Talleyrand. In the hush after the announcement, somebody exclaimed: 'What an event!' 'It is no longer an *event*,' said Talleyrand. 'It is only a piece of news.'

There is no satisfactory, universal definition of news. But even the most proud and venerable newspapers can only survive by spending their time, like the Athenians, in nothing else but hearing some new thing, observing what interests the new generation, and finding new ways to tell it.

# OLD WIVES' TALES

## Man is a credulous animal
## and must believe something

'He had been kicked in the head when
young and believed everything he read in
the Sunday papers.'
*The America of George Ade*, 1962, by George Ade

I don't know why we blame old wives for our gullibility about
ridiculous tall stories. In my experience old wives tend to be
hard-headed and cynical. The phrase is another example of the
ingrained sexism of our language and attitudes. If you want to
point the finger at the real culprits for broadcasting bunk, you
should call them old hacks' tales. Journalists, because of the
speed at which they work, their consequent dependence on
clichés, and their need to popularize with striking images and
metaphors, often taken from cartoonists, use phrases that bear
no relation to the real world. Over the years dozens of people
have rebuked them for their popular fallacies, without making
them change their ways a billimillimetre. We need our suicidal
lemmings, our kryptokephalic ostriches, our blubbing crocodiles, our elephants with memories as tenacious as Mnemo-
syne, and the rest of our menagerie of chimeras, to serve the
Great Goddess Cliché.

We ought to rehabilitate the lemming. The popular notion
that the little rodents commit mass suicide by plunging off the
Arctic shore and swimming out to chilly sea is deeply ingrained
folklore. It is repeated in such respectable reference books as
my (admittedly 1958 edition) *Encyclopaedia Britannica*: 'None
returns, and the onward march of the survivors never ceases
until they reach the sea, into which they plunge and are
drowned.' There is even a romantic theory that the lemmings
are seeking not death, but an extension of life in a far-off place
known to their ancestors, perhaps Atlantis.

Like most popular folklore this is pure nonsense. No credible

233

observer has ever recorded the mass suicide of the lemmings. The most that can be said is that on their periodic emigrations to escape from overcrowding lemmings cross rivers and lakes tumultuously, like migrating ants, and many are drowned. Nor is there any serious evidence for John Masefield's myth that lemmings are following instinctively in ancestral footsteps from the Miocene period, when the Baltic and North Seas were dry land.

It is all bunkum. Lemmings simply do not do what they are supposed to do. The only animal that regularly commits mass suicide is *Homo sapiens*. But evidently we have a rhetorical need for some vivid metaphor from nature to illustrate the human propensity to self-destruction. The poor, bleeding lemming has been adopted as a cliché to fit the description; and scientific facts have nothing to do with rhetoric or journalism.

It makes no difference to a bull whether you wave a red, blue, or green rag at it. Bulls are colour blind, as are all cattle. By AD 45 Roman writers were referring to the use by Spanish bull-fighters of skins and cloaks to confuse the bull and wear him down. It was not until about 1700, when bull-fighting had become a stylized dance, that Francisco Romero from Andalusia introduced the *muleta*, the red worsted cape folded over a short stick. The red was chosen not to excite the bull, but to protect the machismo of the bull-fighter, and camouflage any blood that was spilt. In spite of the facts, a red rag to a bull remains a popular cliché for old journos.

Ostriches do not bury their heads in the sand. If they did, they would have become extinct ages ago, like the dodo. Flightless birds have a hard time in this wicked world. The dodo was all right until Western explorers discovered Mauritius and Reunion Island. Then, although its flesh tasted disgusting however it was cooked, the sailors soon exterminated the dodo for fun. The ostrich, the biggest and ugliest bird on earth, survives because it keeps its head up, runs very fast, and kicks very hard. However, it suits the rhetoric of journalists, particularly cartoonists, starting with Pliny in the first century AD, to portray the ostrich as a silly bird, which believes that because it cannot see its attackers, with its head buried in the sand, they cannot see it.

Pound for pound, elephants have proportionately smaller

brains than beagles, Jack Russells, or cats. Contrary to the rhetorical cliché, elephants have very bad memories. Crocodiles do not weep, not even crocodile tears. The crocodile grunts and moans in satisfaction as it eats: somebody suffering from a bad attack of the Pathetic Fallacy might suppose it to be weeping. The nerve supply to the parotid and salivary glands (saliva) and that to the lacrimatory glands (tears) are similar and situated close together in the crocodile, though not in man. When the crocodile is presented with a mouth-watering chef's special of the day, water comes out near its eyes. But it is saliva, not tears.

Neither Herodotus, nor Strabo, nor other early crocodile-watchers, recorded crocodiles weeping. The best guess is that at some time in the Dark Ages somebody thought he observed a crocodile weeping while in fact it salivated, or some monk invented the fable with an improving moral to adorn his bestiary. The earliest known reference to crocodile tears occurs in the work of Photius, the Patriarch of Constantinople, who lived from about AD 810 to 895. His most important work, the *Bibliotheca* or *Myriobiblion*, describes several hundred books, often with exhaustive analyses and copious extracts, and is an invaluable mine of strange information. It reproduces a homily of Asterius the Sophist, the Arian theologian, who died after AD 341: 'Forget the pleasures of the table and practise fasting, thereby imitating Christ. If you are still attached to Jewish things, what good is fasting to you? Are you bent on imitating the crocodile of the Nile? They say that these crocodiles mourn over the human heads they devour and weep over the remains of the dead – not from motives of repentance, but from regret that the head has no flesh they can eat.' This first allusion to the legend is agreeably scientific in attributing crocodile tears to greed not hypocrisy.

Nero did not fiddle while Rome burned. For one thing the violin was not invented until fifteen centuries after his death. For another thing, the rumours that Nero had something to do with the great fire of AD 64 were put about by that great historian, great black propagandist, Tacitus. Tacitus remarks that Nero profited from his country's ruin by building his new palace on the prime site made vacant by the fire: 'But neither human resources, nor imperial munificence, nor appeasement of the gods, eliminated sinister suspicions that the fire had been deliberately started. To suppress this rumour, Nero invented scapegoats – and punished with every refinement the notoriously depraved Christians.' And here is Gibbon, another great historian, great dramatist: 'But all the prudence and humanity affected by Nero on this occasion were insufficient to preserve him from the popular suspicions. The voice of rumour accused the emperor as the incendiary on his own capital; and, as the most incredible stories are the best adapted to the genius of an enraged people, it was gravely reported, and finally believed, that Nero, enjoying the calamity which he had occasioned, amused himself with singing to his lyre the destruction of ancient Troy.' Nevertheless, the image of the demon artistic emperor fiddling while his capital city burns on his instructions, while he sheds crocodile tears, suits the simple rhetorical purposes of journalism. It is no good hoping that we are going to give it up.

Our Society for Onomastic Rehabilitation (for which I predict nil success) will have to do something about poor old King Canute. It is an engaging paradox of the whirligig of time that in careless rhetoric Canute has now been widely adopted as the example of an infatuated and arrogant reactionary, who seriously believes that he can turn back the tides, usually those unpersuasively historicist currents, the tides of history. Politicians and other noisy persuaders evidently feel the need for some such dummy figure to insult. And Canute has drawn the short straw. In the great Boat Club in the sky he must be spitting with righteous indignation that he is slandered down here every day as a silly megalomaniac who seriously believed that he could stop the flowing tide.

What happened was the exact opposite. Canute (c. 995–1035) was the great sea-king of Denmark and England. His fleets ruled the waves, and, under his personal command, defeated the Swedish fleet at Stangebjerg, and the combined Norwegian-Swedish fleet at the mouth of the Helgeaa, both in 1028. He was the last man to waive the rules of seamanship. If any contemporary knew about the tides and other ways of the sea, it was Canute.

The story of Canute and the tide is recorded only by Henry the Archdeacon of Huntingdon, who wrote his *Historia Anglorum* a century after Canute's death. Henry says that Canute sat on the muddy bank of the Thames at Westminster (other tidal resorts have subsequently claimed the honour of being the place where this happened or did not happen), and commanded the rising tide to go back as a dramatic rebuke to his sycophantic court. He got his feet wet on purpose, as a parable to demonstrate to his magnates that there were forces in the world greater than kings and war, and to prepare them for his unpopular submission to the Pope. Henry of Huntingdon adds that, as a gesture of humility, Canute would never afterwards wear his crown: he hung it, instead, on the head of an effigy of the crucified Christ. The story is found nowhere else. It reads like a pious ecclesiastical legend with homiletic intent rather than news or history. That is not going to stop us using it as a handy label.

Cloud-Cuckoo-Land is another old journo's tale, grossly misunderstood, widely misused, and useful for the instant images that politicians and pop papers manipulate. It has become a derogatory vogue word, supposed to mean a silly sort of place, part away with the birds, part cuckoo, part castle-in-the-air, and wholly undesirable. Before the process is complete, it is worth recalling that Cloud-Cuckoo-Land was originally a very desirable and highly successful state.

*The Birds*, by Aristophanes, was first performed at the Great Dionysia of 414 BC. Its plot concerns an ingenious Athenian called Peisthetairos, 'Persuader', who persuades the birds to build themselves a city in the clouds, and so compels the besieged gods to accept humiliating terms. Like all comedies by Aristophanes, it combines witty and fantastic farce with distinctly sharp satire and schoolboy scurrility about prominent Athenians. Even the slowest member of the audience could grasp the satirical connection between the visionary ambitions of the birds and the imperialist ambitions of Athens, which had just launched against Sicily the most formidable armament that had ever issued from a Greek harbour: on collision course with disaster. Perhaps Aristophanes' masterpiece took only second prize because it outraged Athenian jingoism, or even Athenian chauvinism.

Nephelococcygia, Cloud-Cuckoo-Land, was indeed fantastic; but in the play it was crowned with brilliant success. It is shown to be in many ways a better place than either Athens or Heaven. For example, common informers, sophists, and other plagues of contemporaneous Athens are refused entry: Miss

World herself comes down to marry Peisthetairos, bringing with her, in addition to Zeus's capitulation, good counsels, happy laws, sound common sense, and all the other blessings that were fast disappearing from fifth-century Greece, not forgetting vegetarianism, at least as far as concerned the flesh of birds.

The abuse of Cloud-Cuckoo-Land as a vague derogatory metaphor, with an imposing ring of spurious learning, is comparatively recent. Victorian politicians, who knew their classics, never used it so. The first Victorian translation rendered the place, less euphoniously, as Cuckoo-Cloud-Land and Cloudcuckoobury. In 1899 the first use of Cloud-Cuckoo-Land as a depreciatory metaphor was recorded: 'All his thinking processes fade off into the logic of Cloud-Cuckoo-Land.' On the contrary, Cloud-Cuckoo-Land was conceived originally as being in many ways more logical than the real world or heaven. Evidently the cuckoo component of the name accentuates for English speakers the craziness of the Never-Never, happy, far-off, paradisal, and infinitely desirable Cloud-Cuckoo-Land. So it has now become an overused vogue word for a silly and unpleasant fantasy. Robert Graves captured poetically the unfashionably desirable and beautiful nature of the place when he wrote:

> Kingfishers, when they die,
> To far Cloud-Cuckoo pastures fly.

But then, he knew his classics.

It would be going too far to insist that journalists, politicians, advertisers, and other users of language to persuade should be exact and scrupulous in every image they use. That is not how the chattering classes work. But, if we use metaphors too wildly, people laugh at us, which may not be what we want.

# PARADOX

## Paradoxically, the word is overused

'He who confronts the paradoxical exposes himself to reality.'
*The Physicists*, 1962, by Friedrich Dürrenmatt

'Paradoxes are useful to attract attention to ideas.'
*Life and Letters*, 1904, by Mandell Creighton

Journalists, students, and the loquacious classes are the pirates
of language. We take the stuff, and use it to attract attention,
without bothering too much about what we are saying. Having
vulgarized a precise word such as 'ironically' until it now
means no more than a grunt, we have turned our flibbertigib-
bet attention to the fine old word 'paradox' and its derivatives,
and are giving them a dreadful mauling. Paradox and its family
are enormously popular among students and hacks as smart
and knowing epithets. With the virtual disappearance of Greek
in schools (and we are already ruing the day) most of the chaps
and chappesses who use the paradoxical words in their pieces,
leaders, and essays are driving in a screw with a hammer.

My historian don friend broke off from marking a very good
essay (on women in Tolstoy) when he stumbled over the
following: 'Anna's ability to see good on both sides of a
question of morality or conduct is what distinguishes her from
Dolly and Kitty, and, paradoxically, marks her as a woman of
the world.' The time has come to turn our attention to a
paradox, a paradox, a most ingenious paradox.

Hoisting the black flag of philosophy, let us declare that a
paradox, considering the roots, look you, if only you had learnt
Greek, means, etymologically, something that is against belief.
A full-blooded paradox shakes the foundations of logic. It
happens when, from a number of premises all generally
accepted as true, a conclusion is reached by valid deductive

argument that is either an outright contradiction, or conflicts with other generally held beliefs. Your true paradox is a philosophical stinker: both vexing and disturbing.

Let us have some examples of the ugly beast. The most famous and oldest of the creatures is the Liar Paradox. There was this Cretan called Epimenides, who asserted: 'All Cretans are liars.' Is Epimenides telling the truth or not? One or other must be the case. But, if it is indeed the case that all Cretans other than Epimenides are liars, both cases lead to contradictions. Are you still with me? Good. That sort is called a semantic paradox. Put it another way: 'This statement is false' seems to be false if true, and true if false.

Zeno's paradoxes are other classic philosophers' puzzles. Zeno was a disciple and friend of Parmenides. They came from Elea on the Tyrrhenian coast of southern Italy in the fifth century BC, and were known as the Eleatics. Zeno's paradoxes were devised to disprove positions contrary to Parmenides' philosophy that only the unchanging one exists, and hence nothing moves. They proposed to show that the concepts of many (plurality), motion (change), and place (space) were inherently contradictory, and led to absurdities; and therefore could not be used to explain the universe and its phenomena. The most famous is Achilles and the Tortoise. Achilles and the tortoise arrange to have a race. Swift-footed Achilles gives the tortoise a start. He takes some time to reach the tortoise's starting line, by which time the tortoise has moved at least some distance. While Achilles covers this new distance, the tortoise has moved on some more. And so *ad infinitum*. Although the successive stages get shorter, and are covered ever more quickly by the sprinting Achilles, at the end of any given stage Achilles is still behind the tortoise. He can never win, and retires to sulk in the changing-room. Zeno's Flying Arrow Paradox argues that, since at any moment an arrow shot from a bow occupies a definite position, and since between two moments there is nothing but other moments, the arrow can only be *in* positions and never move from one position to another. The Grain of Millet argues that a single grain of millet makes no noise when it falls and hits the ground, but a thousand grains make a dull thud; so a thousand nothings become a something, which is absurd, or a *reductio ad absurdum* as the philosophers call it.

Another famous and more modern brute is Russell's Paradox, named for Bertrand. It is important in Set Theory and the foundations of mathematics. Some classes are members of themselves, but most are not. For instance, the class of cats is not a member of itself, since it is a class and not a cat. However moreover and whereas, the class of non-cats is a member of itself, and the class of classes is a class. Is the class of all classes that are not members of themselves a member of itself? If yes, no. If no, yes.

Of course, the term and word 'paradox' are not the exclusive property of rigorous philosophers. Relativity has its Clock Paradox, and mathematics the Skolem Paradox. Even such less strenuously theoretical studies as literary criticism use the term 'paradox' in a more malleable way than the philosophers to describe a statement, which though it seems to be self-contradictory at first glance, yet contains a germ of truth. Your literary paradox makes the reader blink and recognize a truth behind the absurdity, as when Shakespeare says, 'Cowards die many times before their deaths'; and Wordsworth, 'The Child is father of the Man.' In this stanza from 'Rabbi Ben Ezra' Browning used the notion of paradox throughout:

> For thence, – a paradox
> Which comforts while it mocks, –
> Shall life succeed in that it seems to fail:
> What I aspired to be,
> And was not, comforts me.
> A brute I might have been, but would
> not sink i' the scale.

Here is an example of a more recent literary paradox, from John Gardner's *Grendel*: 'I knew, for one, that the brother-killer had put on the Shaper's idea of the hero like a merry mask, had seen it torn away, and was now reduced to what he was: a thinking animal stripped naked of former illusions, stubbornly living on, ashamed and meaningless, because killing himself would be, like his life, unheroic. It was a paradox nothing could resolve but a murderous snicker.'

On his deathbed Hegel, that master of paradox or at any rate obscurity, complained, 'Only one man ever understood me.'

He fell silent for a while, and then added, 'And he didn't understand me.' These are deep and dark philosophical waters. The best advice for amateurs is: do not use paradox or paradoxical unless you are sure of what you are on about. That is to say: do not use them.

Irony is easier because it is more widely diffused among the general public, and because philosophers do not use irony as a technical term of jargon, only as a mode of discourse to put down their students or opponents. Irony in Greek means dissimulation. The *eiron* was a stock character in Greek comedy, the dissembler. Being a puny weakling, he resorted to various forms of deception to overcome the *alazon*, the braggart soldier. The fox was described as *eiron* in Greek fables. Socratic irony was the infuriating way that Socrates in discussion used to adopt another person's viewpoint or argument in order finally to ridicule it and do a dance of derision on the pieces.

Dramatic irony was invented by the Greek tragedians. The plots of most Greek plays were the nursery tales of every Athenian child, and therefore well known to the audience. But the characters on the stage, Agamemnon, Oedipus, Pentheus, and the rest were in the dark. One of them could make some remark that on the surface sounded trivial to the dramatis personae, but sent a frisson of horrified expectation through the spectators, who knew that it was pregnant with doom. The irony of Fate is a concept invented by cynics who always expect the worst (or at any rate the unexpected) and are seldom disappointed.

The modern literary use of irony and ironic is much looser. These are trendy words of Lit. Crit. Irony can mean the use of words to suggest, through tone, stress, understatement, or overstatement, the opposite of their literal meaning, often sarcastically, sardonically, or cynically. It means mocking disingenuousness. It means writing that conveys something opposite to what is ostensibly expressed. It means an event or remark that casts a strange or sad light on what has happened before. *Falling In Place* by Ann Beattie: 'She was thinking about what she was going to do: she was going to talk about irony to students who, ironically, were too stupid to perceive irony.'

When Daniel Defoe, in *The Shortest Way With Dissenters*, 1702, demanded the total and savage suppression of dissent, he was using irony in his notorious pamphlet. He was himself a Dissenter. Swift is the great master of sustained irony in English. Remember *A Modest Proposal*, *The Battle of the Books*, and, for that matter, *Gulliver*. F. R. Leavis analysed Swift's irony in *Determinations*:

> Swift's irony is essentially a matter of surprise and negation; its function is to defeat habit, to intimidate and to demoralize. What he assumes in the *Argument Against Abolishing Christianity* is not so much a common acceptance of Christianity as that the reader will be ashamed to have to recognize how fundamentally unchristian his actual assumptions, motives and attitudes are. And in general the implication is that it would shame people if they were made to recognize themselves unequivocally. If one had to justify this irony according to the conventional notion of satire, then its satiric efficacy would be to make comfortable non-recognition, the unconsciousness of habit, impossible.

'Irony' is an old word and, though its meaning has been extended and loosened so that it is nearly a weasel word, there are still occasions when it can be used meaningfully. The journalistic overuse of it to mean 'oddly enough' or 'it's a rum thing that' or 'there's nowt so queer as folks' mishandles it and erodes its usefulness.

# POLITICAL EPONYMS

## Slagging Maggie

'When they circumcised Herbert Samuel,
they threw away the wrong bit.'
David Lloyd George, on his fellow Liberal, 1930s

We take people's names and turn them into general words. It is a common process, going back to Adam and Eve, caesarean sections (it is folklore and legend that J. Caesar was delivered by surgical incision through the abdominal and uterine walls), and martial arts. Politicians, being celebrities on everybody's lips and television screens, lend themselves particularly to eponymy. Most of the words derived from politicians' names are used, somewhat boringly, merely to describe their adherents or policies, as Gladstonian Liberal, Churchillian (applied both to Lord Randolph and Sir Winston), Lloyd-Georgian, Rooseveltian (applied both to Teddy and F.D.), Kennedy kitchen cabinet, and so on. Most politicians are shooting-stars, brilliant for a short spell, but soon forgotten, and leaving no permanent mark on the language.

Margaret Thatcher is one of the longest serving Prime Ministers in British history. There is some evidence that her name is undergoing eponymy of a more interesting sort than the purely descriptive. Thatcherism and Thatcherite have for some time been used to describe her form of populist, activist, and radical Toryism, which is meant to cut government expenditure and intervention in business and industry, bring down inflation by control of the money supply, beat the drum for British interests in the world more loudly, increase defence expenditure, reduce the corporate power of the trade unions, and move away from the consensus politics of the Fifties. Lord Boyd-Carpenter offered a gnomic definition in his autobiography, *Way of Life*, in 1980: 'The Thatcherite view accepts the thesis that equality of opportunity means opportunity to be unequal.'

In Labour and radical circles Thatcher and Thatcherite have developed pejorative connotations, and are becoming terms of abuse, ever since as Secretary of State for Education and Science between 1970 and 1974 Mrs Thatcher stopped free milk for school-children, and was serenaded, 'Thatcher, Thatcher, milk (or baby) snatcher.' 'Thatcher's girls' is slang for prostitutes, because her economic policies are believed by opponents to have caused widespread unemployment, especially in the north and other old industrial heartlands of the United Kingdom. In consequence many women on the bread-line travel south to London to look for work; and in many cases the only 'work' available is in the sex industry. Defiantly, they call themselves Thatcher's girls. Another name for the same phenomenon is 'have it away day', in jocular reference to the day-return ('Away Day') train tickets on which an increasing number of women are travelling to London in order to earn money as prostitutes.

If this goes on, we may look forward to foul-mouthed people shocking respectable citizens with, 'Thatcher off!', 'By Thatcher!', 'Go to Thatcher!', and 'Thatcher you!' Yet it is a harmless, rural, traditional English name. Thatcher is the preferred form in the south, with Thacker showing Scandinavian influence in the north, and Theaker from the Old Norse word 'to cover' in Yorkshire and Lincolnshire. Thaxter has been noted only in Norfolk, where it still survives. It is just as well that Margaret Thatcher does not have a name that sounds more violent and explosive, like Pitt, Cripps, Pym, or Horatio Bottomley. In any case, nobody can be entirely hated who is widely known by the nickname Maggie. I do not think that Mrs Thatcher should feel too wounded by the process. It happens all the time, and is evidence that she is leaving her mark on the dictionary as well as the economy.

Ronald Reagan too has left his name in the lexicon. When he announced that he was running for President, Jack Warner commented: 'No, No! Jimmy Stewart for President, Reagan for best friend.' Reaganite and Reaganism describe his policies and supporters, which could be defined as extremism in defence of Fordism. He won his elections on a call for a return to traditional American values of self-reliance, individualism, and private enterprise, backed up by deflationary policies to reduce social expenditure, especially on welfare, cut back taxes, reduce government intervention, and stimulate economic growth. These old-fashioned policies were renamed eponymously Reaganomics, or 'supply side' economics, as distinguished from management of demand. But whatever chance of success they may ever have had was denied by the combination of a world recession, rising unemployment, and a flood of imports, particularly from Asia.

Neil Kinnock has not been at the top of politics for long enough to have given his name to the vocabulary. But I think that he needs to be more parsimonious in having himself photographed surrounded by assorted babies. This brings irresistibly to mind the Hon. Samuel Slumkey, the successful candidate at Eatanswill. 'He's kissing 'em all,' screamed the enthusiastic little gentleman. And, hailed by the deafening shouts of the multitude, the procession, and the English language, moved on.

Eponymous fame for politicians is cruelly short. Who now but elderly political groupies can define the Nixon Doctrine (a foreign policy that maintains US involvement in the affairs of the world, but in a way that requires allies to bear the manpower burden of their own defence); or Nixonomics (it means that all the things that should go up – the stock market, corporate profits, real spendable income, productivity – go down, and all the things that should go down – unemployment, prices, interest rates – go up). Eisenhower Syntax was once used to mean convoluted extemporaneous remarks and ad libs that appeared confused. The Gettysburg Address as ad-libbed by Ike runs: 'I haven't checked these figures, but 87 years ago, I think it was, a number of individuals organized a governmental setup here in this country . . . Well, now of course we are dealing with this big difference of opinion, civil disturbance you might say, although I don't like to take sides or name any individuals . . . But if you look at the overall picture of this, we can't pay any tribute – we can't sanctify this area – we can't hallow, according to whatever individual creeds or faiths or sort of religious outlooks are involved, like I said about this particular area. It was those individuals themselves, including the enlisted men – very brave individuals – who have given this religious character to the area . . . We have to make up our minds right here and now, as I see it, they didn't put out all that blood, perspiration and – well, that they didn't just make a dry run here, that all of us, under God, that is, the God of our choice, shall beef up this idea about freedom and liberty and those kind of arrangements, and that government of all individuals, by all individuals and for the individuals shall not pass out of the world picture.'

Theodore Roosevelt, the most ebullient and energetic of presidents (1901–9), has left his eponymous tracks in the dictionary. Teddy bear, as the name for the child's cuddly toy, is said to be a humorous reference to Roosevelt's passion for hunting bears, or anything else on four legs. The earliest references support this etymology. *Daily Chronicle*, 1907: 'While Europe is sending aloft the diabolo, America is playing with bears. The sudden delight in these mere things of the toy-shop is due to their name – Teddy-bears.' The name stuck longer than most political eponyms, so that A. A. Milne could immortalize it for middle-class nurseries in *When We Were Very Young*, 1924:

> They said, 'Excuse me,' with an air,
> 'But is it Mr Edward Bear?'
> And Teddy, bending very low,
> Replied politely, 'Even so!'

There goes your proto-Pooh.

Theodore Roosevelt's bear-hunting expeditions inspired a popular comic poem, accompanied by cartoons, in the *New York Times* of 7 January 1906, concerning the adventures of two bears named Teddy B and Teddy G. These names were transferred to two bears (also known as the Roosevelt Bears), presented to the Bronx Zoo in the same year. What seems to have happened is that enterprising American toy dealers turned these events to their profit by naming toy bears imported from Germany 'Roosevelt bears'. They became an instant fashion and spread around the world.

Teddy Roosevelt was certainly an enthusiastic hunter, indeed an enthusiast generally. Shortly before leaving the White House in 1909, he began to make plans for a hunting trip to Africa. Hearing that a famous English big-game hunter was in the United States, he invited him to come to Washington to give him some pointers. After a two-hour conference with the President, the Englishman came out of his office dazed. 'And what did you tell the President?' asked an inquisitive bystander, probably from the Press. 'I told him my name,' replied the exhausted visitor. It was when he left on this visit that J. P. Morgan, the banking tycoon and old opponent of Roosevelt, exclaimed: 'Health to the lions.'

When they first landed in France in the First World War American troops were originally called Teddies. They disliked the nickname as much as Sammies, and it was soon dropped. But this was clearly another eponymous reference to Roosevelt. Ezra Pound, in a letter dated 25 August 1917: 'The *Morning Chronicle* assures me my compatriots are called "Teddies", which is one in the eye for Mr Woodie Wilson.'

Remarkably Roosevelt may have given his name to a third eponymous object in addition to words for describing his politics: the woman's undergarment combining chemise and panties. A dictionary of *American Speech* published in 1929 describes it: 'There is an article of feminine wearing apparel, a sort of overall piece of underwear, I believe, which is known as a *teddy*. I would suppose that this was so-called from its real or fancied resemblance in general shape (or shapelessness) to the teddy-bear.' The *Hartford Courant* of Connecticut gives a more scientific description: 'Teddys are no longer synonymous with teddy bears alone. They also represent the sexiest lingerie around. The teddy is a camisole and pants set combined. The chemise bodice, often fashioned after a camisole, unbuttons either in the front or the back. The all-in-one feature of teddys has made them more popular as sleepwear.' I can think of no other politician who has given his name to such diverse objects. Napoleon was the eponymist of, among other things, a coin, a top-boot, a cannon, a code, a card game, and an allegedly old kind of brandy. Gladstone gave us a leather portmanteau, and a name for cheap French plonk. But nobody has the marvellously wide range of Teddy Roosevelt's eponymous words.

There is no damned merit in which politicians become eponyms. It helps to have made a great stir in the world, like Napoleon. Longevity and long service help, as with Gladstone. But chance can make a second-division and long-forgotten name immortal. For example, the illuminated amber globes that mark street crossings in the United Kingdom are still called Belisha beacons, because they were introduced when Leslie Hore-Belisha, a second-rank Liberal in the long eye of history, was Minister of Transport between 1934 and 1937. The eponymists of the useful sandwich and cardigan were not the best or most celebrated public figures of their periods. Some great men are remembered for trivial things: it is surprising that the great name of Giuseppe Garibaldi is remembered for a loose red blouse worn by women, and a type of British biscuit with currants in the centre, also known as 'squashed flies'. Certain periods or events are paradoxically prolific with eponyms. Think of the Crimean War, not the most important war that Britain has fought in the past two centuries, which nevertheless enriched the lexicon with cardigan, balaclava helmet, and raglan overcoats, with sleeves that continue to the collar instead of having armhole seams. Their eponymist, Lord Raglan, the Commander of the British troops in the Crimea, had had his arm amputated without anaesthetic after Waterloo, and persisted in calling the enemy in the Crimea the French instead of the Russians. There seems to be no connection between his amputation and his choice of sleeve design.

Names of institutions as well as persons can be taken as descriptive or abusive eponyms. It happened once to *The Times*. In the struggle over the Reform Bill in the 1830s William Cobbett fought a war with no holds barred with *The Times* over who spoke for the public. He called the newspaper 'the vile *Times*', and 'the stupid and beastly old *Times*'. Those were days of brisk abuse, livelier than anything we can imagine today. *The Times* was registered at the Stamp Office in the names of two sisters of the proprietor (those were still days when it was imprudent and dangerous to be known as a newspaper proprietor). This gave Cobbett an opportunity for some male chauvinist abuse: 'Swift very justly lays down, that when women quit the behaviour of their sex and behave like bullying men, they are to be treated like bullies and kicked down stairs accordingly. Every word contained in this indecent and atrocious newspaper must be deemed and taken to be the words of these two women. I do not at present know the persons of the audacious termagants. When I do, I shall be by no means sparing in descriptions of their paunches and such other parts belonging to them that I may think worthy of description.'

In the war of words, Cobbett and the Chartists adopted *The Times* as an eponymous verb, meaning to calumniate in a libellous and lying manner, as in: 'If you don't look out, I'll *Times* you.'

# PRONUNCIATION

## Pronounced discrepancies

'You can't be happy with a woman who
pronounces both ds in Wednesday.'
*Sauce for the Goose*, 1982, by Peter De Vries

Pronunciation is a feature of English that permits even more
variety than orthography, grammar, semantics, or vocabulary.
We are diffident about criticizing other men's pronunciation
these days. But we are confident that we, and those who
pronounce as we do, are intelligible and euphonious. A century ago there was something called Received Pronunciation
or Standard English. It was defined by the inventor of the
name as, 'a class dialect rather than any local dialect – the
language of the educated all over Britain'. British upper-
middle-class Received Pronunciation, non-regional and transmitted through boarding schools and universities insulated
from the localities where they are situated, has lost is unique
prestige. It is still preferred for most British newsreaders, in
the same way that the Middle American pronunciation known
as network English is preferred for newsreaders on US radio
and television.

Some regional pronunciations have a lowly status, particularly those that diverge pronouncedly from the average: for
example, thick Ulster, in which a lake means a hole in a kettle;
and braid Glescaranto, in which 'Amphora' is an expression of
choice, as in, 'Amphora glessna pint', which means, 'If you
twist my arm, I shall accept a large whisky and a pint of
heavy.'

We tend to feel threatened or cross when pronunciations
change. But it happens all the time, as it is bound to in a living
language. You have only to read Shakespeare, or any old poet
who used metre and rhyme, to be continually bumping into
pronunciations that have changed since he wrote. Commend-

able sounds right today with the stress on the second syllable, '-mend'. In Shakespeare's time the stress was evidently on the first syllable:

'Tis sweet and cómmendable in thy nature, Hamlet.'
'Silence is only cómmendable
In a neat's tongue dried and a maid not vendible.'

When Noah Webster, the great American philologist and lexicographer, published his spelling book in 1783, he offended religious decency by insisting that the suffixes -tion, -sion, and -cion be pronounced as single syllables. Supporters of the old two-syllable pronunciation were outraged. The story goes that a Scottish Presbyterian elder in western Pennsylvania rode furiously into town one morning and called out: 'Have ye heard the news, mon? Do ye ken what's gaen on? Here's a book by a Yankee lad called Webster, teaching the children clean against the Christian religion.' 'How so?' 'Why, ye ken ye canna sing the psalms of David without having salvation and such words in four syllables, sal-va-si-on, and he's making all the children say salvashun.'

'Niche' is a word that is changing its pronunciation fast, as are thousands of others in the mysterious currents of fashion and language. It is increasingly pronounced 'neesh'. Presumably this is a consequence of pronouncing foreign-looking words in a foreign way, to show that we too have been to Alicante, and have slides to prove it if you would like to see them. This new pronunciation disregards the rude old limerick about the Abbess of Chichester, whose beauty made saints in their niches stir. But then, the English have never been too sure about how to pronounce Chichester.

It would amuse Noah Webster to observe that another word that is changing its sound is 'consortium'. Politicians and businessmen, and other classes who talk about consortia or consortiums, tend to say 'consorshum'. At first I though they were just having trouble with their false teeth. Then I took it to be yet another consequence of the disastrous decline in the study of Latin in the United Kingdom. And then I remembered the customary way we pronounce 'nasturtium', and shut up. I still think 'consorshum' is ugly.

Another speaking tendency that is changing pronunciation is for specialists, particularly scientists, to pronounce words in a different way from the rest of us, perhaps to show off that they are using the words in a specialized way, superior to that of the common herd. There is nothing particularly modern about this tendency. Remember Holofernes, and, for that matter, Don Adriano de Armado. But the change is more rapid, because there are more specialists around 'mispronouncing' the language.

Thus specialists in the know pronounce cervical cancer with a long 'i'. We ignorant outsiders always thought it had a short 'i' and are becoming a bit uneasy about our pronunciation, in case there is something in it that our best friends don't dare tell us. Similarly profane amateurs pronounce the science chĕmistry with a short 'e' in the first syllable, as we learnt to do years ago in Stinks. The initiates pronounce fermentation systems with stabilized chemistry as kēēmostats, and treatment of patients with chemical drugs as kēēmotherapy. Micro and semi-micro chemistry are becoming fashionable: by the experts they are pronounced mickro and semi-mickro. Thank Asclepius that mickroscope has not yet become the way to pronounce it. It will, it will, vexing the Greek scholars. Cȳcles have spawned sicklical. Titration has produced a mickro method that has minced its way into scientific and medical usage as the mīcrotītre, pronounced mickroteeter, method.

These specialist variations display the closed shop of the pronouncer. But they take the words farther away from their etymological pronunciations, and help further to confuse those who speak English as a second language, and even ourselves, native here, and to the mannerisms of British pronunciation born.

We have become much more relaxed about pronunciation in the United Kingdom over the past twenty years, as class distinctions have been eroded, and we hear rich varieties of English pronunciation all around us, in the streets and on the air-waves. The fetish that the only correct way to pronounce the Queen's English was that indoctrinated at the great public schools and older universities has been exploded. The myth of BBC English has been dissipated, so that a distinctive regional accent, even an Ulster accent, is a positive asset for a broadcaster. But there is one area left in which it still matters to pronounce words correctly. And that is the area of names of people and places. We are defensive about our proper names.

Who steals my purse, steals trash. But he that mispronounces my good name, causes mortal offence.

We make it pretty easy to cause mortal offence in the United Kingdom, with astonishing vagaries and idiosyncrasies of nomenclature. Horatio Bottomley (1860-1933), the British journalist, financier, and con-man who ended up in prison, called to see Lord Cholmondeley. 'I wish to speak to Lord Cholmondley,' he said to the butler. 'Lord *Chum*-ley, sir,' said the butler, putting his pronunciation right, and Bottomley down. 'Oh, all right,' said Bottomley. 'Tell him that Mr Bumley would like to see him.'

We go out of our way to complicate our names, out of snobbery or that old English eccentricity. Take the family Pepys, for example. Its members pronounce their name variously as peppis, pips, peeps, and pepps. And woe betide the uncultivated slob who pips a pepps. Peppis is appropriate for the family name of the Earl of Cottenham. Peeps, as far as we can judge, was the way that the great diarist Samuel pronounced his name, the dear man whom his friend John Evelyn remembered as 'a very worthy, industrious and curious person, none in England exceeding him in knowledge of the navy . . . universally beloved, hospitable, generous, learned in many things, skilled in music, a very great cherisher of learned men'. Not a bad epitaph. And Peeps is the pronunciation used today by the Pepys Cockerell family, lineal descendants of the diarist's sister, Paulina.

Take those names, presumably Norman French, that begin with Beau. They offer as much variety in pronunciation as there are vowels to choose from: Beauchamp (beetcham), Beauclerk (boklair), Beaulieu (bewli), and Beaudesert in Warwickshire (either bodezert or, just to be difficult, belzer). These variations are not pure perversity and blue-blooded snobbery to distinguish owners of such names from the common herd. Pronunciations change all the time, diverging from their original spellings; and Norman names have undergone nine centuries of change.

Even names that look plain sailing have quicksands and reefs, and barking Scylla and maelstrom Charybdis, for the unwary. Meyer looks a simple enough name. Nothing to it really. But some Meyers pronounce the name my-er, others mair, others may-er, and others meer; and, if you get it wrong, they will put you right. Are the Powells you know powel (like the film critic, journalist, and broadcaster Dilys Powell), or po-el (like Anthony *A Dance to the Music of Time* Powell and Lord 'Be Prepared' Baden-Powell)? Palgrave of *The Golden Treasury* liked to be called palgrayv; other Palgraves prefer pawlgrayv. Some people called Onions pronounce their name like the vegetable (as did the great C. T. Onions, philologist, grammar-ian, and editor of the *Oxford English Dictionary*); others avoid the vegetable sound by calling themselves oni-onz, with the stress on the 'i'. Similar motives of avoiding the common or disagreeable persuade some people called Death to pronounce themselves de-ath.

To help its staff and the rest of us through this minefield of nomenclature, the BBC regularly publishes its *Pronouncing Dictionary of British Names*. It represents more than fifty years of cumulative research into the tricky business of British names, and lists more than 20,000 difficult names, with their pronunciations drawn from the Corporation's pronunciation unit.

The BBC knows from bruised experience that a mispron-ounced name causes more offence even than a properly pro-nounced improper word. And it goes to considerable pains to ensure that its announcers get this kind of pronunciation right. 'Right' in this context means that surnames should be pro-nounced as the bearer of the name herself or himself prefers, and that place-names should be pronounced as the local inhabitants pronounce them. The trouble with the latter prin-ciple is that the local inhabitants often disagree vehemently about the pronunciation of their place. The BBC usually con-sults the post office, the vicar, the library, or the police station, to establish exactly how the people who live there pronounce their village or town name. People with difficult personal names are invited to pronounce them definitively for the rest of us.

These are tricky and tongue-twisting territories, my masters, with names such as Feaveryear (fev-yer), O'Cathain (o-ka-hoyn), and MacGillesheatheanaich (mach-gille-he-haneech, with the stress on the 'he' and the ch as in 'loch'), living in places called Postwick (pozzick), Costessey (kossi), Braughing (braffing), Flawith (flawith or floyth), Saughall (sawkl), Culzean (killayn), Kirkudbright (kurkoobri), and Troedrhiw-fuwch (Oh, forget it).

Not even the BBC can establish the truth in all these matters of pronunciation punctilio. Of Bobingworth in Essex all that its *Pronouncing Dictionary* can bring itself to assert, enigmatically, is: 'The post office is Bovinger.' It is a useful little word-book of etiquette. On the other hand, it might so inhibit one with the terror of names that one would never dare call anyone by his or her name again, making do with 'dear boy' and 'dear girl'.

# QUOTATIONS

## Wit half as old as time

> 'Hush little bright line,
> Don't you cry,
> You'll be a cliché
> By and by.'
> Fred Allen, 1961

Quotation is the sport of the sedentary classes. It is probably too late to run a mile in under four minutes, though I impressed myself, and alarmed the conductor, with a long sprint off the crown of the last bend to catch a number 27 bus the other day. I no longer seriously expect a telephone call from the West Indies to join the England touring party in order to add some biff to their middle-order batting; though, in my opinion, they are wet not to think of it.

But we can all quote; and we do, Oscar, we do.

> If, with the literate, I am
> Impelled to try an epigram,
> I never seek to take the credit;
> We all assume that Oscar said it.

Dorothy Parker's versicle from *Sunset Gun*. Next to being witty ourselves, the best thing is to quote another's wit. It is the English vice; an irritating form of showing off; and between friends and on the right occasion a way of sharing pleasure. The apt and amusing quotation in a book or an article is a way of making the readers feel they are part of a club of *cognoscenti*. But it needs to be done with some discretion. Frequent quotation marks are a form of hanging out one's banners on the outward walls: I think that you do better with veiled references, which will gratify those who recognize them, and not disturb those who miss them. As Lionel Trilling wrote, pinching the idea from somebody else: 'Immature artists imitate. Mature artists steal.' Classical quotation is no longer the parole

256

of literary men all over the world. You need to be jolly careful about letting a particle of Greek or Latin slip out these days, for fear of seeming élitist and an intellectual snob.

Richard Porson, the great Cambridge classical scholar and textual critic, was as famous for his outstanding memory as for his prodigious capacity for booze (an unusual combination). There are stories to confirm the observation that Porson would drink ink rather than not drink at all. One day he was travelling in a stagecoach, when an Oxford undergraduate let slip a quotation in Greek, in order to impress the ladies present, and asserted that it was from Sophocles. Porson was not impressed. He pulled a pocket edition of Sophocles from the recesses of his coat, and challenged the young man to find him the passage.

With the presence of mind and sang-froid for which Oxford is famous, the undergraduate said that he had made a mistake, and that the quotation was in fact from Euripides. Porson immediately produced a text of Euripides, and repeated his challenge. In a desperate attempt to save face in front of the giggling girls, the young man declared that the quote must have come from Aeschylus. When the inevitable text of Aeschylus popped out from the folds of Porson's coat, the undergraduate shouted up: 'Coachman, let me out! There's a fellow here has the whole Bodleian Library in his pocket.' The anecdote illustrates well the different qualities of the two universities: pedantry versus style.

All writers crib, borrow, adapt. You have only to read any play by Shakespeare with care to find a hundred echoes from his predecessors and contemporaries. The genius lay in how he improved them. If you steal from one author, it's plagiarism; if you steal from many, it's research, or Princess Michael of Kent's form of historiography. Wilson Mizner said that, but I suspect he stole it from somebody else. I put it in without inverted commas to con the unwary into thinking that I had invented it myself.

Frank Harris, the journalist who was at the heart of *fin de siècle* literary London, was an unashamed plagiarist in his conversation. The only 'ism he believed in was plagiarism, as Dorothy Parker said cattily about a woman writer. Harris once related as his own an anecdote that everyone in his audience recognized as the property of Anatole France. There was a slightly embarrassed silence. Then Oscar Wilde broke it by saying: 'You know, Frank, Anatole France would have spoiled that story.'

Plagiarism is as old as literature. The word itself has an interesting history, being derived from a man-hunting net for catching slaves. Ancient Rome ran on a slave economy. Prisoners of war, debtors, and law-breakers were turned into slaves to keep the Republic and then its Empire working. A popular and profitable crime was to kidnap freemen and use them or sell them as slaves. This crime was known as *plagium* from *plaga*, the hunting net which was used to catch these unfortunate victims. The *Lex Fabia* of the second century BC was the first of many laws designed to prevent such profiteering in flesh.

As early as 84 AD the scurrilous epigrammatist Martial used plagiarism to describe stealing words rather than people. In his first book of epigrams, LII, he addressed his friend Quintianus, asking him to protect his poems against a plagiarist, probably a Fidentinus, who is a frequent target for Martial's poisoned darts.

The poems are represented as in bondage to the plagiarist, and Quintianus is asked to reclaim them as the freed men of Martial:

> Hoc si terque quaterque clamitaris,
> Impones plagiario pudorem.

'If you shout out three or four times that the verses are my freed men, you will shame the plagiarist.'

*Plagium* came into English Civil Law in 1577 as the term for kidnapping or man-stealing, and continues in use as the technical term. Ben Jonson anglicized the word as plagiary to describe literary theft in his *Poetaster*, attacking Dekker and Marston, 1600–1: 'Why the ditt' is all borrowed; 'tis Horaces: hang him plagiary.' The form was extended by the addition of 'ism and 'ist, creating the modern term for the appropriation of another's work or ideas as one's own.

We resent being plagiarized. But to be occasionally quoted, if only on 'What The Papers Say', is the supreme fame for scribblers. To make it into the *Oxford Dictionary of Quotations* is to have a monument that will last longer than bronze. The fascinating ones are the one-quotation men: those whose literary memory rests on a single quotation. The classic example is John William Burgon (1813–88), Dean of Chichester, who, as an undergraduate, wrote in his entry for the Newdigate Prize:

> Match me such marvel save in Eastern clime,
> A rose-red city half as old as Time.

Burgon was actually echoing Samuel Rogers, the banker who became a popular poet, in *Italy, A Farewell*:

> By many a temple half as old as Time.

Plagiarism apart, his single line has lived, unlike anything else that J. W. Burgon wrote. After his undergraduate effort in *Petra*, the rest of his life as a writer must have been anti-climax, like that of an infant prodigy who is burnt out at the age of fourteen.

The Reverend Cornelius Whur wrote the amiable couplets:

> On firmer ties his joys depend
> Who has a polish'd female friend!
>     . . .
> While lasting joys the man attend
> Who has a faithful female friend!

The *Oxford Dictionary of Quotations* misspells his name Whurr, and conflates the two verses to:

> What lasting joys the man attend
> Who has a polished female friend.

Nothing beside remains of his writing. Garbled, plagiarized, and misquoted, his is still a memorable solo quote.

Dr Martin Joseph Routh, President of Magdalen College, Oxford, for sixty-three years, said: 'You will find it a very good practice always to verify your references, Sir'; and apparently nothing else of note worth remembering. It does not seem much to show after all those years as president of a famous Oxford college. What is extraordinary is that he made his solo quotation to Dean Burgon, that other monoquote expert, who recorded it in the *Quarterly Review* and his book *Lives of Twelve Good Men* (1888). Never mind. It is a good quote, worth being remembered for. It only goes to quote.

# QUOTES AND SIC

## Oh my giddy quote

'The thought of foolishness is sin: and the
scorner is an abomination to men.'
*Proverbs*, xxiv, 9

Controversialists, resourceful hacks, and the chattering and
scribbling classes can get a big rhetorical punch out of the
smallest words and punctuation marks. Take, for example,
those damned inverted commas in the air, quotation marks, or
quotes, as we call them in the trade. They are nothing but
grief. The new printing technology of photocomposition has
peculiar difficulty in getting them right, single or double,
upside down or right way up, inside or outside the final point.
And just you try cutting a spare set of quotes out of otiose
copy and sticking it in the place you need it. It is like picking
up a mustard seed with chopsticks. To do that sort of job, you
need fingers as neat as Queen Mab's. In fact, most old-
fashioned compositors have fingers the size and consistency of
bunches of over-ripe bananas. One of the benefits of the recent
revolution in the printing industry is that for the first time
people with small, tidy hands, such as women and the young
of all races, have been allowed to get their fingers in the
printers' pie.

Dictating copy over the telephone always causes trouble
with inverted commas. The hack dictates 'quotes', and it ends
up in his pieces as 'goats', giving the prose an unintended
surrealist flavour. By then the queue waiting indignantly for
the public telephone is tapping menacingly on the windows of
the call-box with tenpenny pieces. (Parenthesis: two impatient
housewives, fed up with the unconscionable length of the
article, once dragged me still dictating from the telephone-box
on Windsor railway station, cut off and left dangling in the
middle of moving purple stuff about the Garter Ceremony.)

Note: the full stop goes inside the parenthesis if it is a complete sentence, but outside the final bracket if the parenthesis is part of a larger sentence (like this). The most embarrassing misquote by homophone over the telephone I ever suffered was in a learned piece I dictated about the Dead Sea Scrolls, before they became as well-known as they are today. They went into every edition of *The Times* as the Dead Sea Squirrels, causing me humiliation and grief, and starting a sarcastic correspondence to the Editor that ran for some weeks in the bottom right-hand corner.

In the inky trade we call inverted commas 'quotes'. When dictating copy to a telephonist, we say: 'Quote . . . Unquote.' We use quotes to corral direct quotations, which are an essential part of any good news story. We use deprecatory quotes around slang or vulgarism to demonstrate our superiority to common people who use such words indiscriminately, without realizing that they are being common, so eating our cake and having it, or having a whipping-boy and doing the whipping ourselves. We use quotes rhetorically in spoken English these days. There is a common gesture of marking inverted commas in the air with one's fingers, to indicate to the audience that we are using words sarcastically or ironically.

When a columnist writes that somebody 'resigned' in quotes, what he means and says is that somebody was invited to resign rather than be sacked. The Champagne Bureau, which campaigns to restrict the use of the eponymous word 'champagne' to sparkling white wine made in the Champagne region of France, is vexed by the use of quotes to get around its monopoly of the word. Publicists write of local Portuguese 'champagne'. When the champagne purists object, the lawyers for Portuguese 'champagne' write back: 'As we feel quite sure you are aware, the effect of inserting this word or phrase in inverted commas – a normal and frequent practice – is to give that word/phrase a special meaning.'

There is a problem for lawyers about proprietary names and trade marks. I am aware that I should use 'biro' to describe only ballpoint pens made by the firm of Biro-Bic, and named after their inventor, the Hungarian László Biró. I am aware that 'thermos' ought to be used to describe only vacuum flasks made by the firm of Thermos. It is just that 'biro' is handier to write and say than ballpoint pen; and in the United States 'thermos' has been judged by the courts to be legally a generic name for more than twenty years. 'Biro' is neat, with its rhyme with giro; and 'thermos' is warmly gratifying to Greek speakers. Let us leave the problem to the lawyers. The language belongs to us as well as them; and on the whole we speak it better than they do. It is difficult to overestimate the pedestrian speech and stupidity of the average English lawyer. The Oxford lexicographers tread warily around the minefield of proprietary names: 'Their inclusion (of proprietary words like 'biro') does not imply that they have acquired for legal purposes a non-proprietary or general significance, nor is any other judgement implied concerning their legal status.'

It is a modern idiom to use quotes all the time in the spoken language. It has always been done to a small extent by accent and stress and intonation. But the anti-establishment generation of the Sixties has taken over the language of the previous straight decades, and poked fun at it, by placing words and phrases within invisible inverted commas. Thus 'charming' is used to damn something or somebody that is by no means charming; and 'chum' and 'mum' are pejorative. 'Nice', that most slippery of adjectives, is no longer a compliment if put between invisible quotes. It may be going too far to call this use of invisible quotes a revolution. Maybe we should put 'revolution' in quotes. There are a lot of the little beasts around. Unquote.

To get down to the vulgar practicalities of punctuation: it is economical to use a single comma, thus, '. . .', for your first quotes; and to use double inverted commas, thus, '. . . ". . ." . . .', for internal quotes. After that you are on your own. But economy suggests that you should revert to single quotes rather than triple. As for the point or full stop: if what you have shrouded in inverted commas is a mere word or phrase, put the stop after the quotes. He called her 'a silly old cow'. But, if the quotation is a complete sentence, put the quotes after the stop. He said: 'She is a silly old cow.'

Notice the use of quotation marks to sneer. Antony Flew, the philosopher, uses the felicitous expression 'sneering quotes' to describe the practice. The writer sticks a word or phrase in the pillory, for his audience to throw rotten tomatoes at, by enclosing it in quotes. The quotes announce: 'Look at this illiterate or ignorant usage. God, I thank thee, that we are not as other men are. Ho, ho, har, har.' The scoffing style of punctuation occurs particularly in 'theological' and 'philosophical' 'works', to illustrate it three times in one sentence, which is over-egging the pudding even in polemical writing. I give you a less artificial example, as it occurs all the time in controversial writing. (The subject of this example is a philosopher, by no means the admirable and learned Flew, but some nameless logic-chopper whom we want to patronize, put down, and put the boot into.) 'I don't think much of his "philosophy": I suspect that he is a "logician" who doesn't see the distinction, like Abelard.'

The sneering quote is analogous to the use of sic as a cheap and compendious linguistic stiletto. The 'proper' use of sic is to confirm that we are quoting accurately, or that we mean precisely what we have written, in spite of doubts or suppositions of misprint that might occur to the discerning reader. Sic says: 'Yes, she did say that, or misquote it that way. I know it's wrong, but that's what she said. Yes, I do mean what I wrote, in spite of your natural doubts.' It says: 'I know that this is going to make you stumble. But stumble not. I mean exactly what I wrote, neither more nor less. Now read on.' For example: 'The three most enterprising industrial companies in the United Kingdom are ICI, Unilever, and Howard's Hooray Henry Green Wellies, plc (sic).' The sic is needed because the third name is a surprise and not a household name like its predecessors.

But sic can also be used to sneer, to exclaim: 'What an idiot!' or 'What a hypocrite!' or 'What a liar!' For example: 'The Chief Constable said that he intended to rectify the mistake (sic) committed by the CID.' 'The Minister said that his Bill was designed to improve (sic) the lot of the workers.' In both examples, the writer butts in and comments disparagingly on what is being said. In spoken English we convey such sneers by nod, wink, tone of voice, and exaggerated pronunciation.

The other little rhetorical links and codes can also be used sarcastically, though not as conveniently as sic. E.g. is *exempli gratia*, for example, and gives an exemplary instance to explain. I.e. is *id est*, that is, and is normally used to paraphrase some previous expression that may be obscure or might mislead. 'They read nothing but bum-fodder, i.e. trashy literature.' Viz. is an abbreviation of *videlicet*, and means 'you may see' or namely. But, rather than paraphrasing, it expands or gives a more particular statement of what has been vaguely described. 'I have three crunching arguments, viz. 1 . . . 2 . . . 3.' Sc. is an abbreviation of *scilicet*, and means 'you may understand or know'. It is found in academic and learned rather than popular writing, and its most characteristic use is to introduce a word or phrase that has not been expressed, but left to be understood. 'The ultimate end of the universe, sc. to know and love God.' 'They shall stamp the same on the one side with these letters (*scilicet*) C. R. for *Carolus Rex.*' *Scilicet* is a term particularly favoured by classical scholars in their textual glosses. It can also be used sarcastically. Here is an example from Oliver Cromwell: 'That holy (*scilicet*) father of Rome.'

Fowler and other lovely purists condemn the sneering use of sic, and would condemn the sneering quote. I am not sure that we can go the whole hog with them in disapproving of the practice. Sneering and sarcasm are, indeed, unkind, uncharitable, and beastly. But controversy, whether political or academic, is an important and can be an angry and unkind business. Getting at the truth matters; and so does putting our point of view. Sneering quotes and sic may be unfair weapons. But in the war of words we are likely to turn to any weapon that comes to hand. I doubt whether we can completely disarm controversialists of such useful little darts. But they should be used with finesse, or they rebound on the user.

# SOD'S LAW

## Buttering up Lady Luck

*Est-il heureux?* ('Is he lucky?'), question asked of
all men who applied for service under him, by
Cardinal Jules Mazarin (1602–61), successor to
Richelieu as prime minister of the queen regent
of France, Anne of Austria, Louis XIII, and
Louis XIV, and founder of the splendid library
in Paris, the Bibliothèque Mazarine

Every day in every way things get worse and worse. Or so the
old bores grumble. And God, they are boring! But at least in
one matter there is an improvement. We are less superstitious
than we used to be, aren't we? We no longer tremble at
thunder, thinking it is God in a bad temper, or making obscene
apotropaic gestures to ward off the evil eye. There is still as
much folly and sin around as drove Juvenal to verse: but at
least there are fewer fortune-tellers, augurs, entrail-
interpreters, prophets, haruspices, weather forecasters, public
opinion pollsters, psephologists, and other such charlatans.

We are rational grown-ups these days, who no longer make
detours to avoid walking under ladders, or blench to sit down
thirteen at a table. The feeble-minded may read their horo-
scopes in the feather-headed blats; but they claim sheepishly
that they don't really believe the rubbish, and look at it only
for a laugh.

Of course, some superstitions are not irrational, but plain
common sense. It is indeed very unlucky to put the sugar in
before the milk when pouring a cup of tea. It has a terrible
effect on your life. My Aunt Cassandra once put the sugar in
first, and over the next fifty years all her teeth fell out. And
even the most hard-headed rationalists have feet of clay, with
their toes crossed, about superstition. Niels Bohr, the Danish
nuclear physicist who was one of the fathers of the Bomb, and
a serious man of science, kept a horseshoe hanging in his

country cottage. A friend teased him: 'Can it be that you, of all people, believe it will bring you luck?' 'Of course not,' replied Bohr, 'but I understand it brings you luck whether you believe or not.'

As Cardinal Mazarin, the French statesman who believed in having around him men who were lucky, lay dying, the night skies of France were lit up by a comet. The superstitious whispered that this portended Mazarin's death. When Mazarin was told about the gossip, he remarked: 'The comet does me too much honour.'

Some beliefs that look superstitious at first are really hard facts that can be demonstrated empirically. One of these is the Aggravating Transport Law of Inverse Urgency. This states that public transport arrives promptly only when it doesn't matter, but is always late when you really need it. When you have all the time in the world, the Circle Line train pulls up as you step onto the platform, and the 27 bus arrives at the stop simultaneously with you, you have the right change, the driver smiles, the traffic lights are green, there is no other traffic about, and you get to work an hour before anybody else. Conversely, when you have an important conference with the Big Boss, and are running a bit late anyway, the bus accelerates away just as you arrive at the stop, and no other comes for half an hour, when three arrive in convoy, frequent District Line trains infest the platform, with never even a rumour of the Circle Line, and the announcer continues his inaudible, or enigmatic, or ungrammatical proclamations about the delay being due to an earlier incident on the line. This is scientific fact, not bad luck or superstition.

It is merely a variant of Murphy's or Sod's Law, a name humorously given to various aphoristic expressions of the apparent perverseness and unreasonableness of things. It states that anything that can go wrong will go wrong; and, to give it its final gloss, if it can't go wrong, it might. This view that the cussedness of the universe tends to a maximum is a pessimistic version of the Pathetic Fallacy.

Murphy's or Sod's Law is the force in nature that causes it to rain mostly at weekends, that makes you get 'flu when you are on holiday, and that makes the 'phone ring just as you've got into the bath. There are numerous variations of the Law, which is said to have been invented by George Nichols in 1949.

Nicols was then a project manager working in California for the American firm Northrop, and developed the axiom from a remark made by a colleague, Captain E. Murphy, of the Wright Field-Aircraft Laboratory. The earliest quotations appear to support this aeronautical explanation: *Aviation Mechanics Bulletin* May–June 1955: 'If an aircraft part can be installed incorrectly, someone will install it that way.'

Murphy's First Law of Biology states: 'Under any given set of environmental conditions an experimental animal behaves as it damn well pleases.' Mrs Murphy's Law states: 'If anything can go wrong, it will, and Murphy won't be at home.' Murphy Junior's Law states: 'It works better if you plug it in.'

Murphy's Law, and its clauses and codicils, are merely scientific formulations of a much earlier universal law about human affairs, the Buttered Side Principle, first set down by James Payn, the editor of *Chambers's Journal* and *The Cornhill Magazine* in 1884:

> I never had a piece of toast
> Particularly long and wide,
> But fell upon the sanded floor,
> And always on the buttered side.

Payn was parodying Thomas Moore's 'The Fireworshippers' (1817):

> I never nurs'd a dear gazelle,
>   To glad me with its soft black eye,
> But when it came to know me well,
>   And love me, it was sure to die.

There are numerous variants of the Buttered Side Principle. Buttered bread falls buttered side down – and if it's a sandwich it falls open. If you drop something from your plate it will just miss your napkin. And so on. A Jewish man once dropped his buttered slice of toast, and it fell with the buttered side *up*. He rushed to tell his local Rabbi, who in turn was astounded, and sought help from higher authority: this sudden contradiction of all the laws of God and man had to have some rational explanation. Eventually a conference of learned Rabbis came to the only possible conclusion: the toast had originally been buttered on the wrong side.

Paul Jennings has reported the famous Clark-Trimble experiments of 1935, which first placed the graduated hostility of things on a scientific basis. Clark-Trimble arranged four hundred pieces of carpet in ascending degrees of quality, from coarse matting to priceless Chinese silk. Pieces of toast and marmalade, graded, weighed, and measured, were then dropped on each piece of carpet, and the marmalade-downwards incidence was statistically analysed. The toast fell right side up every time on the cheap carpet, except when the cheap carpet was screened from the rest (in which case the toast did not know that Clark-Trimble had other and better carpets). But it fell marmalade-downwards every time on the Chinese silk. Most remarkable of all, the marmalade-downwards incidence for the intermediate grades of carpet was found to vary exactly with the quality of the carpet. We need say little here of the similar experiment of Noys and Crangenbacker, in which subjects of all ages and sexes, sitting in chairs of every conceivable kind, dropped various kinds of pencils and biros. In only three cases did the pencils come to rest within easy reach. In most cases the pencil not only broke, but rolled out of sight, or into some crevice that could be reached only by lying prone and stretching in the dark, so demonstrating the essential hostility of objects to man.

The underlying truth of this principle goes back much further. Indeed, it has been built into the human condition since Adam and Eve. With Murphy's Law and the Buttered Side Principle ruling the world, there is no room for superstition.

# SPELLS

## There's life in the old quote yet

'I don't know if you happen to be familiar with a poem called "The Charge of the Light Brigade" by the bird Tennyson whom Jeeves has mentioned when speaking of the fellow whose strength was as the strength of ten . . . the thing goes, as you probably know,
Tum tiddle umpty-pum
Tum tiddle umpty-pum
Tum tiddle umpty-pum
and this brought you to the snapperoo or pay-off which was "someone had blundered".'
*Jeeves and the Feudal Spirit*, 1954, by P. G. Wodehouse

'I might repeat to myself, slowly and soothingly, a list of quotations beautiful from minds profound; if I can remember any of the damn things.'
*The Little Hours*, 1944, by Dorothy Parker

English idiom is changing all the time. At the same time much of it is remarkably durable, and older than we think. Take *The Relapse, or Virtue in Danger,* by Sir John Vanbrugh, dramatist, architect and wit, first produced in 1696, with Sir Novelty Fashion, newly created Lord Foppington, one of the comic roles of the English stage. Better still go to see it, and you will sit up with a start to hear an idiom or catch-phrase that sounds too modern for a piece written in the seventeenth century. 'Virtue is its own reward,' says somebody, sententiously. 'That's funny,' one muses; 'I should have guessed Dickens, or one of the other Victorian moralists, as the originator of that smug platitude.' So one looks it up, and discovers that it is far older than Vanbrugh. It is recorded in English in 1509 in Barclay's *Ship of Fools*: 'Virtue hath no reward.' But you can take it back fifteen centuries earlier than that. Ovid (who else?)

wrote *Pretium sibi virtus*, or, as we say in the trade, 'Virtue is its own reward.' Vanbrugh was recycling a proverbial cliché with moths and rust on. A bit later in *The Relapse* somebody says: 'That's thinking half-seas over', and we sit up again. In this case Vanbrugh was one of the earliest to use the phrase metaphorically in a transferred sense. But 'half-seas over' had been around as a literal idiom for a century and a half before that. Raleigh himself, that great half-seas over sea-dog, used it, when he wrote of sailors riding it out at anchor, 'half-seas over between England and Ireland'.

A little later in *The Relapse* one of those seventeenth-century comedians remarks: 'So, matters go swimmingly'. You could still say, 'Oh, things are going swimmingly,' today, without sounding hopelessly old-fashioned. So you look it up, and discover that things had been going swimmingly long before Vanbrugh used the phrase as contemporary slang in his play; which means that fashionable people had been using the vogue commendatory adverb for even longer, before anybody thought of writing it down. It also means that Vanbrugh had a good ear for contemporary idiom and quotation: writers of comedies have to. It is not the case that there is nothing new under the sun in language. But slang is often older than it seems.

'I don't mind if I do!', which Tommy Handley turned into a raging catch-phrase in the wartime radio programme ITMA, was actually the revival of a saying that had been around since *circa* 1700. The criminal and disaffected classes had been calling police officers pigs two centuries before the young of the Demonstration Generation rediscovered the slang in the Sixties. 'My feet are killing me' is at least a century old. 'I'll have your guts for garters' may sound like a twentieth-century coinage by a sergeant-major. Sergeant-majors certainly still use the phrase with thunderous emphasis. But it has a long literary history, going back at least to Robert Greene's *James the Fourth*, 1598: 'I'll make garters of thy guts, thou villain.' We are continually using what we think are new words and idioms for old. But quite often they are not as new as we suppose.

Some of these well-worn tags are devilish hard to track down. Take that old *L'homme moyen sensuel*, which journalists tend to drop into their pieces to suggest polyglot cultivation. If asked where it comes from, they think: 'Easy-peasy; it will be one of those quotable Frog Ms who crowd the quotation dictionaries – Molière, Montaigne, Montesquieu, or de Musset.' Failing them, La Rochefoucauld? Apollinaire? Flaubert? Pascal? Gide? Help. Then you look in the quotation dictionaries. Then you take a trip to the British Library, and look in bigger and better quotation dictionaries. Then you ask your friends with memories like a data base, whose heads are crammed with gobbets of useless information. Then you telephone literate French friends. Then you ring the French embassy. Then you panic. Somebody must have written it or said it. It does not have the ring of an *anonyme* maxim, or a piece of proverbial folklore. It is very odd that the author of such a well-worn quotation is so elusive. No doubt he is well known by every French schoolchild. In that case, the French schoolchildren you have tried must have been exceptional.

You get a clue when the French claim never to have heard of the phrase, and to find it rather silly. And, if you persevere, you will find that Matthew Arnold coined the phrase in *Irish Essays*: 'But this whole drama may be best described as the theatre of the *homme sensuel moyen*, the average sensual man, whose city is Paris, and whose ideal is the free, gay, pleasurable life of Paris.'

Matthew Arnold liked his phrase so much that he used it several times more, for example in his essay on George Sand: 'How should she faint and fail before her time, because of a world out of joint, because of the reign of stupidity, because of the passions of youth, because of the difficulties and disgusts of married life in the native seats of the *homme sensuel moyen*, the average sensual man . . .'

Other English writers picked up the shiny phrase like magpies, transposing it to the *homme moyen sensuel*. It never caught on in the supposedly sensual land of France. Montesquieu in his *Lettres persanes* number 106 has: *Paris est peut-être la ville du Monde la plus sensuelle, et où l'on rafine le plus sur les plaisirs*. The expression *homme sensuel* occurs in Rousseau's *La nouvelle Héloïse*, part II, letter 15, and no doubt in many other places. The *homme moyen sensuel*'s finest hour in literature came when he was cited for the criterion of decency in the courts of the United States, when Judge Woolsey decided to remove the ban on *Ulysses*. But he never made it into the quotation dictionaries, and his proud originator is neglected.

Man is a quoting animal. It depends on one's idiosyncrasy which quotations linger in the memory, and make the hair at the nape of the neck bristle. I am haunted by lines that were penned in a summer-house by Lake Geneva two centuries ago: 'It was among the ruins of the Capitol that I first conceived the idea of a work which has amused and exercised nearly twenty years of my life, and which, however inadequate to my own wishes, I finally deliver to the curiosity and candour of the public.' Finishing a book brings the relief and sense of loss of giving birth. For a daily hack there is something godlike about spending twenty years on a single piece. Gibbon then took a walk in his avenue of acacias. The air was temperate, the sky was serene, the silver orb of the moon was reflected from the waters, and all nature was silent: 'I will not dissemble the first emotions of joy on recovery of my freedom, and, perhaps, the establishment of my fame.' Marvellous. Almost as hair-bristling as his account of the beginning of *The Decline and Fall*, with the barefooted friars singing Vespers in the Temple of Jupiter. Those are haunting lines. But, as it happens, Gibbon nodded. It was the Temple of Juno in which the barefooted friars were singing Vespers. The Temple of Jupiter was the ruin in which Gibbon was sitting.

The only proem to a work of prose to compare with Gibbon's is the opening of *The Golden Bough*. 'In this sacred grove there grew a certain tree round which at any time of the day, and probably far into the night, a grim figure might be seen to prowl. In his hand he carried a drawn sword, and he kept peering warily about him as if at every instant he expected to be set upon by an enemy. He was a priest and a murderer . . .' There you have the priest who slew the slayer, and shall himself be slain. And, if he does not make your hair bristle, you have remarkable sang-froid, or no imagination.

F. McEachran, 'Mac', of Shrewsbury School, a latter-day Mr Chips, used to call these haunting tags of incantatory and concentrated poetry, asking to be declaimed by small boys, 'spells'. Some authors are more prolific with great single-liners than others; though, of course, *chacun à son* quote. I have never been able to get to the end of *Finnegans Wake*'s streams of consciousness without skipping. But it contains haunting spells: 'Suffoclose Shikespower Seudodante Anonymoses', the latter the prolific poet Anonymous, the whole suggesting the grain of corruption that runs through the most beautiful things.

> The flushpots of Euston and the hanging gardens of Marylebone.

> No birdy aviar soar any wing to eagle it.

This just shows that I enjoy puns, a deplorable taste, no doubt. But some good men, including Shikespower, shared the taste.

Sometimes a single-liner gets distorted and misquoted by its appropriators. It was not 'Blood, sweat, and tears' that Churchill had to offer the House; but 'Blood, toil, tears and sweat.' In my list of spells for a desert island, or a bad day at the office, I'm having:

> *Ariane, ma soeur, de quel amour blessée*
> *Vous mourûtes aux bords ou vous fûtes laissée.*

That must be the only occasion in literature that the absurd tense the French Past Historic is used to stunning effect. I'm having:

> *Giù per lo mondo senza fino amaro.*

A great book is more than a congeries of glittering quotations. But there is comfort and pleasure in the great spells:

> But if the while I think on thee, dear friend,
> All losses are restor'd and sorrows end.

# SYNONYMS

## The treasure of words

'One forgets words as one forgets names.
One's vocabulary needs constant fertiliza-
tion or it will die.'
*Diaries*, by Evelyn Waugh

Life, particularly for the scribbling classes, sometimes seems to
consist of one long hunt for the *mot juste*, the parole that
conveys the nuance most precisely, the word that rings up
three bells on the word processor, provoking a shower of
coins, the locution, the vocable, the cliché, the expression, the
utterance, the exact way to convey meaning that brings a thin
smile to the lips of the oldest sub-editor, and has the readers
letting go of the straps on the Underground to applaud and
falling over. But all of us get stuck for a word sometimes, not
just when we are doing the crossword. The question is: what
do we do then?

We can sing out to a colleague: 'What's the fourteen-letter
word for the head of a human joined to an animal body?
Begins with A. It's on the tip of my tongue.' But he, being
busy too, probably replies crossly: 'Artichoke.' I find it a help
to concentrate on something else, so that when the *mot juste*
thinks I am not looking, it sneaks furtively out of the undergrowth of my subconscious, and I can pounce. But sometimes
the word does not emerge, or comes too late, after the piece is
away, or in the middle of the night, when it would be more
fun to be sleeping. For this perplexity, we have the thesaurus.

There is a euphemism for you. *Thesaurus* is the Latin for a
treasure or treasury, as in Horace, *Odes* III, 24: 'Richer than the
intact thesaurus of the Arabs.' What a thesaurus means in
modern English is a book of information about a particular
subject, especially a book of words grouped according to their
meaning. When stuck for a word, you grab a thesaurus and

inspect the field. A more straightforward name for the thing is a word-finder. But we feel a bit shifty about using so plain a name, since it announces bluntly that we have failed; that our vocabulary is not as well-endowed as Dr Johnson's or Bertie Russell's, and that we are having to cheat by looking it up in a thesaurus, word-book, journo's crutch, enchiridion, or Roget.

Peter Mark Roget (1779–1869), physician, polymath, and inventor, was the originator of the English thesaurus. He was the son of a Swiss pastor, and, like many doctors, he had an insatiable curiosity about language as well as physiology. After a long and eventful career as physician, professor of physiology, popular lecturer, and inventor of the first slide-rule and other mechanical gadgets, in his retirement he published his *Thesaurus of English Words and Phrases, classified and arranged so as to facilitate the expression of ideas, and assist in literary composition*. In his introduction to the first edition of 1852, Roget explained: 'The present Work is intended to supply, with respect to the English language, a desideratum hitherto unsupplied in any language; namely, a collection of the words it contains and of the idiomatic combinations peculiar to it, arranged, not in alphabetical order as they are in a Dictionary, but according to the *ideas* which they express.' Roget's words are grouped in categories measureless to man, such as 'General social volition' and 'Intellect: the exercise of the mind.' Stalking a word through his thickets is a jolly hunt if you have the time; and, with a bit of luck, while you are engaged on it you will remember the word you were looking for in the first place. The book evidently filled a pressing need. It reached its twenty-eighth edition during Roget's lifetime, and has now sold more than thirty million copies. Its title has been shortened.

The thesaurus is a two-edged weapon. It needs to be used with precision, like a sniper's rifle, to pot the exact *mot juste* that you have forgotten for the moment: not as a blunderbuss to pepper your prose with elegant variation, obscure words, and pudder. It is a primitive fallacy (held in part by Roget himself, to judge from his overweight prose) that a copious vocabulary necessarily makes good writing. A vocabulary of more than 20,000 words (many of them coined by himself at the ink-well) surges through Shakespeare's bustling work. Racine deploys only about a tenth of the number: he was writing a very different kind of tragedy.

The mistake is to suppose that there are synonyms, that one word is as good as another. There are no exact synonyms in English, or in any language. By definition, each word has a peculiar origin, history, and cluster of connotations around it. London Pride and *Saxifraga umbrosa* are the same pretty little plant, but the names have quite different uses and connotations. Undernourishment is not quite the same thing as malnutrition, and impartiality is not quite the same thing as disinterestedness. Gorse, furze, and whin are all names for the same prickly shrub, *Ulex europaeus*, with bright yellow flowers, which the golfer avoids if possible. Shakespeare, that living thesaurus, used two of them in the same line in *The Tempest*, IV, 1, where Ariel is describing the dance he has led Caliban and his conspirators: 'Tooth'd briers, sharp furzes, pricking goss and thorns.'

But, although gorse, furze, whin, and, for that matter, *Ulex europaeus* are synonyms or the same names in one sense, they are not interchangeable. Gorse and furze are both Old English, the former first recorded in 725, the latter in 888 in King Alfred's translation of Boethius's *De Consolatione Philosophiae*. Whin is probably Scandinavian, and is first found in place names of the Danelaw and Scandinavianized areas, such as Whinburgh in Norfolk, and Whinfell in Cumbria. In the linguistic atlas of Britain, isoglosses would demarcate those areas that use gorse, those that use furze, and those, mostly in the North, Scotland, and Ireland, where they say whin. Even in second-division poetry, such as Francis Thompson's *Daisy*, you cannot substitute one synonym for another without altering the poem:

> Where 'mid the gorse the raspberry
> Red for the gatherer springs,
> Two children did we stray and talk
> Wise, idle, childish things.

The opposite of the thesauran fallacy that sesquipedalian orotundity equals good writing is the fallacy that short words are necessarily best. One version of this is called Saxonism, which is the attempt to increase the proportion of Anglo-Saxon words in English. Saxonists form new derivatives from English words to replace established words of Latin or other descent: bodeful (1813) for ominous, birdlore (1930) for ornithology, and foreword (1842) for preface. They revive obsolete or archaic English words as substitutes for the 'alien' words that have replaced them: happenings for events, betterment for improvement, english for translate into English. Where synonyms survive side by side, Saxonists pick the Anglo-Saxon: burgess or burgher for citizen, belittle for depreciate. The insistence on the short, sharp English word is just as silly as the love of the long word, abstractitis, avoidance of the obvious, and use of such cotton-wool words as adumbrate, eventuate, situation, ameliorate. There is no golden rule for writing English, such as 'use short words', because there are so many Englishes that we want to write and speak.

For some registers, for example giving orders in the field, what is needed are short, sharp words that admit no misunderstanding or double meaning, unlike the notorious 'fourth order' issued to Lord Lucan on the day of Balaclava: 'Lord Raglan wishes the cavalry to advance rapidly to the front – follow the enemy and try to prevent the enemy carrying away the guns. Troop Horse Artillery may accompany. French cavalry is on your left. Immediate. (Sgd.) R. Airey.' The ambiguity of the order that led to the Charge of the Light Brigade was not in the turgidity of the vocabulary, but in the imprecision of the small words 'to the front'. Since then the Army has tried to do better, using for giving orders and directing fire such unambiguous words as bushy-top tree and church with tower. On the other hand some registers, for example a political speech to a mass rally of supporters, seek to spread a general air of authority and success without conveying any precise meaning. For this there are coded hurrah words and expressions to convey emotion rather than sense.

In some registers of English, the last thing that you want is to be understood. The new Chinese ambassador to the Court of St James in Victoria's reign expressed a wish, shortly after his arrival in England, to make the acquaintance of the principal English poets, and Robert Browning was presented to him. The conversation turned to the compositions of the ambassador, who was himself a poet. 'What kind of poetry does His Excellency write?' asked Browning. 'Pastoral, humorous, lyric, or what?' There was a pause. At length the interpreter said that His Excellency thought that his poetry would be better described as 'enigmatic'. 'Surely,' replied Browning, 'there ought, then, to be the deepest sympathy between us, for that is just the criticism that is brought against my own works, and I believe it to be a just one.'

It was Roget's misapprehension that anybody can write well by deploying enough long words. It is a common misapprehension that anybody can write well, if only he can find the Open Sesame. The truth is that writing well is a high skill that can be learnt only by a few with practice and pains. To write with natural genius is given to only one or two in a generation. There are now thesauruses arranged alphabetically, in addition to Roget's idiosyncratic system of classification. Used judiciously and parsimoniously a thesaurus can make you more articulate, fluent, forceful, graceful, moving, persuasive, silver-tongued, stirring, well-expressed. At any rate it may prevent you going bananas while trying to remember the *mot juste* on the tip of your tongue. If what you want is erudite variation, difference, novelty, variety, pass the Roget.

# UNNECESSARY WORDS

## Unicorns and howlers

'Language is a uniquely human characteristic.
Each person has programmed into his genes a
faculty called universal grammar.'
Noam Chomsky, speech to the Royal Society

Mel Brooks (as 2,000-year-old man): 'We spoke
Rock. Basic Rock . . . Two hundred years before
Hebrew, there was the Rock Language. Or Rock
Talk.'
Carl Reiner (as interviewer): 'Could you give us
an example of that?'
Brooks: 'Yes. Hey, don't throw that rock at me!
What are you doing with that rock? Put down
that rock.'
*The 2,000-year-old Man*, by Mel Brooks and Carl Reiner

The language belongs to all of us who use it. We should
welcome new words and new meanings into it with open
arms, since they increase our common stock of vocabulary. If
we do not like them, we do not have to use them. If enough of
us do not like them, they will die of under-use and neglect.

Nevertheless, we need more crusty and opinionated pedants
who are tough enough to say that some new words are otiose,
pretentious, tautologous, and should have their throats cut
without any wet waiting about to see whether they catch on.
The trouble is that we are all terrified of being thought élitist,
and bossy, and intellectually superior. But, when it comes to
using language, it is sensible in most contexts to be élitist: all
that élitist means is picking the best, in this case choosing the
best words to convey your meaning. These useless and unnecessary vogue words have been called unicorns, because they
sound good but do not mean anything, which may be unfair
to unicorns, who have an elegant existence in mythology and
medieval literature. For example, the word 'meaningful' has a

modest but useful role in the jargons of logic and philosophy; when it is used in journalism or sociology and other general registers, it is almost always a unicorn, and meaningless.

The champion unicorn in political jargon at present is 'mandate', which all winners by however small a margin claim to have for whatever they choose to perform from their election manifestos. Politics is a language of argument and propaganda, and politicians tend to prefer the strong word 'mandate' to weaker, more precise words. This is not a new phenomenon. The National Government with Ramsay MacDonald as Prime Minister elected in the United Kingdom in 1931 asked voters for a doctor's mandate. You can even claim a mandate without an election. Walter Lippmann wrote: 'Political ideas acquire operative force in human affairs when they acquire legitimacy, when they have the title of being right which binds men's consciences. Then they possess, as the Confucian doctrine has it, the mandate of heaven.' 'Mandate' is a value word and a matter of opinion. As such it needs watching for unicorn qualities.

In defence jargon Star Wars is a bit of a unicorn to describe the Strategic Defense Initiative, the proposed system of artificial satellites armed with lasers to destroy enemy missiles in space. The phrase, cribbed from a science-fiction film, is misleading, flash, inaccurate, and pure pop journalese wind and *Sun*-spot. It has also become a crashing cliché. Let us resolve not to use it. 'Vertical access device' as pretentious jargon for lift, or, as the Americans call the foul things, elevator, strikes me as a unicorn. You could argue that a vertical access device is a broader category than lift, including for example the paternoster, in which the platforms are attached to continuous chains, and passengers step on and off at each floor while it is moving, and worry about what happens when they get to the top. But I take vertical access device to be unnecessary gobbledygook.

Roundheads of language could take their pruning knives to the suffix 'busters', inspired by the dreadful film *Ghostbusters*, and applied to everything that moves, from inflation-busters to crime-busters. Let us resist the temptation to be trendy, and undertake not to to bung busters on to the end of a word just for effect or neophilia.

'Bare naked' is in vogue in the United States, and is clearly a tautology. 'Significant writedown' is a unicorn and a pretentious euphemism for a big loss. When Nasa pilots are said to 'visually eyeball the runway', I smell the musty scent of unicorn. 'Near miss' ought to be 'near hit': it actually missed, but nearly hit. 'Up to speed' is a vogue phrase in US government jargon, and sounds like a unicorn to me. 'Read' as noun or adjective, as in 'this book is a good read', has become tiresome jargon in the United Kingdom as well as the United States, and is a unicorn that somebody should pick a quarrel with, preferably the kind of quarrel with a four-edged head that you fire from a crossbow.

'Sight unseen' seems to me to be circumlocution and unicorn. 'Unseen' on its own is shorter and simpler. But 'sight unseen' has become idiomatic and smart. When you stop to think about it, it is an odd phrase, a kind of chimera, with the head of a tautology, the tail of a contradiction, and the body of a goat. It has come into the language only recently, but it is recorded in all the latest dictionaries. I guess from the exemplary citations that they give, about buying a car sight unseen, that the phrase comes from the flash and prolific jargon of car sales. Or maybe the dictionaries all give the same example from car sales talk because lexicographers are shameless and hardened plagiarists of each other's definitions. I think 'sight unseen' is a unicorn and an attempt to sound smart. 'Unseen' does the same job more economically. I resolve never to use the phrase myself, and to remove it from the copy of any reviewer.

Much ephemeral slang is a unicorn, strictly unnecessary, though it adds to the gaiety of conversation. The bacterium of deadly Legionnaire's Disease (named after the outbreak at a meeting of the American Legion at Philadelphia in 1976) was recently found in the cooling water system of one of Glasgow's best known breweries. This is the sort of rumour that runs through the bars and saloons like, well, the plague. We had better not mention the name of the brewery. But I am told, and do in part believe, that the latest jocularity in that great city is for a Glaswegian to saunter into his local tavern and, irrespective of what brand of heavy is on offer, to call for 'a pint o' Legionnaire's'. This new phrase illustrates a number of characteristics of slang. It shows how fast the sensational news that is presented in black headlines three inches deep in the pop tabloids affects the language. It illustrates the emollient propensity of slang to mock the distasteful, brighten the gloomy, and say the unsayable. It exemplifies the sharpness of Glesga talk: 'Awawn dunk yer doughnut.' But the local point of the metaphorical use of Legionnaire's means, I think, that this unicorn will not spread as widely around the world as other Glasgow slang, such as the universal, 'X Rules, OK?', which almost certainly originated near Ibrox, one of Glasgow's great gladiatorial football grounds. The tendency towards novelty language is continual and irresistible. Some new phrases are so noisy, like a pint of Legionnaire's, that we notice them at once. Slang unicorns can add colour to social intercourse. A policy of shooting all unicorns on sight, because they are tautologies, or euphemisms, or otiose, would be unduly puritanical. It wouldn't work, anyway. Humans have a sneaking affection for the illogical beast.

Children particularly like unicorns of language. 'During one long hot summer a serious trout hit the country.' That grave fish was invented by a Cypriot student. 'Henry Tutor succeeded Richard III.' There is another typical Cypriot mistake. I know a Greek Cypriot who regularly says 'Coot Cot' instead of 'Good God'. Because of a difference in the phonology of the two languages, Cypriot and Byzantine Greek students have difficulty distinguishing between English ps and bs, ks and hard gs, and ts and ds.

Howlers and bloomers from schools and colleges where foreign students learn English language and literature illustrate the trickiness of English as a foreign language, and also the surrealist beauty of unicorns. Here are some examples from recent exam papers at one of London's biggest and best polytechnics: I don't approve of corpular punishment; I was completely demolarized by the examination; It is a well non fact; I have left this behind me in my infantry; You have to pay 10p for a wash and brush-off; He was insulting me, and using filthy languages; I like adventure books like *Treasury Island*; There was a raping noise at the door; You should follow the ten commitments; Nowadays many women work as men; The Shah of Iran was overthroned; Several people, maybe more, were in the room. The last enigmatic unicorn was written by a Japanese student. When the lecturer fell about with delight, the student was offended by her amusement, and told her stiffly that she had been taught that 'several' meant 'five'.

Here are some creative definitions, unicorns and chimeras, from exams at the same polytechnic:

Listless = too many to list.

A steamroller = something to curl your hair with.

A jockey = someone who tells jokes.

An inhabitant = someone who doesn't live in a place.

Even those of us who are native here have trouble with the crazy obstacle race of the English language. Edward Heath recently gave a talk on aspects of the Third World at Great St Mary's, Cambridge. At one point he spoke of 'the slopes of the Himalayas which have now been consumed as forests'. The secretary who was transcribing his address from the tape rendered this into unicorn and surrealist poetry as: '. . . which have now been hewn into porridge'.

Here are some more unicorns to tease. Question: When do we read modern English idiomatically from right to left? Answer: The favourite won easily at 4–7. That's how we write it, but we say: 'The favourite won easily at seven to four on.'

How can we account for the fact that Blue or Bluey is a common name given to those with red or ginger hair in Australia? Answer: Australians are notorious jokers with language.

Why are surnames such as White, Black, Brown, and Green common; yet we never meet a Mr Red or a Miss Yellow, and only occasionally a Lionel Blue?

Have you noticed how the media have got hold of the wrong end of the sticking-point, which is in danger of becoming a vogue word and a unicorn? They take it to mean something like a bottleneck. Some gnome on television recently referred to a situation having several sticking-points or tricky places where things might go wrong. 'But screw your courage to the sticking-place, and we'll not fail.' The allusion in *Macbeth* seems to be to the screwing-up of the peg of a musical instrument until it becomes tightly fixed in the hole. Echoes of Shakespeare have turned the famous phrase into a unicorn.

# Index

abbreviations, distinguished
from acronyms 14
Achilles, swift-footed, can't beat
a tortoise 240
acronyms, dangers of
misunderstanding 14–16
address, problems of 145–6
admirals, origin of 169
Agul, the alphabet with the most
consonants 137
AIDS, ambiguity of 15–16
alibi, misused 114
*Alice's Adventures in Wonderland*,
by Lewis Carroll (Charles
Lutwidge Dodgson), 1865, and
architecture 28, the gryphon a
cherubim 222
alphabets, punning, unhelpful,
misleading 136–41
American slang 20–4, flaky 30,
hype 77–8, gay slang 87,
losing buttons 93, short
strokes 118–20, white nigger
127, white hat 128
Amharic, complex alphabet
136–7
amphibology, and AIDS 17, with
hopefully 69
antithonyms 193
Apicius, Marcus Gavius (1st
century AD ish, if you believe
that you'll believe anything),
on gravy 64
appellations, and handles 142–7
arbitrage, pejoration of 31–2
Aristophanes (?457–?385),
Cloud-Cuckoo-Land 237–8

Arnold, Matthew (1822–88)
*l'homme moyen sensuel* 271
Augustus, Emperor, Caius
Octavius (63 BC–AD 14) plays
marbles 95
Austen, Jane (1775–1817) forms
of address 123
Australian slang on marbles 95,
there you go 132, abbreviated
words of approval 135
*Authorized Version* of the Bible
(1611) on the Good Samaritan
121–2, folk etymology of
'woman' 142, modernized
215–24
auto-antonyms 189–94

Balfe, Michael (1808–70) on balls
93
Baldwin, James (b. 1924) on
hype 77
Baring, Maurice (1874–1945) on
liberals 112
band-wagon, derivation 65–6
Bennett, Gordon (1841–1918)
eponym of the ejaculation
107–9
Bentham, Jeremy (1748–1832) on
community 39, defines
utilitarianism 113
Berne, Eric defines stroking
119–20
Bible, translated again 215–24
biffing, distinguished from
boffing 30
Big Bang, linguistic
consequences 30